The Sociology of Longevity

The Sociology of Longevity:

Socioecological Factors of Survival Probability

By

Jong In Kim

Cambridge Scholars Publishing

The Sociology of Longevity:
Socioecological Factors of Survival Probability

By Jong In Kim

This book first published 2022

Cambridge Scholars Publishing

Lady Stephenson Library, Newcastle upon Tyne, NE6 2PA, UK

British Library Cataloguing in Publication Data
A catalogue record for this book is available from the British Library

ISBN (10): 1-5275-8062-8
ISBN (13): 978-1-5275-8062-6

I want to express gratitude to my son, who is living in the United Kingdom, and with whose assistance, this book was made possible.

TABLE OF CONTENTS

Preface xi

Acknowledgments xii

List of abbreviations xiii

Part 1: Approach to the survival probability of becoming a centenarian (SPBC)

Chapter 1 2
The concept of the survival probability of becoming a centenarian (SPBC)

1.1 The concept of SPBC and country-local society support (CLSS)
1.2 Impact of CLSS

Part 2: Factors of becoming a centenarian

Chapter 2 16
The socioecological factors (SEFs) of becoming a centenarian

2.1 Increase in survival probability and life expectancy (LE)
- 2.1.1 Personal life improvement (PLI)
- 2.1.2 Difference in CLSS
- 2.1.3 PLI and CLSS
- 2.1.4 Increase in survival probability and LE

2.2 Socioecological determinants of survival probability
- 2.2.1 Estimation of SPBC and SEFs
- 2.2.2 Framework of SEFs impact on SPBC
- 2.2.3 Gross national income (GNI)
- 2.2.4 Health expenditure as a percentage of the GDP (HEPGDP)
- 2.2.5 Fixed telephone and mobile phone subscribers (FTMPS)
- 2.2.6 Basic sanitation services (BSS)
- 2.2.7 Gender inequality index (GII)
- 2.2.8 Urban population (UP)
- 2.2.9 Individuals using the Internet (IUI)

2.2.10 Safely managed drinking water (SMDW)
2.2.11 Services value-added per worker (SVPW)

Part 3: Factors of life expectancy (LE)

Chapter 3 94
Life expectancy (LE) factors related to becoming a centenarian

3.1 LE and SEFs
3.1.1 LE and GNI
3.1.2 LE and SMDW
3.1.3 LE and BSS
3.1.4 LE and GII
3.1.5 LE and IUI
3.1.6 LE and FTMPS
3.1.7 LE and GHE
3.1.8 LE and UP
3.1.9 LE and SE
3.1.10 LE and SVPW
3.1.11 LE and OPR
3.1.12 LE and GI
3.1.13 LE and DCI
3.1.14 LE and HEPGDP

3.2 LE at age 60
3.2.1 Impact on old age LE (OLE) of SEFs
3.2.2 A case study of OLE

3.3 Remaining years of life expectancy (RLE)
3.3.1 Impact on RLE of SEFs
3.3.2 An assessment of RLE (65)

3.4 Inequality in LE (ILE)
3.4.1 Impact on ILE of SEFs
3.4.2 A case study of ILE

3.5 Healthy life expectancy (HLE)
3.5.1 Impact on HLE of SEFs
3.5.2 An assessment of HLE

Part 4: Application of SEFs as determinants for becoming a centenarian

Chapter 4 184
Influence of SEFs on LE and SPBC

4.1 Correlation between LE and SEFs and between SPBS and SEFs
4.1.1 Planning to nurture healthy centenarians
4.1.2 Correlation between LE and SEFs and SPBS and SEFs

4.2 Measures for SPBC
4.2.1 Developing the estimation formula of ISS
4.2.2 Output for ISS
4.2.3 Differences between countries for ISS

4.3 Prediction of the estimates for SEFs
4.3.1 Gross national income (GNI)
4.3.2 Old age pension recipient (OPR)
4.3.3 Secondary education (SE)
4.3.4 Safely managed drinking water (SMDW)
4.3.5 Fixed telephone and mobile phone subscribers (FTMPS)
4.3.6 Basic sanitation services (BSS)
4.3.7 The Gini index (GI)
4.3.8 Urban population (UP)
4.3.9 Gender inequality index (GII)
4.3.10 Individuals using the Internet (IUI)
4.3.11 Government health expenditure (GHE)
4.3.12 Health expenditure as a percentage of GDP (HEPGDP)
4.3.13 Services value-added per worker (SVPW)
4.3.14 Depth of credit information (DCI)

4.4 Application factors of SPBC
4.4.1 Establishment of short-, medium-, long-term plans
4.4.2 PLI: Income, hygiene, drinking water, and use of the ISS
4.4.3 Social environment of mixed CLSS: GII, IUI, and UP
4.4.4 Hospital visit: GHE and HEPGDP
4.4.5 Achievement of the health level and SPBC feasibility review
4.4.6 Healthcare system based on CLSS
4.4.7 Health resource mobilization
4.4.8 Assessment of health level based on CLSS

Part 5: A society wherein people live to be centenarians

Chapter 5 270
Implications from interviews with centenarians

5.1 Ranking impact factors between SPBC (82) and SEFs
5.2 The SEFs affecting centenarians
 5.2.1 BSS
 5.2.2 HEPGDP
 5.2.3 IUI
 5.2.4 FTMPS
 5.2.5 SVPW
 5.2.6 GNI
 5.2.7 SMDW
 5.2.8 UP
 5.2.9 GII

5.3 Humans can live 100 years or more, based on PLI and CLSS for SEFs
5.4 Impact when combined with SEFs in SPBC (82)
 5.4.1 GNI, UP, and SMDE
 5.4.2 BSS, SVPW, and UP
 5.4.3 HEPGDP, FTMPS, and IUI
 5.4.4 FTMPS, BSS, IUI, UP, and HEPGDP
5.5 Summary: Impact of SEFs on SPBC (82)

Completing this book 295

PREFACE

This book documents factors that determine humanity's survival probability of becoming a centenarian (SPBC) as well as the life expectancy (LE) associated with socioecological factors (SEFs).

The data are taken from the Human Mortality Database (HMD), the World Bank and WHO Database, and interviews with centenarians. In particular, SPBC is calculated from the HMD. SEFs and LE are analyzed from the WHO and World Bank Database. In addition, data were collected through interviews with 130 centenarians aged 100 to 108.

The chapters in this book contribute to possibilities for increasing SPBC and LE by applying SEFs analytical strategies to understand trends and patterns in SPBC. The book also includes detailed accounts of 14 factors that affect SPBC and LE.

The book reports on the causes and impact of SEFs on SPBC and LE. A critical finding, confirmed in the analysis of interviews with centenarians, is that SEFs influence LE and SPBC.

As the first time the influence of SEFs on SPBC has been analyzed and described, this book presents evidence of SPBC and LE factors in all countries and contributes to globally applicable knowledge of how to become a healthy centenarian for individuals and country-local societies.

ACKNOWLEDGMENTS

This work was supported by the Ministry of Education of the Republic of Korea and the National Research Foundation of Korea (NRF-2017S1A5 B1020830).

LIST OF ABBREVIATIONS

BSS: Basic sanitation services
CLSS: Country-local society support
DCI: Depth of credit information
FDA: Female dominant authority
FSE: Female secondary education
FSP: Female survival probability
FTMPS: Fixed telephone and mobile phone subscribers
GI: Gini index
GEI: Gender equality index
GHE: Government health expenditure
GII: Gender inequality index
GNI: Gross national income
HEPGDP: Health expenditure as a percentage of the GDP
HLE: Healthy life expectancy
ILE: Inequality in life expectancy
IUI: Individuals using the Internet
LE: Life expectancy
MDA: Male dominant authority
MSE: Male secondary education
MSP: Male survival probability
OLE: Old age life expectancy
OPR: Old age pension recipient
OPW: Output per worker
PHL: Personal hygiene-oriented leadership
PLI: Personal life improvement
PSL: Public sanitation-oriented leadership
RLE: Remaining years of life expectancy
SE: Secondary education
SEFs: Socioecological factors
SMDW: Safely managed drinking water
SPBC: Survival probability of becoming a centenarian
SVPW: Services value-added per worker
UP: Urban population

PART 1

APPROACH TO THE SURVIVAL PROBABILITY OF BECOMING A CENTENARIAN (SPBC)

Part 1 introduces the concept of the survival probability of becoming a centenarian (SPBC) and socioecological factors (SEFs), including country-local society support (CLSS). By explaining the correlation between SEFs and SPBC, I emphasize the impact of CLSS on SPBC. In addition, the relationships between CLSS and SPBC and between CLSS and life expectancy (LE) are demonstrated using survival probability graphs. Finally, the lifespan graphs of SPBC and LE (based on increasing/decreasing SEFs) are presented.

CHAPTER 1

THE CONCEPT OF THE SURVIVAL PROBABILITY OF BECOMING A CENTENARIAN (SPBC)

Can we live to be 100 years of age? Is it feasible? If so, how many people can survive to age 100? Is there any way for all humans to live to this age? This book attempts to use a socioecological perspective to answer these questions.

In addition, this book explains the relationship between SPBC, an indicator of the healthy survival of citizens of each country until the age of 100, and the SEFs that affect countries around the globe. Furthermore, the socioecological factors related to LE are discussed, and the research work that identifies them is presented. Based on the results of this study, we propose making efforts toward building a country wherein individuals can live to be 100 years of age. Moreover, if the government utilizes and applies the contents of this book, it is possible that humanity can reach this milestone.

1-1 The concept of SPBC and country-local society support

We hope to live healthily to 100 years or more. The longevity of humans has been affected by various factors. These longevity factors involve both a microscopic and a macroscopic perspective. Microfactors are innate, natural elements. However, macrofactors are influenced by social circumstances. In this regard, we need to consider the sociological perspective for the longevity of humanity. In particular, this book intends to examine the factors of human longevity from a socioecological perspective.

A society of longevity refers to a community where human beings live healthily beyond 100 years. These 100-year-old people are called centenarians. By observing the lifestyle and social environment of centenarians, we can find the root of longevity in the socioecological aspects. Therefore, the sociology of longevity is a social science that studies societies wherein human beings can live healthily beyond 100 years. We aim to contribute to the healthy longevity of humanity by observing socioecological factors (SEFs) that heighten the survival probability of becoming centenarians (SPBC) for all people.

There are both inherent and acquired factors that affect human life. For instance, genetic factors are intrinsic, and if they are constant, the level of acquired characteristics can affect human lifespan. Furthermore, acquired factors primarily consist of lifestyle habits and national and community factors. Therefore, if these factors affect SPBC, it is necessary to recognize them as an essential issue and conduct a systematic study.

The concept of SPBC introduced in this book is crucial for identifying SEFs and establishing a national strategy for helping people reach the milestone of 100 years old. Specifically, SPBC refers to the number of survivors who turn 100 on a given date, divided by the corresponding cohort size of the specified year (Kim & Kim, 2014a, 2015, 2017a).

For instance, suppose we estimate that individuals who are 70 years old in 1980 will reach 100 in 2010. In that case, the calculation is the number of centenarians in 2010 divided by the corresponding cohort size of 70-year-olds in 1980. SPBC also includes the advantage of controlling for other potential confounding factors (e.g., infant mortality) that affect the centenarian population and overcoming the migration problem inherent in the change of nationality.

Health is influenced by several dimensions from a socioecological perspective, including individual, community, and public policy factors (Kim & Kim, 2017). This book focuses on (1) individual perspectives, (2) community-related perspectives, and (3) public policy perspectives on health promotion. However, it broadly uses the socioecological model from (1) personal life improvement (PLI) and (2) country-local society support (CLSS). Therefore, the socioecological perspective has broadly been classified into the PLI and CLSS domains. The socioecological structure organized in this way may include the following factors (Kim, 2013, 2014b, c, Kim & Kim, 2014a, 2015, 2016, 2017a, b, 2018, 2019).

(1) PLI includes factors such as income, secondary education level, safe drinking water, personal hygiene, mental stress by gender discrimination, personal favorite phone, and Internet use. (2) CLSS includes factors such as the urbanization rate of the population, labor productivity, and the share

of health costs in GDP. In addition, major factors, such as the income inequality phenomenon, ratio of pensioners to population, government medical expenditure, and national credit index, can be classified as CLSS factors. From this point of view, in this book, SEFs had been set up with PLI and CLSS.

First, Point C in Fig. 1.1 shows the following. Until the age of 65, individuals receive good healthcare protection, including the following:

- Vaccinations and nutrition from their parents since infancy
- Programs aimed at ensuring that young adults reach adulthood without suffering from severe illness
- Physical activity and exercise promotion after marriage

Individuals reach the age of 75 without illness by exercising, not smoking, and consuming limited alcohol. In other words, up to the age of 75, an individual can live a healthy life without being too affected by the local community or national health policy. However, individuals beyond this age are inevitably affected by CLSS. In this regard, support and social structure changes can influence an individual's lifespan and survival probability.

As Fig. 1.1 illustrates, survival probability is affected by SEFs such as unique social living environments and eating habits, national health policies, and social structural change. Curve A shows survival probability beyond age 75 among all age groups. After birth, the younger generation maintains a horizontal curve. However, the survival probability after age 75 rapidly decreases due to CLSS and social change. As shown in Curve B, individuals generally maintain their health through personal eating habits and healthy lifestyles until around 75.

However, the survival probability after this age can significantly increase or decrease based on CLSS. Thus, there is a difference between Curves A and B. Specifically, the size of the survival probability scale is determined by CLSS and the rate of personal life change. In addition, the degree of personal–society and CLSS changes (quantitative and qualitative) indicates the range of the increase or decrease in survival probability of an aging society. As for the SEFs, their influences are as follows.

In Fig. 1.1, Curve A shows the relationship between an individual's health level and longevity. For instance, if an individual dies at the age of 100, their survival probability curve is downward and slopes to the right. However, suppose an individual lives with insufficient water and unsanitary drinking water in a nation with a poor national income and impoverished health sanitation welfare. In that case, personal lifestyle and country-local social factors threaten their survival in both the short and long terms. Therefore, the SEFs of individuals and countries may shorten the survival probability of individuals.

In Fig. 1.1, the CLSS of Curve B shows the implementation of the following SEFs:

· Innovative health and social policies
· Implementation of national health insurance
· Community and national government support life expectancy
· National and local healthcare policies and support
· Innovation of national and community health programs
· The local community provides disease prevention programs
· Investments for creating a healthy society
· An increase in the local government's healthcare expenditure support ratio
· Realization of public interest in health
· Implementation of a gender equality society
· Changes in the social health consciousness structure
· Growth in the population of large cities
· Local hospitals equipped with adequate healthcare systems

Therefore, these SEFs will increase the nation's LE and SPBC; that is, the survival probability curve rises to the right. For instance, the implementation of national health insurance can reduce the burden of national medical expenses. In addition, health promotion projects in the local community can prevent diseases, thereby extending individuals' lifespans.

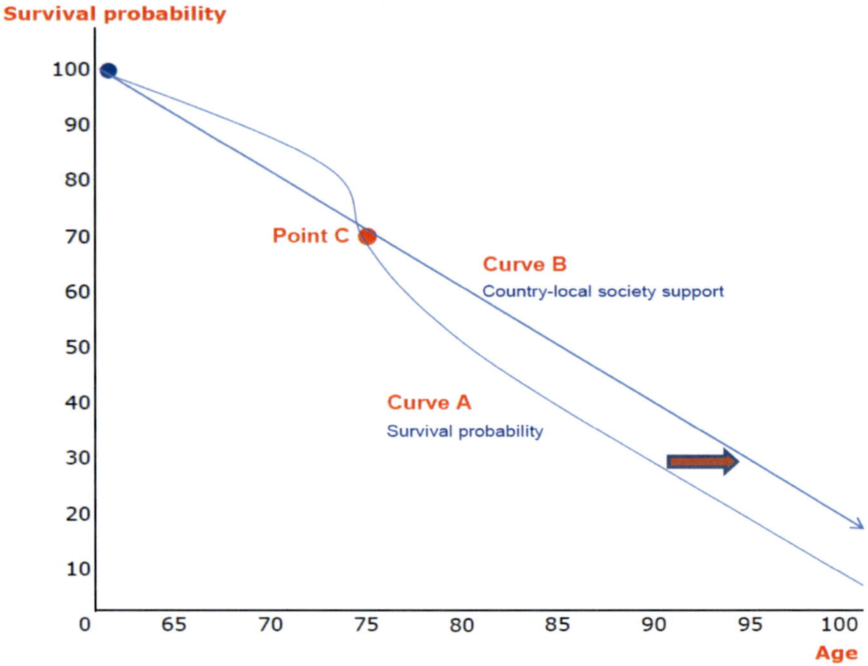

Fig. 1.1. Survival probability and CLSS

1.2 Impact of CLSS

Fig. 1.2 presents CLSS by country, where the Y-axis is the level of survival probability, and the X-axis shows age according to CLSS. For instance, individuals in a country with CLSS 1 have a 50% chance of surviving to age 65, whereas those in CLSS 2 countries have a 50% chance of surviving until 75. Then, in CLSS 3 countries survive up to the age of 100, whereas CLSS 4 countries, 30% survive up to the age of 90.

Fig. 1.2 shows the difference in the survival probability by age in each country based on quantitative and qualitative levels of CLSS. As mentioned earlier, the curve in Fig. 1.1 represents personal health and LE. Accordingly, an individual's survival probability decreases with age. However, in this reality, when a national economy develops, the level of social consciousness changes, and innovative investments are made in the healthcare sector. In addition, an individual's survival probability can vary depending on CLSS. In other words, from CLSS 1 to CLSS 4, the difference in survival probability by age is based on the aging population and level of CLSS. Therefore, because of the country's aging, the survival probability will create a gap in the national economic status and the ratio of healthcare expenditure to total expenditure.

In addition, as shown in Fig. 1.2, CLSS 3 countries have the highest proportion of survival rates until the age of 100. Compared with other countries, the survival probability until age 65 is similar. However, one can infer an aging society, such as those in CLSS 3 countries, to be a country with a well-established national welfare system for the elderly. In other words, it can be considered to have a national social welfare system that provides effective support, including (1) retirement pensions, (2) specialized hospitals and nursing facilities for the elderly, (3) adequate sanitary facilities, and (4) safe drinking water, all of which are the bases of good health for the elderly. Moreover, suppose a country includes effective medical systems that can transport patients to a general hospital within 30 minutes in an emergency. In that case, the survival probability will inevitably be higher.

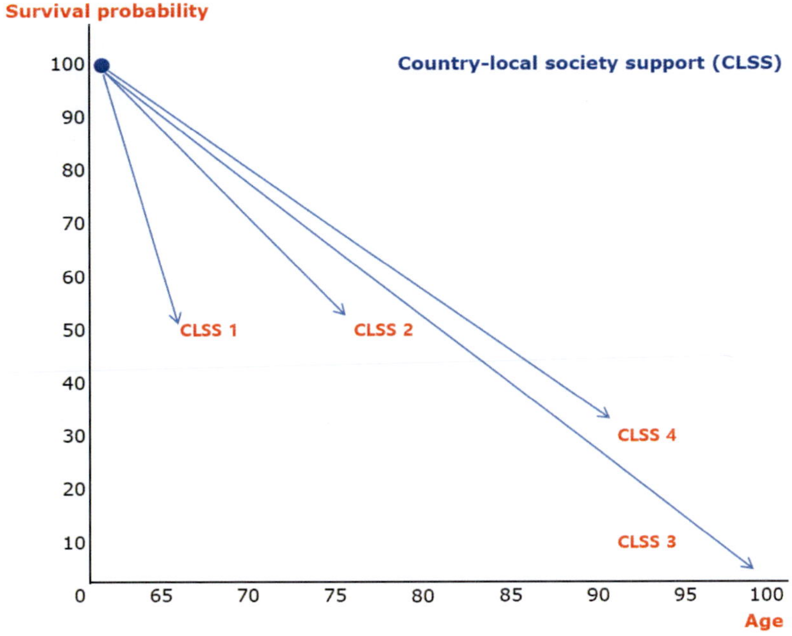

Fig. 1.2. Survival probability and CLSS

Meanwhile, in Fig. 1.3, the Y-axis is LE, whereas the X-axis is SEFs. For instance, in CLSS 1 countries, the CLSS 1 is approximately 50% of the SEFs, with an LE around 60 years of age. However, advanced CLSS 3 countries have an LE of 87 years of age, with 85% of the SEFs used as a national social support system that invests in the healthcare sector. Therefore, CLSS 1 and CLSS 3 countries have a gap in LE because of conflicting national social support systems and changes in social structure.

Fig. 1.3 also explains the close correlation between LE and CLSS. In other words, it assumes that the higher the CLSS, the higher the LE. In addition, from CLSS 1 to CLSS 4, we can hypothesize that the difference in LE occurs according to the SEFs in the countries. For instance, the higher the share of healthcare expenses in government spending, the more significant the difference in LE. This figure shows that CLSS 2 countries include a structure that can predict LE to around 75, based on a healthcare expenditure input of 60%. However, CLSS 3 countries have a national structural system that can predict LE to around the age of 88, based on a healthcare expenditure input of 86%. This indicates that the correlation between the input of SEFs and LE is relatively close.

Due to national economic development and innovative investments in the health sector, LE has been extended from 65 to 70. However, because its input cannot be increased indefinitely, LE cannot be extended similarly. This is because human survival probability and LE include specific limitations. For instance, according to recent data, the lowest LE of any country is 53 years of age, whereas the highest of any country is 85 (an average of 73). Therefore, reducing the differences between these countries is necessary to extend the LE beyond 73 years.

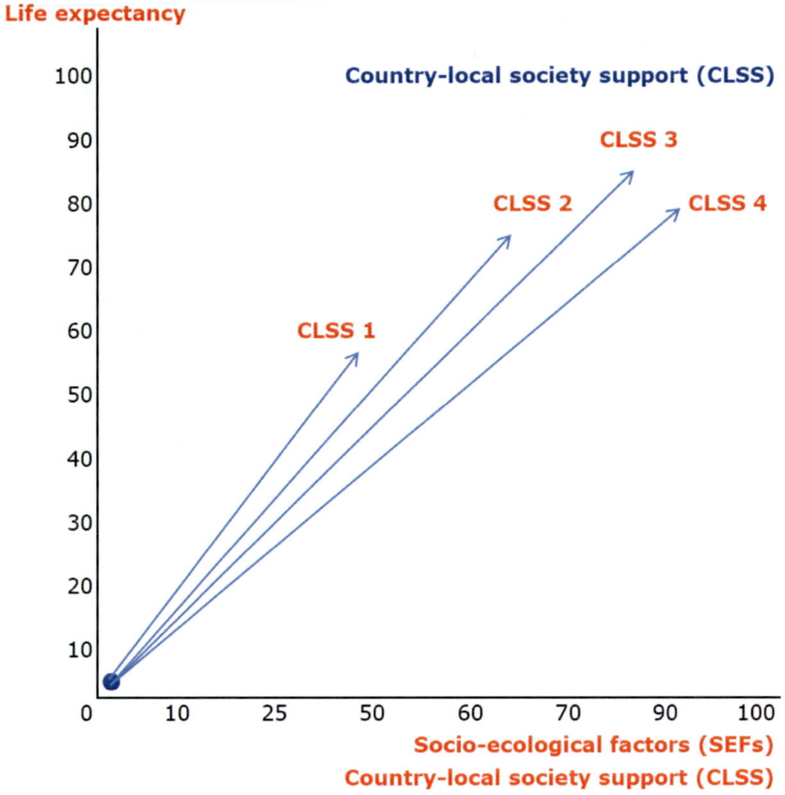

Fig. 1.3. LE and CLSS

Fig. 1.4 shows the quantitative levels and LE of the SEFs, which is an opposing graph to Fig. 1.3. In other words, the SEFs indicate a negative (−) direction. Hence, LE is higher because the value of the SEFs is relatively minor. Alternatively, it suggests that the higher their value, the lower the LE. For instance, if the gender discrimination index is high, the LE will inevitably be low because the socio-structural change is undesirable. Therefore, as for the value of life expectancy, the larger the SEFs that are socially and structurally undesirable, the lower the LE.

It is noteworthy that even if an individual is born with a genetically healthy constitution, they (from the age of 65) may develop diseases due to inadequate healthcare. However, the case of reaching the age of 75 in good health is similar to what is shown in Fig. 1.1. Therefore, realistically, if a national government intensively allocates medical resources to the healthcare sector, the impact can be enormous. In other words, the influence of an individual's healthy lifespan extension will increase their survival probability and LE the most, as shown in CLSS 3 countries. For instance, at 100 years of age, the survival probability will increase from 5% to 10%, whereas LE will also increase from 75 to 80 years. This indicates that healthcare projects carried out by state and local communities are more effective than individual efforts at maintaining health.

Finally, CLSS 3 countries have an advanced state-led health and welfare system that guarantees a prosperous retirement for an aging society. These developed countries can teach lessons to developing countries, which have low survival rates. For instance, they can provide healthcare information by revealing the reasons for such longevity and the SEFs that affect LE and survival probability the most. In addition, humanitarian efforts should support public health and medical projects in developing countries, which will significantly increase survival probability. SEFs can have a decisive effect on an individual's lifespan; we hope that influential variables can reduce the gap between countries.

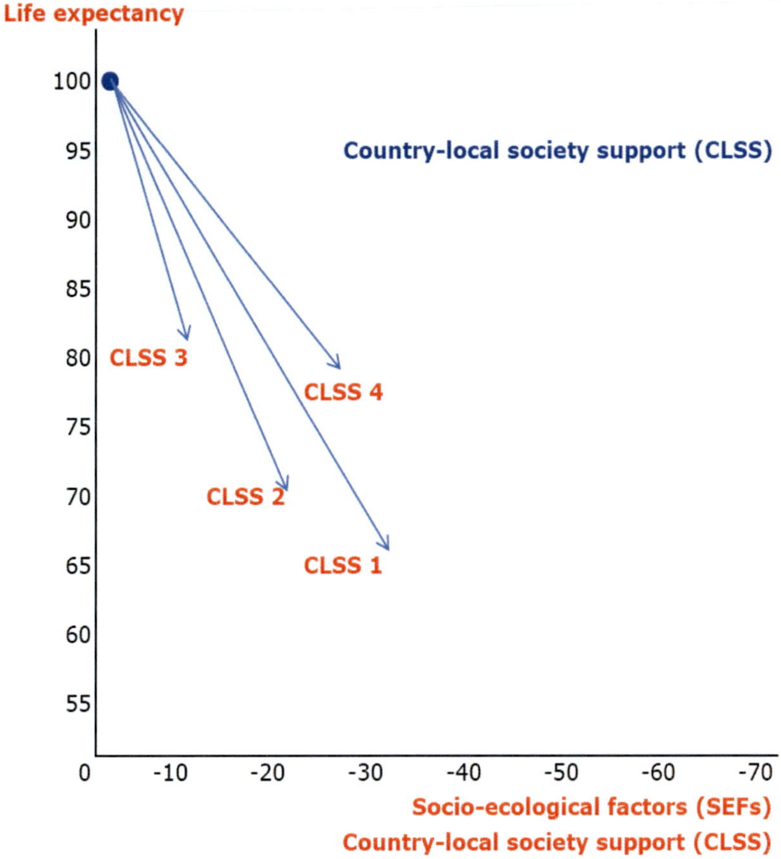

Fig. 1.4. Reverse LE and CLSS

Fig. 1.5 shows the relationship between survival probability and SEFs. In other words, the SEFs indicate a negative (−) direction. Hence, survival probability is higher because the value of the SEFs is relatively minor as in Fig 1.4. Alternatively, it suggests that the higher the (−) value of SEFs, the lower the survival probability. For instance, if the gender discrimination index is high, the survival probability will inevitably be lower because of mental stress. Therefore, as for the value of survival probability, the larger the SEFs that are socially undesirable factors, the lower the survival probability.

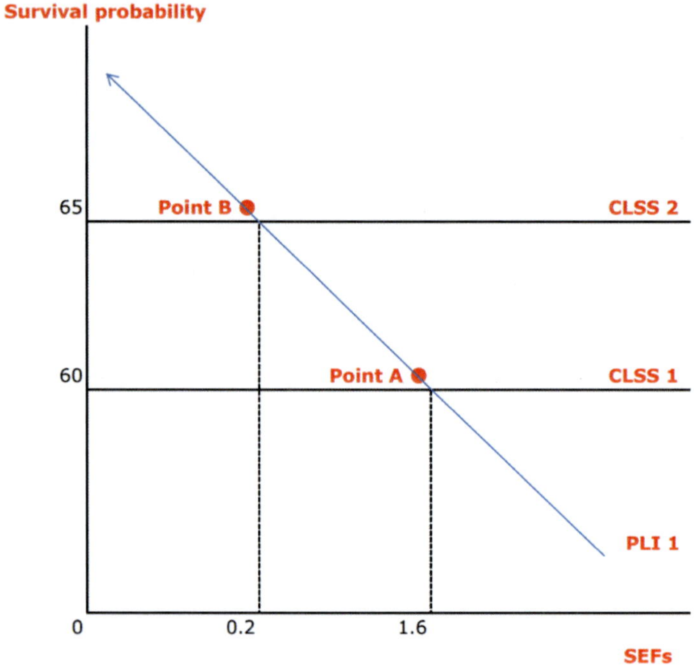

Fig. 1.5. Survival probability and GII of SEFs

If PLI is the gender discrimination index (GII) in Fig.1.5, as the GII factor increases, the GII of SEFs continues to deteriorate, and the survival probability decreases. In terms of CLSS, the survival probability is 60 years old when the sex discrimination index is 1.6 in a CLSS 1 country, with a very high sex discrimination index in the current national society (point B). However, in a CLSS 2 country, the gender discrimination index is 0.2, and the probability of survival is 65 (point A). Thus, the difference in survival probabilities between these countries is a 5-year gap.

However, in Fig.1.6, PLI is upward sloping. Because if the PLI in this case is basic sanitation services (BSS), the survival probability increases as BSS increases. In Fig.1.6, in a CLSS 1 country with a very low BSS in the current national society, when BSS is 80%, the survival probability is 75 years old (point B). However, in a CLSS 2 country, when the BSS is 90%, the survival probability is 80 years old (point A). Therefore, the difference in survival probabilities between these countries is a 5-year gap.

Thus, an increase or decrease in GII and BSS of SEFs leads to an increase or decrease in the survival probability of humanity. This book will empirically explain these outcomes using various studies in each chapter.

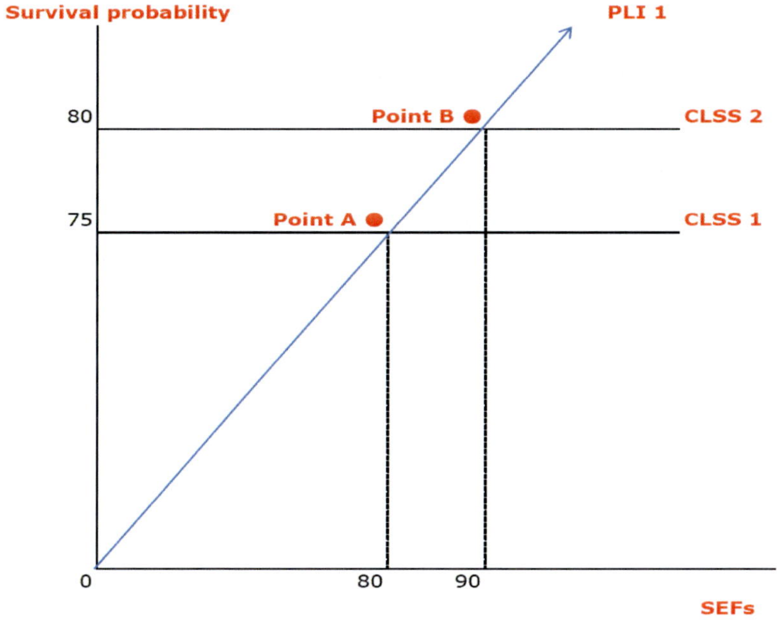

Fig. 1.6. Survival probability and BSS of SEFs

References

Kim JI. Social factors associated with centenarian rate (CR) in 32 OECD countries. *BMC International Health and Human Rights.* 2013; 13(1), 16.

Kim JI. Association between social factors of health ageing and longevity: determinants of the longevity index (LI) in OECD countries. *Ageing International*. 2014c; 39(2): 97–105.

Kim JI, Kim G. Factors affecting the survival probability of becoming a centenarian for those aged 70, based on the human mortality database: income, health expenditure, telephone, and sanitation. BMC Geriatrics. 2014a; 14(1), 113.

Kim JI, Kim G. Labor force participation and secondary education of gender inequality index (GII) associated with healthy life expectancy (HLE) at birth. *International Journal for Equity in Health. 2014b;* 13(1), 1–8.

Kim, JI, Kim G. country-level socioeconomic indicators associated with healthy life expectancy: income, urbanization, schooling, and internet users: 2000–2012. *Social Indicators Research. 2016a;* 129, 391–402.

Kim JI, Kim G. Social Structural influences on healthy aging: Community-level socioeconomic conditions and survival probability of becoming a centenarian for those aged 65 to 69 in South Korea. *The International Journal of Aging and Human Development.* 2015; 81(4) 241–259.

Kim JI, Kim G. & Choi Y. Effects of air pollution on children from a socioecological perspective. BMC Pediatrics. 2019; 19, 442.

Kim JI, Kim G. Effects on inequality in life expectancy from a social ecology perspective. BMC Public Health. 2018; 18, 243.

Kim JI, Kim G. Socio-ecological perspective of older age life expectancy: income, gender inequality, and financial crisis in Europe. Globalization and Health. 2017b; 13, 58.

Kim JI, Kim G. Country-level socioeconomic indicators associated with survival probability of becoming a centenarian among older European adults: gender inequality, male labor force participation, and proportions of women in parliaments. *Journal of Biosocial Science.* 2017a; 49(2) 239–250.

Kim JI, Kim G. Relationship between the remaining years of healthy life expectancy in older age and national income level, educational attainment, and improved water quality. *The International Journal of Aging and Human Development.* 2016b; 83(4), 402–417.

PART 2

FACTORS FOR BECOMING A CENTENARIAN

Part 2 presents the conceptual graphs of survival probability and examines the correlations between SPBC and PLI and CLSS in SEFs. Further, it focuses on the SPBC at 82 years of age and explains significant SEFs.

CHAPTER 2

THE SOCIOECOLOGICAL FACTORS (SEFS) OF BECOMING A CENTENARIAN

Chapter 2 introduces the SEFs that determine SPBC. As explained in Part 1, SPBC is affected by SEFs' increase and decrease through CLSS and PLI. Thus, this chapter shows the synergistic effect on SPBC when CLSS and PLI are combined. However, there is a gap in SPBC, depending on the increase/decrease in these two aspects. In this case, nine variables of PLI and CLSS are used to express the influences of SEFs in 39 countries. Moreover, the association between SPBC and these variables is described using data from the 'Human Mortality Database.'

2.1 Increase in survival probability and life expectancy (LE)

2.1.1 Personal life improvement (PLI)

The factors that determine an individual's survival probability can initially be found in their diet and lifestyle (i.e., food, clothing, hygiene, and shelter). Fig. 2.1 presents a curve regarding the association between SPBC and PLI. For example, the 85-year-old PLI 1 curve shifts to the 90-year-old PLI 2 curve, thus extending the lifespan. As a result, the 90-year-old's survival probability improves by 20%, from 10% to 30% (Fig. 2.1). This is due to the formation of triangle ABC, which indicates that the survival probability can increase by improving an individual's income, hygiene, living environment, lifestyle, diet, and stress levels. Specifically, the survival probability increases by 20% by vertically moving from Point A to Point C and extending from 85 to 90 years by horizontally moving from Point B to Point C. In addition, this chapter empirically discusses a case in which a 70-year-old can become 100 years of age based on improved income and living environment.

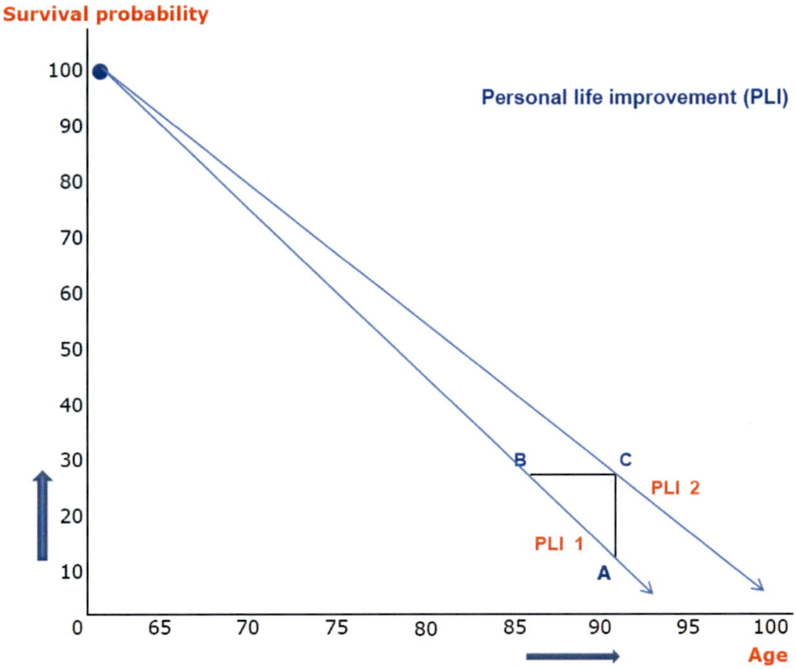

Fig. 2.1. SPBC and PLI

2.1.2 Difference in CLSS

What role does the national government play when determining the survival probability of an individual? Fig. 2.2 shows that the CLSS change curve includes the same meaning as the survival probability curve of countries. In other words, their survival probability curve moves downward and to the right. It is also a CLSS change curve that can predict the survival probability of citizens up to the age of 100.

For example, a CLSS 1 country has a 50% chance of survival at age 65, while a CLSS 2 country has a 50% chance of survival at 75. However, a CLSS 3 country has a 30% chance of survival at age 95 (Fig. 2.2). Thus, the difference in survival probability and age between these countries is that various factors are at work, the cause of which can be found in SEFs.

As for the difference in survival probability between CLSS 1 and CLSS 3 countries, advanced countries maintain the top group in CLSS 3. However, some countries in CLSS 1 of Asia, Africa, and Eastern Europe with low incomes and living standards have low survival probability until 100. In addition, the development of the national economy and socio-cultural level and the improvement of living environments and lifestyles can also affect the difference in survival probability and LE.

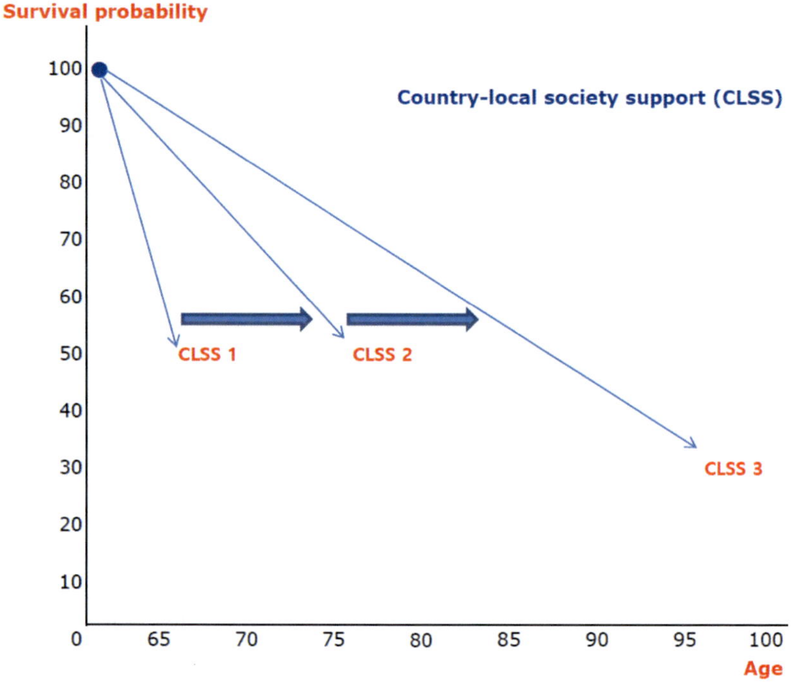

Fig. 2.2. SPBC and CLSS

It is assumed that the CLSS and PLI curve, which increases the survival probability (SPBC) and LE, includes the following properties (see Fig. 2.2 and 2.3):

· SPBC and LE gradually rise to the right in countries where the quantity and size of CLSS and PLI increase in SEFs.

· As the number of CLSSs and PLI increases, the SPBC (survival probability) and LE do not sharply drop but gradually lowers to the right. The extent of this drop depends on the amount of change in the CLSS and PLI curves.

· The increase/decrease in the PLI and CLSS curve of SEFs affects survival probability (SPBC) and the increase/decrease in LE.

· Some SEFs affect the probability of survival up to the age of 100. However, the extension of SPBC and LE includes a property that all SEFs affect.

· If LE is extended up to 100 years, it depends on the capacity of change in PLI and CLSS. This is because improvements in income and living standards have the effect of extending SPBC and LE.

For instance, PLI in SEFs includes an individual's economic level, Internet usage, and cellphone subscription rate, all of which can affect LE and SPBC. The related research and their relevance are presented in Chapters 2 and 3.

2.1.3 PLI and CLSS

How does LE relate to PLI and CLSS? In this regard, note Fig. 2.3, in which CLSS and PLI form a rising curve, respectively. Here, the CLSS curve extends LE to 90 years of age. This is the result of extending LE based on the quantitative scale of social structural change and the input of the national healthcare sector. In other words, the national income and the ratio of healthcare expenditures in the gross domestic product (GDP) at the national level affect the increase in human lifespan.

In the same figure, PLI raises LE to 70 from 50 years of age. This can occur when fundamental life improvements such as safe drinking water and personal hygiene facilities, are affected. Thus, if CLSS and PLI are simultaneously carried out in a country with social change, an increase in

LE will bring about a synergistic effect (Fig. 2.3). In other words, the rise in LE means that individual and country social factors act dually, making room for a significant increase. For example, suppose the increase in the ratio of healthcare expenses in the GDP is considered CLSS, and personal hygiene facilities are considered PLI. In that case, this book clarifies that SEFs can transform 70 and 82 years of age into 100 years.

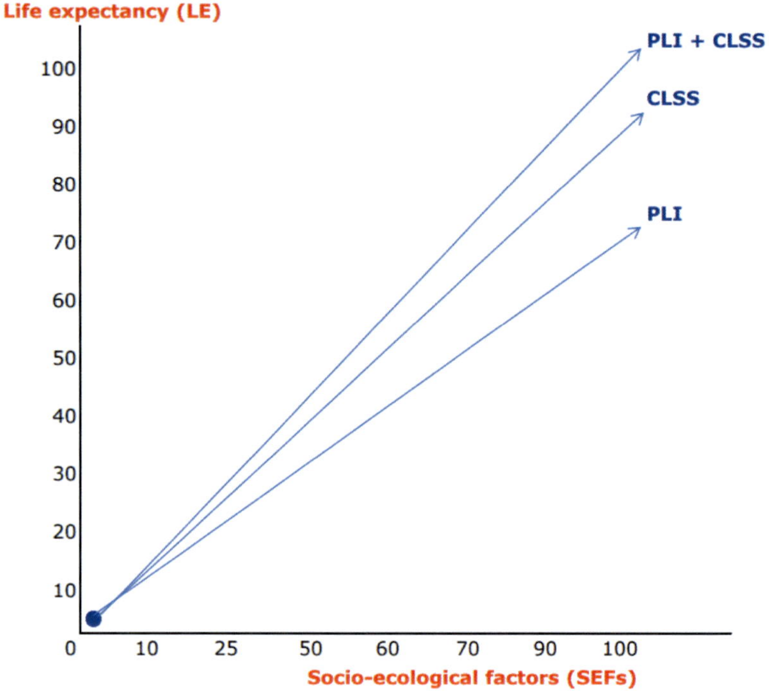

Fig. 2.3. PLI and CLSS

2.1.4 Increase in survival probability and LE

How will SEFs curves determine survival probability at the ages of 70 and 80 at the individual and social level? First, let us introduce their comprehensive curves. Fig. 2.4 shows the curves in which SEFs successfully improve survival probability and LE by increasing PLI and CLSS. In other words, it assumes that the PLI and CLSS survival probability curves shift upward, thus assuming that the PLI and CLSS curves survive to the age of 100. In addition, PLI 1 and CLSS 1 curves increase the survival probability by 59% due to an increase by 60% in SEFs. The PLI 4 and CLSS 4 curves improve by 90% by inputting more than 99% (Fig. 2.4). Therefore, the increase in survival probability and LE can be predicted by the increase/decrease in SEFs.

For example, from an individual's point of view, if hygiene problems are improved, LE will increase. In addition, from a national and social point of view, a change to a society without gender discrimination can increase LE and survival probability. Therefore, provided that the countries' public health expenditure increases, sanitation problems are improved, and a change to a society without gender discrimination occurs, the probability of survival to 100 years of age is expected to increase.

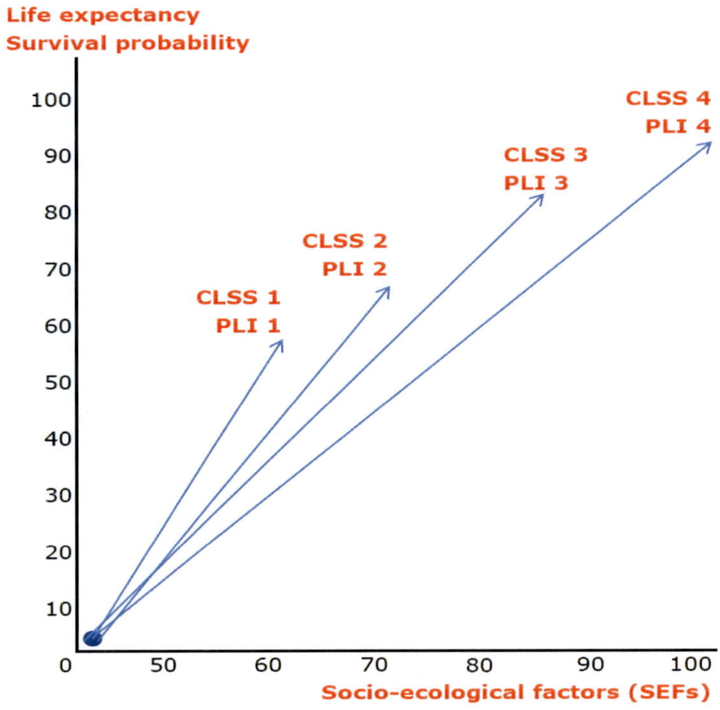

Fig. 2.4. LE, SPBC, and SEFs

2.2 Socioecological determinants of survival probability

2.2.1 Estimation of SPBC and SEFs

Is there a correlation between SEFs and SPBC? What factors influence SPBC in their age groups? Will these factors include income, medical expenses, cell phone use, or sanitation services? In many countries, especially for women, the odds of surviving to 100 years of age have increased over the past few decades. Although survival rates to 100 years are improving, it is impossible to determine whether natural lifespans have increased, at least in some countries (Kannisto, 1988). However, SPBC may be influenced by the aforementioned SEFs indicators. Hence, a review of case-control studies may help uncover the factors associated with SPBC and healthy aging.

Today, the 100-year-old population is steadily increasing worldwide (Byass, 2008), with dramatic increases in this demographic over the past half-century (Berr et al., 2012). Thus, SPBC defines the production estimate for the population of 100-year-olds (Kim & Kim, 2014). Meanwhile, SPBC (82) refers to the probability of surviving to age 100 for the population of 82-year-olds. It should be noted that SPBC (82) is not associated with fertility because the study cohort had already reached 82 years of age.

Conversely, survival probabilities are expressed as numbers. The 100-year-olds proposed in previous research were used as healthy aging indicators, yielding longevity indices applicable in certain countries (Robine, 2005; Kim, 2013, 2014; Kim & Kim, 2014). Therefore, these case studies investigated the relationship between SEFs and SPBC (82) as an independent variable. The present study can estimate the influence of the nine variables by determining how SEFs affect SPBC (82) from the PLI and CLSS in 39 countries (see Fig. 2.5.1~4).

Overall, this study estimates the association between SPBC (82) and SEFs using Pearson's correlation coefficient and multiple regression models. In particular, this chapter identifies the differences in SEFs related to SPBC (82) in 39 countries. As stated earlier, SPBC (82) is the number of survivors who turn 100 years of age on a given date, divided by the corresponding cohort size for that age (Kim, 2013; Kim & Kim, 2014, 2016, 2017). In this case, 82 is the age used for all countries from 2000 to 2018, divided by the cohort size for that age. For these calculations, this study utilized the Human Mortality Database (HMD, 2018).

As shown in Fig. 2.5. 1–4, it is essential to consider what policies are necessary for increasing the survival probability to 100 years of age. Under the premise that other factors are constant, CLSS and PLI can increase/decrease the survival probability (SPBC) and LE by increasing/decreasing SEFs. Note that the PLI and CLSS curves in Figs. 2.5.1, 2.5.2, and 2.5.3 are upward and to the right. It indicates that the survival probability and LE increase when individuals improve their lives, and the countries promote health policies and related projects. In other words, the survival probability and LE increase when CLSS (UP; HEPGDP; SVPW) and PLI (GNI; BSS; SMDW; IUI; FTMPS) increase. However, there are factors in which the sign of SEFs operates in the negative (−) direction. For example, in Fig. 2.5.4, the curve is downward and to the right. In practice, the gender inequality index (GII) should also decrease. Then, individuals in their 70s and 80s can reach the age of 100 and maintain a healthy lifespan.

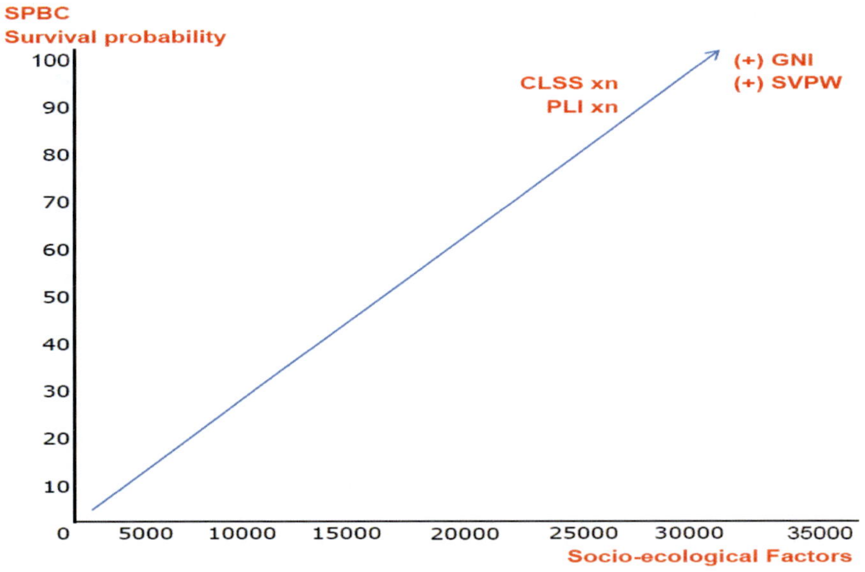

Fig. 2.5.1. Relationship between SPBC, and GNI and SVPW in SEFs

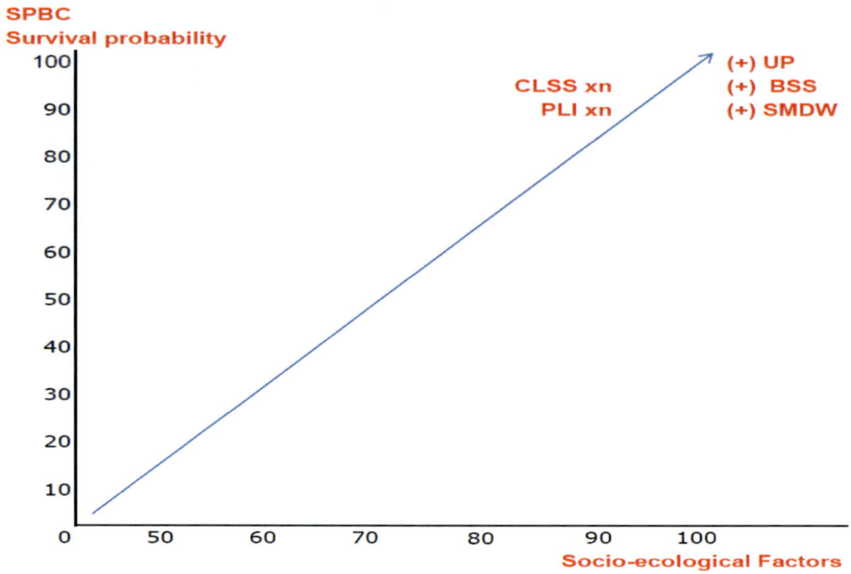

Fig. 2.5.2. Relationship between SPBC, and UP, BSS, and SMDW in SEFs

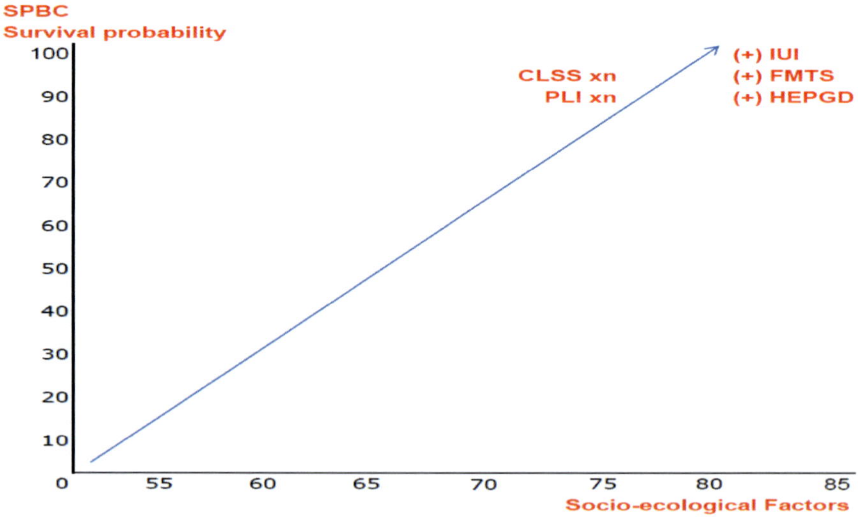

Fig. 2.5.3. Relationship between SPBC, and IUI, FTMPS, and HEPGDP in SEFs

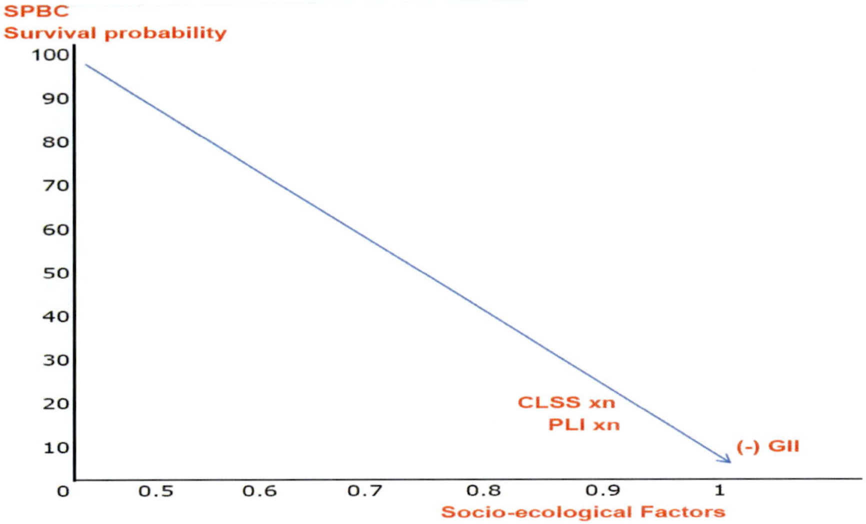

Fig. 2.5.4 Relationship between SPBC and GII in SEFs

2.2.2 Framework of the impacts on SPBC

At this point, the proposed research framework describes the SEFs for SPBC (82) in Fig. 2.6. The primary hypothesis is that all conditions are constant. However, the influence of genetic factors on SPBC (82) is excluded. Thus, the factors related to SEFs are as follows. The factors GNI, FTMPS, BSS, GII, IUI, and SMDW are assumed in PLI. However, from the CLSS perspective, the elements like HEPGDP, SVPW, and UP are set. The significant, influential variables are analyzed under the premise that they are related to SPBC (82), PLI, and CLSS.

Consequently, from the perspective of PLI, it is hypothesized that the better the national income, telephone use, basic hygiene, gender equality without gender discrimination, users of the Internet, and safe drinking water, the greater is the probability that 82-year-olds will reach 100.

From the CLSS perspective, it is hypothesized that the proportion of health and medical expenses in the GDP, value-added productivity, and a national society with better urbanization can increase the probability of surviving from age 82 to 100.

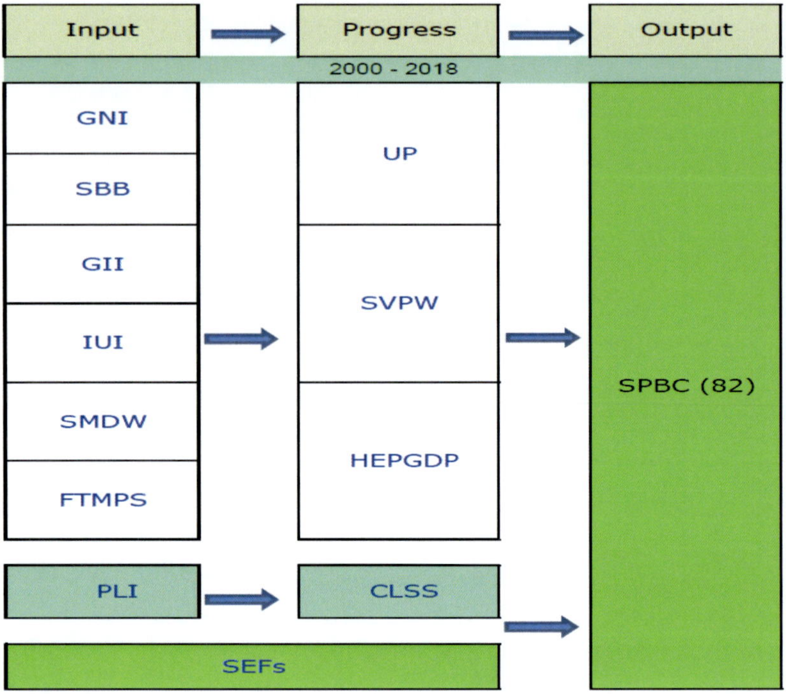

Fig.2.6. Conceptual framework of the SEFs for SPBC (82)

Fig. 2.6 indicates the determinants that affect SPBC (82). The factors are GNI, HEPGDP, FTMPS, BSS, GII, SVPW, IUI, UP, and SMDW.

For example, GII showed a negative effect among these variables, while HEPGDP, IUI, and BSS showed more than 50% correlations in Table 2.1. The results of these nine variables are as follows: In a country with an LE of 82 years, if eight variables increase and one variable decreases, the probability of survival to 100 years of age increases.

Overall, this chapter focuses on the correlation between the nine variables, while the estimated regression formula of SPBC (82) for those variables is described in Chapter 4.

Table 2.1. Correlation coefficient for SPBC (82) and SEFs

Variables		Correlations coefficient	p-value
	GNI	0.487	0.002
	SMDW	0.482	0.002
	BSS	0.554	0.000
	UP	0.481	0.002
SPBC (82 to 100)	GII	-0.471	0.003
	IUI	0.535	0.000
	HEPGDP	0.544	0.000
	SVPW	0.491	0.002
	FTMPS	0.493	0.001

2.2.3 Gross national income (GNI)

One significant SEF that can affect the survival probability of an individual's healthy lifespan is basic income.

The food, clothing, and shelter consumed as income are fundamental for maintaining a healthy lifespan. In other words, if there is no basic income, then it is impossible to maintain an essential livelihood. Besides, if the national income level is high, there is a high possibility that the healthcare system is well-equipped, and it will quickly respond in the case of an emergency. In addition, families with high-income levels have a higher quality of life than those of low-income households, and they are more likely to maintain a healthy lifespan and reach 100 years of age.

Fig. 2.7 presents a graph showing the association between GNI and SPBC (82). As a country's GNI increases, its SPBC (82) increases. For example, the probability of survival from 72 to 102 years of age gradually increases as the GNI increases.

In this figure, the probability of survival at 82 is 15% at Point B, the survival probability at the age of 92 is 25% at Point C, and the 102-year-old survival probability is 30% at Point D. In this case, their survival probabilities increase as the GNI increases. However, as the age increases, the rate of the rise in the survival probability decreases. Specifically, from 82 to 92, the increase is +10%, but from 92 to 102, the growth is only +5%. It is the result of aging and the level of health.

In addition, in low-income countries with low LE, the survival probability until the age of 72 is 10% at Point A, while until the age of 82 it is +5%. This confirms the close relationship between the survival probability and the national income level.

After all, the GNI is the most critical variable among the SEFs. This is because the GNI can improve health with economic support and the human lifespan can reach 100 years of age. Furthermore, we can confirm that the lower the income level, the lower the probability of survival. This is the main reason why research on the improvement of each country's economic level, sustainable economic development, and extension of human lifespan should continue.

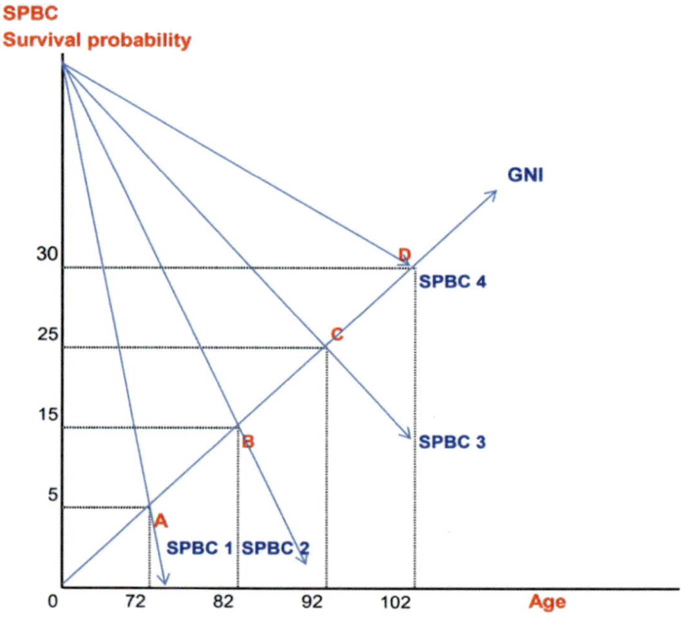

Fig. 2.7. SPBC associated with GNI

Fig. 2.8 does not extend the human lifespan, but it increases the survival probability at 82 years. Specifically, from Point A1 to Point A2, i.e., at 82, the survival probability increases by +10%, i.e., from 50% to 60%. This is due to advancements in medical technology, including the following:

· Artificial oxygen respirators
· Improvement in heavy-equipment operating rooms
· Artificial intelligence diagnoses and procedures
· Use of cutting-edge medical equipment
· Improvement in the efficacy of herbal ingredients
· Improvement in vascular procedures
· Improvement in cerebrovascular systems
· Development of new drugs, etc.

In this regard, such medical developments are the result of economic support. Thus, it is a collective approach to the development of socioecological healthcare by the national government and medical field, which, in turn, can increase the survival probability of the older population.

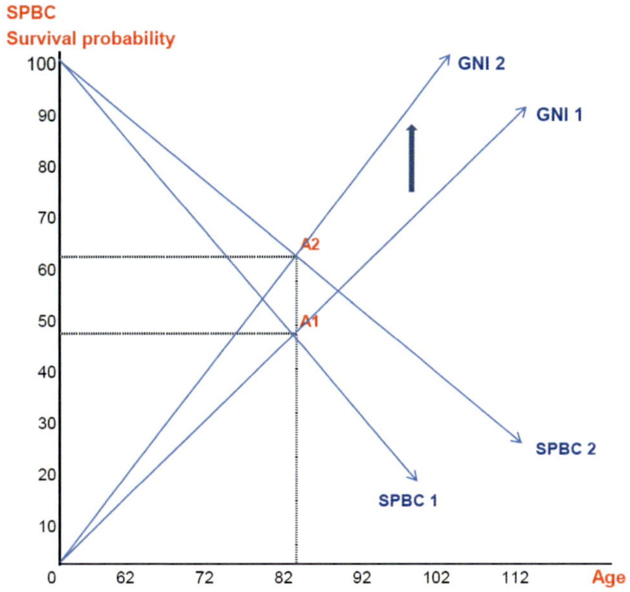

Fig. 2.8. Increase in SPBC and GNI

Fig. 2.9 shows the extension of a healthy lifespan. In this case, it does not increase the odds of survival at 82 years of age, but it extends the lifespan from Point A to Point B. Specifically, at 82 years of age, the survival rate is constant at 60%, but it is a case of extending the healthy lifespan by five years from 80 to 85. This indicates that it is a product of cutting-edge medical development that has extended the human lifespan with economic support. Specific examples are as follows:

· Robotic treatment
· Video-call treatment
· New medical technology that prevents and treats diseases, customized to individuals
· Generalization of artificial organs
· Treatment of geriatric diseases with brain disease treatment technology
· Remote surgery through u-health technology
· Disease treatment by robots

Such state-of-the-art medical development is not achieved by the passive healthcare administration of the countries. Instead, it is achieved through unprecedented health and economic support by the countries' health and medical services. Furthermore, it can reach by making radical innovations such as performing state-of-the-art robotic medical procedures. Therefore, human lifespan extension is only possible when the national income level improves and medical science advances.

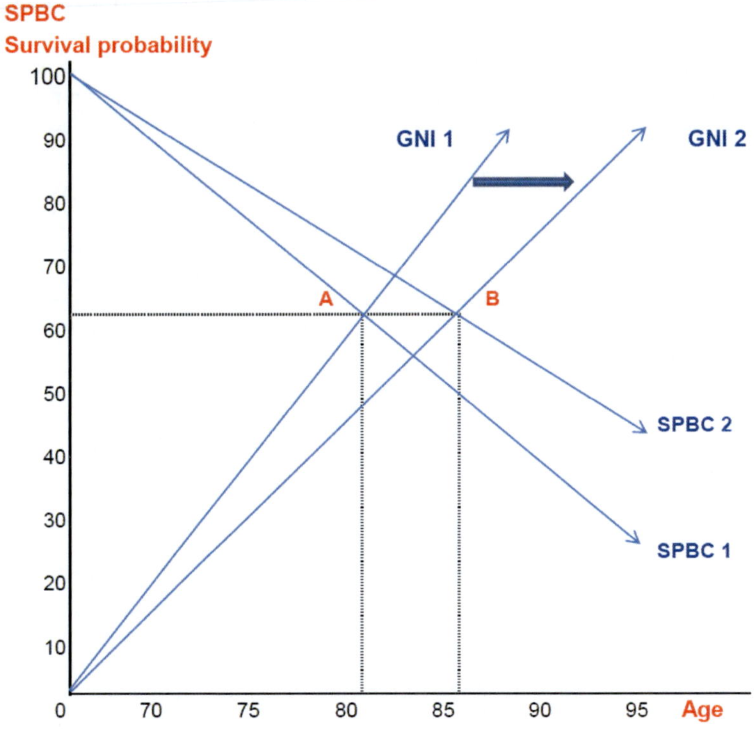

Fig. 2.9. Extension of SPBC and the increase in GNI

> GNI is defined as income per capita converted to U.S. dollars, divided by the midyear population. Thus, GNI is the sum of value-added by all residents, in addition to any product taxes not included in the valuation of output and net receipts of primary income from abroad. GNI, calculated in national currency, is usually converted to U.S. dollars at official exchange rates (WB, 2021a).

Since GNI is the sum of the country's citizens in return for participating in domestic and foreign production activities or providing the necessary assets for production, it is possible to conclude that the GNI is proportional to the health level of the country. In addition, the lowest SPBC (82) among the 39 countries surveyed shows Ukraine. Specifically, the country's income level (i.e., the GNI per capita) in 2020 was $3,540, while that of the European Union in 2019 was $35,873, and that of Central Asia in the same year was $25,246. Consequently, Ukraine's GNI level is low. Therefore, countries with low-income levels have low national health levels.

Meanwhile, tuberculosis (TB) mortality rate can be used to measure the health level of individuals and countries, compared to a country's income:

> The incidence of TB is the estimated number of new and relapse cases in a given year, expressed as the rate per 100,000 people. In this case, all forms of TB are considered, including issues of individuals living with HIV (WB, 2021b).

The 2019 incidence of TB in Ukraine, with the lowest SPBC (82) among the 39 countries surveyed, is 77 (per 100,000 people). In 2019, the TB death rate in Europe and Central Asia was 27. Compared to Ukraine, the United States included three people, while the United Kingdom had eight. Thus, the gap between these countries was 26 times and ten times, respectively.

Tuberculosis is known to be a common disease in underdeveloped countries. There is also a gap in the incidence/prevalence of TB according to the country's economic level. In other words, TB is a common disease in emerging countries with low national economic standards. For TB, long-term drug use and adequate nutrition are essential. In particular, getting sufficient nutrition and taking long-term TB drugs for more than six months is only possible when the national income level and hygiene standards are high. In addition, the national income level can be proportional to the intake of essential nutrients to strengthen immunity. This being the case, GNI is highly correlated with national health. Thus, it is significant SEFs in the survival probability of reaching 100 years of age.

Fig. 2.10 shows a graph in SPBC (82) increases as GNI increases. Based on this hypothesis, Ukraine has 21 people (per 10,000 people) in SPBC (82), while Japan has 185 and France has 153 (see Additional File 1). This figure shows that the estimated value calculated is SPBC 1 for Ukraine, SPBC 2 for France, and SPBC 3 for Japan. Thus, SPBC 1 country is approximately seven to nine times lower than SPBC 2 and SPBC 3 countries.

As mentioned earlier, even if the national economic level is high, if diseases, such as TB, are widespread, the probability of survival to the age of 100 is inevitably low. However, it is possible to state that the health level can reach 100 years of age if it overcomes common infectious diseases and diseases like cancer, cardiovascular disease, diabetes, and high blood pressure.

Consequently, if a significant population suffers from an underlying infectious disease, then the probability of survival at the age of 100 will be even lower.

From a macro perspective, the national income level (especially a high-income level) affects the probability of survival to 100 years of age. Conversely, a country with a low-income level will not consider national social support without state aid. The problem is that there is a need for strategies to respond to healthcare services. However, even if interest, support, or outsourcing for the health of world countries is at the national level, alternatives (e.g., personal medical services and health policies) that can improve one's personal life must be legislated.

Overall, socioeconomic support is necessary for improving the national health level. First, if the economic status of underdeveloped countries is to improve, foreign aid and loans from advanced countries are required. However, suppose a country's national health policy is not pursued as the top priority. In that case, it will be challenging to achieve a healthy lifespan and the probability of survival to 100 years of age. Thus, the best method to maximize such survival probability is prioritizing national health and medical policies and providing economic support. Second, the next priority is to prepare legislation for the nation that can be practiced by the state and individuals, even if the economic support of the national government aims to solve such health problems. Based on this point, healthcare and health education should continue so that the citizens can improve their standard of living.

A high national income level is observed in SEFs that exerts a significant influence on improving the health of citizens and increasing the survival probability to the age of 100. In other words, individuals with high-income levels can actively prevent diseases through, for example, personal hygiene and safe drinking water management and improve their quality of life without gender discrimination. In addition, countries with high national income levels can enhance the health of their citizens by revitalizing medical production and health services through the economic support of the nations. Thus, preventing diseases, improving individuals' quality of life and health, and receiving medical aid from the countries are attributable to GNI.

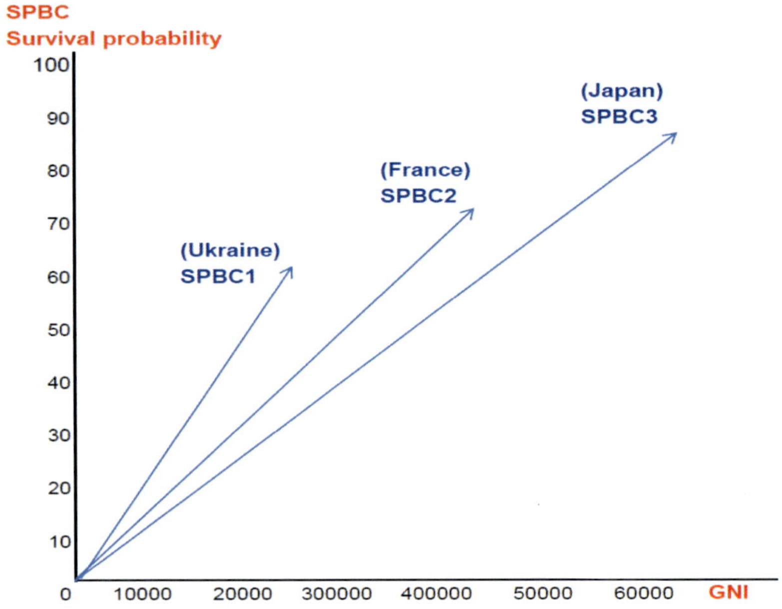

Fig. 2.10. Difference in SPBC and GNI

Fig. 2.10.1 shows SPBC and GNI by country. In a previous study (Kim & Kim, 2014, 2018), GNI also affected SPBC (70) in the 32 surveyed countries, confirming that the SEFs of GNI are essential in the production of SPBC.

In SPBC (82 to 100) of this book, the GNI per capita, Atlas method (current US$), 2018 of Switzerland (83,730), Iceland (67,890), Norway (80,640), Australia (53,190), Luxembourg (70,910), and United States (63,170) were from 53,190 to 83,730. Switzerland's GNI was the highest among the 39 countries. That country corresponds to Point A (SPBC 1, survival probability 91–112) in Fig. 2.10.1.

Additionally, the GNI of Austria (49,080), Finland (48,280), Italy (33,840), Germany (47,050), the Republic of Korea (32,730), New Zealand (42,110), United Kingdom (41,770), and Israel (40,860) are from 32,730 to 49,080 categories. Therefore, their Point B groups fall under the SPBC 2 (survival probability 78–108) classes.

Lastly, GNI of Czech Republic (20,520), Greece (18,970), Slovak Republic (18,350), Lithuania (17,460), Latvia (16,540), and Hungary (15,020) are from 15,020 to 20,520 categories. These countries fall under the categories of Point C groups (SPBC 3, survival probability 42–97).

Thus, we confirm that GNI is critical in raising SPBC (82 to 100) from Point C and B to Point A countries.

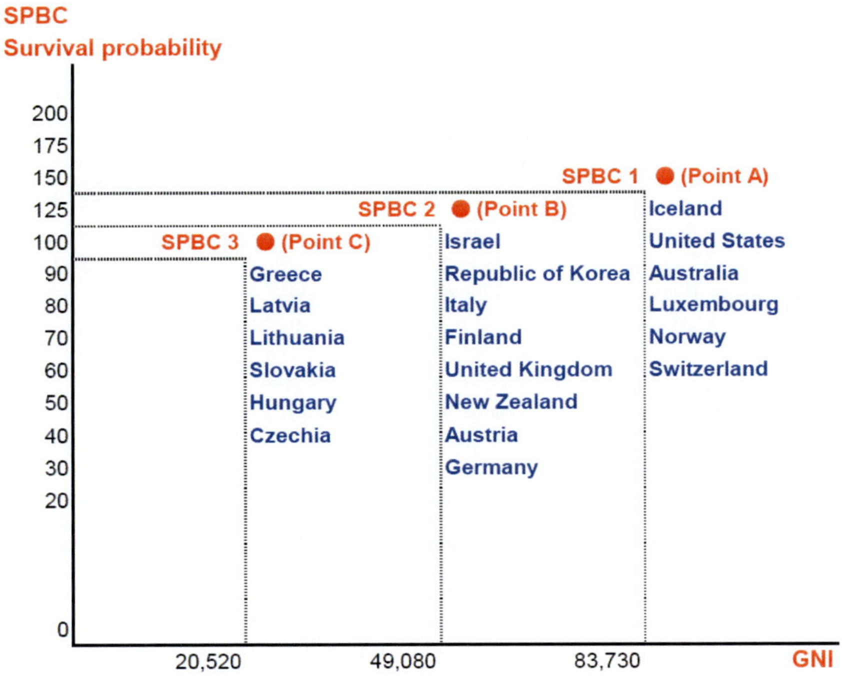

Fig. 2.10.1 SPBC (82) associated with GNI

In addition, this book of 2021 shows the correlation coefficient for SPBC (82) and GNI in 39 countries (r = 0.487). Table 2.2 presents research proving that SPBC (82) is associated with GNI. This means that if it is an increased GNI, SPBC (82) will also increase. Therefore, if the national income level increases, centenarians' probability of survival will increase.

Table 2.2. Correlation coefficient for SPBC (82) and GNI (N = 39)

Variables		Correlations coefficient	p-value
SPBC (82 to 100)	GNI	0.487	0.002

Conversely, the human development index (HDI) can evaluate a country's education level, GNI, and LE. If all three indicators are high, the survival possibility of reaching 100 years of age is very high (Kim, 2013). However, the problem is the level of the country's HDI. If we prioritize these three factors, we will need a strategy that simultaneously raises our income and education levels because countries with higher income and education have higher LE. Therefore, if HDI is high, the survival probability of reaching 100 years of age is very high.

Kim, Jong In. Social factors associated with centenarian rate (CR) in 32 OECD countries. BMC Int Health Hum Rights 13, 16 (2013).

2.2.4 Healthcare expenditure as a percentage of GDP (HEPGDP)

The share of national medical expenditure in the GDP, the proportion of health and medical expenditure among government expenditure, and public medical expenditure are significant factors. This indicates that the countries play an important role in maintaining the healthy lifespan of individuals up to 100 years of age. Therefore, the countries' HEPGDP should be the top priority in maintaining or increasing LE.

Even in a country with a small national budget, if the proportion of healthcare costs is high, then the health of its people can be improved. This indicates that citizens' health can be determined by how much healthcare and medical expenses are spent, rather than the size of the total national budget. In addition, the higher the proportion of investments in healthcare and medical expenses in the national budget, the more advanced the healthcare and medical system. Accordingly, it is possible to increase the LE of the population and maintain a healthy lifespan up to the age of 100.

Conversely, Fig. 2.11 presents SPBC (70) as the survival probability of reaching 100 at 70 in the 32 countries surveyed (Kim & Kim, 2014). In this case, personal living standards, GNI, and HEPGDP significantly affect SPBC (70) (Kim, 2013; Kim & Kim, 2014, 2016). Thus, as confirmed by the author's previous study (Kim & Kim, 2014, 2016), an increase in GNI and HEPGDP can increase both SPBC (70) and SPBC (82). In other words, it considers that HEPGDP and GNI are essential factors for the survival rate at 100 years of age.

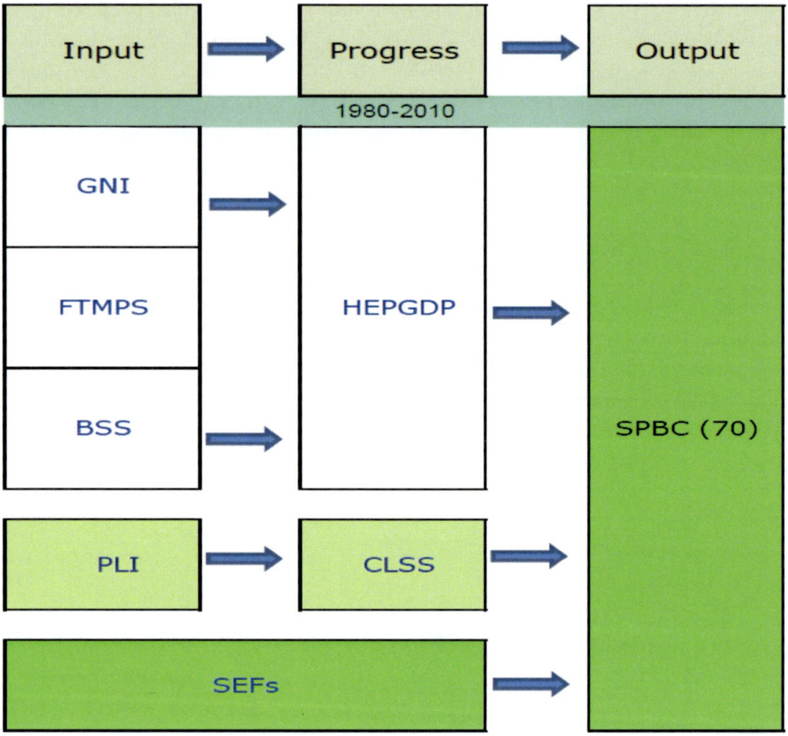

Fig. 2.11. Conceptual framework and SPBC (70)

SPBC (82) confirmed that the countries with the lowest SPBC had higher incidences and morbidity in primary infectious diseases such as TB. It showed that such aspects were closely related to basic sanitation facilities and primary healthcare services. The countries with the lowest SPBC (82) had lower income levels and low HEPGDP. Consequently, the incidences and morbidity of infectious diseases were inevitably high (Theou et al., 2013).

If we look at the history of disease worldwide, malaria is an infectious disease carried by the Astragalus mosquito. This disease infects 200–300 million people and kills millions every year. In this regard, it is important to take anti-malarial medications before traveling to certain areas. As for other examples, common diseases in Burundi, Africa, include malaria, pneumonia, and typhoid fever (Guthmann et al., 2007). In fact, in 2015, roughly 1 out of 10 children in Burundi died before the age of five from preventable and treatable illnesses such as pneumonia and malaria (Kim & Kim, 2019). Interestingly, in 2013, Burundi spent 8% of its GDP on healthcare (W, 2021). Meanwhile, in high-income countries, the prevalence of infectious diseases is low, and LE is high. This indicates that individuals in high-income countries tend to live longer than those in low-income countries (Theou et al., 2013; Kim & Kim, 2014, 2019).

For SPBC (82) and SPBC (70), respectively, the model predictor relationship between HEPGDP and GNI is significantly positive, indicating that such factors contribute to the probability of surviving to 100 years. Developed countries with high national incomes have a much faster rate of medical technology development than less-developed countries. On the other hand, countries with a low national income have a slower rate of medical technology development. Thus, there is a high correlation between the national economic level and the speed of medical development (Kim & Kim, 2014). In addition, the higher the HEPGDP, the higher the national health level. However, developing countries with low-income groups lack the power to invest because the budget is limited. This indicates that only improvements in economic status can increase the health levels of citizens.

In sum, if the national economic level is high, but medical development technology and the proportion of HEPGDP is low, there is insufficient capacity to contribute to the survival probability of reaching 100 years of age. Conversely, when the national income level and the proportion of national medical expenses are high, the probability of reaching the age of 100 is high (Kim & Kim, 2014). Meanwhile, if the intensity of labor increases to increase national income, then the level of health decreases. On the other hand, if the power of labor increases with a balance between the number of leisure and working hours, individuals' health will likely improve. Moreover, if a national political leader increases the share of healthcare and medical expenses in the GDP, the dream of being 100 years of age can be realized (Kim & Kim, 2014).

Based on Fig. 2.12, it appears that when HEPGDP increases, LE is extended from the age of 82 to 92 years. However, an increase in HEPGDP does not increase the probability of survival at 82 years of age. Put precisely, although the survival probability moves from Point A to Point B, it moves horizontally at a constant level of 70%, with no change. Yet, from 82 to 92 years of age, the LE is extended by ten years. This indicates that the LE can be extended by increasing modern medicine and the government's healthcare expenditure.

As stated earlier, if the GDP is high and the healthcare expenditure increases, it will help extend individuals' LE. However, even if the GDP is high, if investment in public healthcare and medical expenses or government spending in the public health sector is low, then the extension of LE cannot be expected. This raises the following question: What would happen if the government has a high GDP, a solid will to invest in the public sector, and significant public healthcare and medical expenditure? It will result in cutting-edge medical technology and development (e.g., robotic surgery, generalization of artificial organs, treatment for infectious diseases, etc.) that will help extend the human lifespan.

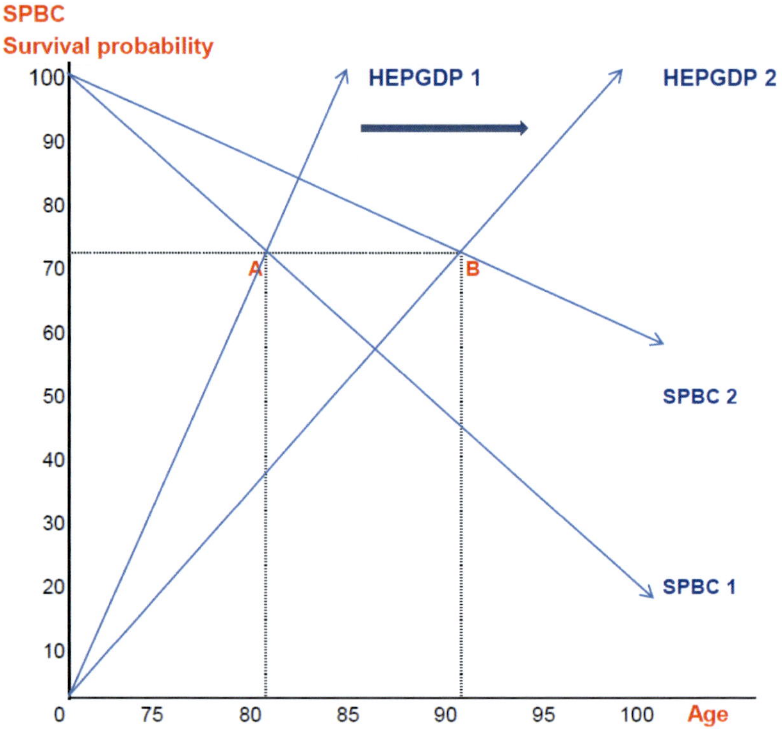

Fig. 2.12. Extension of SPBC and an increase in HEPGDP

Fig. 2.13 shows that by increasing the share of HEPGDP, the LE can be extended from 82 to 92 years old, and when the lifespan of the same age group increases, it can reach 100 years of age. This is also a case in which the survival probability of the patient rises from 70% to 80%. For example, in Japan, the number of 82-year-old women reaching the age of 100 was 237 (per 10,000 people) in 2018 (see Additional File 1). Meanwhile, Japan's HEPGDP was 84%, the second highest among the 39 countries surveyed. Conversely, Ukraine was the country with the lowest HEPGDP, at 48%. Additionally, the number of 82-year-old women in the country reaching the age of 100 was the lowest at 23. In sum, the production of 100-year-olds in Japan is ten times the countries' investment and approximately 1.8 times the expenditure in the public sector.

This comparison is based on the assumption that the conditions of SEFs affecting different lifespans are constant. We must pay attention to the fact that a country's GDP should be increased to raise national productivity and investments in the public health sector.

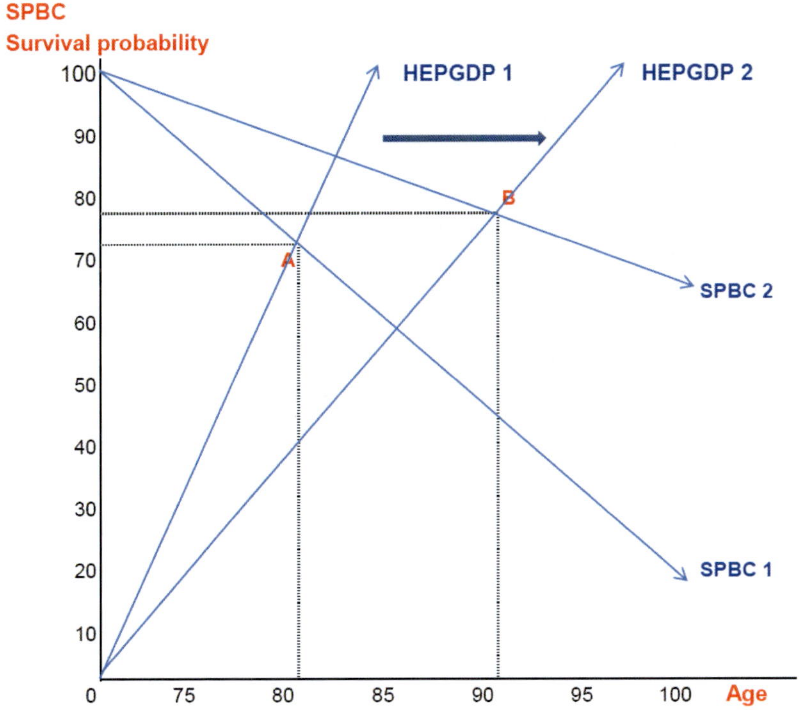

Fig. 2.13. Increase in SPBC and HEPGDP

Fig. 2.14 presents a graph in which SPBC (82) increases as HEPGDP increases. For example, among the 39 countries surveyed, Ukraine has 21 SPBCs (82) per 10,000 people. In comparison, Japan has 185 people, while Iceland has 122. Therefore, the figure's estimated value is SPBC 1 in Ukraine, SPBC 2 in Iceland, and SPBC 3 in Japan.

In this case, the SPBC (82) of the SPBC 1 country, compared to that of the SPBC 2 and SPBC 3 countries, is approximately 5.8 times and 8.8 times lower, respectively. What is the reason for this? As mentioned earlier, the low level of the national economy is preventing the countries from investing in the public health sector.

The national health level of the country should rise, even if it receives a country's loan. However, in countries with a high GDP, the share of public health expenditure may still be below. This indicates the neglect of the health levels of the country's people and highlights a severe health policy error.

Consider the following example. Country A has economic strength and a high GDP. In addition, the political leader of Country A is interested in the health of the citizens. However, if the investment priority in the public health sector is low, then national health will be uncertain.

On the other, the leader of Country B, who lacks the resources of the GDP, has a strong desire to invest in the public health sector and is constantly working to raise financial resources to improve people's health.

In addition, although the GDP is at the country's lowest level, the leader of Country C receives foreign economic aid to improve national health and make bold investments in the public health sector.

Based on these examples, what type of leader would we prefer?

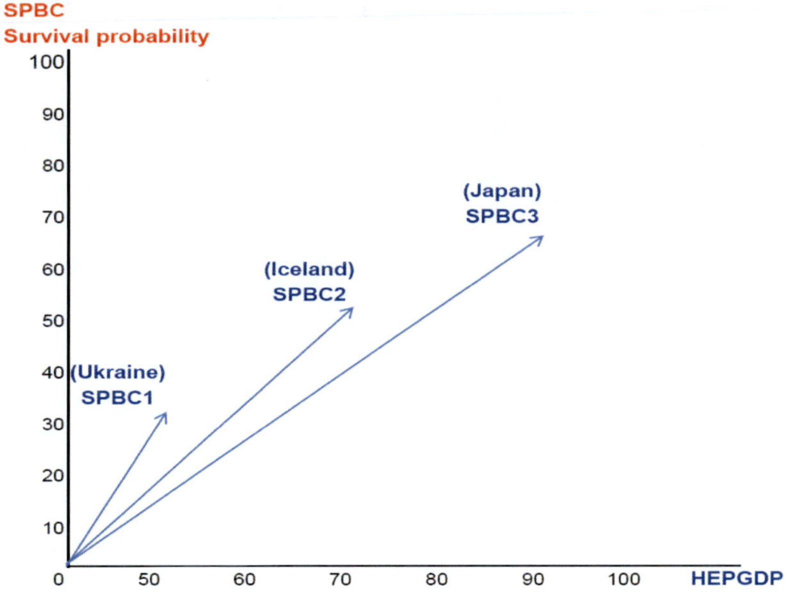

Fig. 2.14. Difference in SPBC (82) and HEPGDP

For reference, in a study published by the author in 2014, SPBC (70) of the subjects of the multiple regression analyses were GNI and HEPGDP in 32 countries (Kim & Kim, 2014). Fig. 2.15.1-2 presents research graphs proving that SPBC (70) increases when GNI and HEPGDP increase.

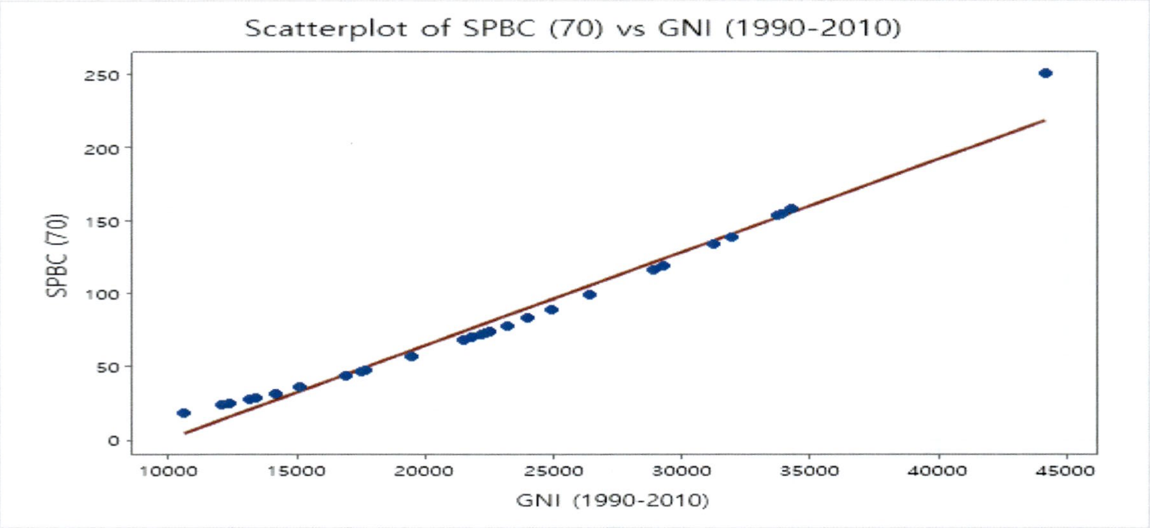

Fig. 2.15.1. SPBC (70) associated with GNI

Jong In Kim & Gukbin Kim. Factors affecting the survival probability of becoming a centenarian for those aged 70, based on the Human Mortality Database: income, health expenditure, telephone, and sanitation. *BMC Geriatrics* 2014; 14:113.

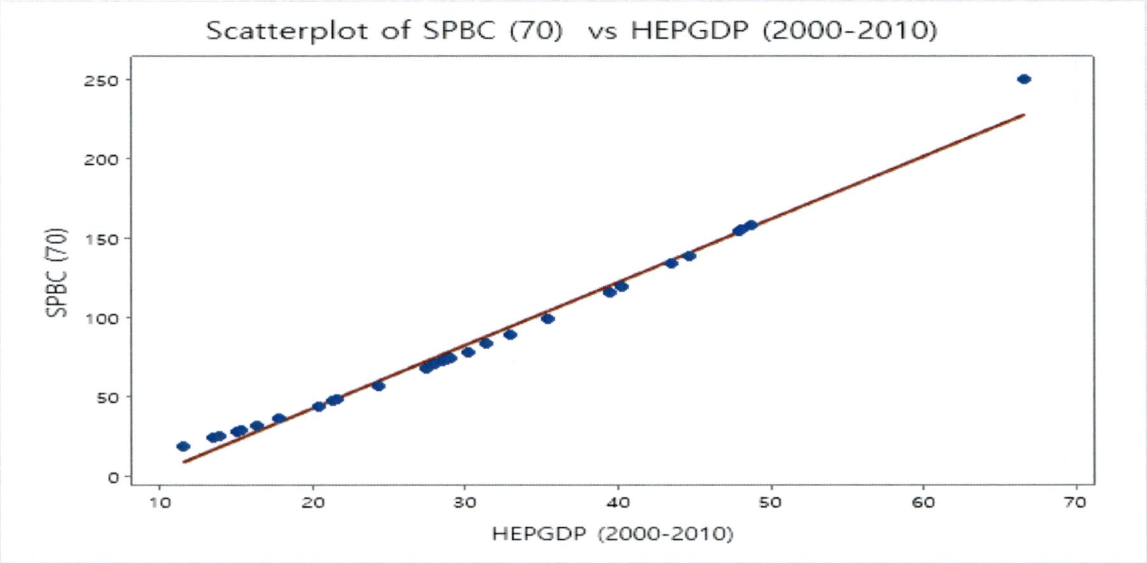

Fig. 2.15.2. SPBC (70) associated with HEPGDP

Jong In Kim & Gukbin Kim. Factors affecting the survival probability of becoming a centenarian for those aged 70, based on the Human Mortality Database: income, health expenditure, telephone, and sanitation. *BMC Geriatrics* 2014; 14:113.

Fig. 2.15.1 shows HEPGDP by country. In a previous study (Kim, 2031, Kim & Kim, 2014), HEPGDP affected SPBC (70) in 32 countries and the centenarian rate (CR, 50-54) in the 32 OECD countries that were surveyed, confirming that the SEFs of HEPGDP are essential in the production of SPBC.

In SPBC (82 to 100) of this book, the current health expenditure as a percentage of GDP, 2018 of United States (16.89), Switzerland (11.88), France (11.26), Japan (10.95), Canada (10.79), Belgium (10.32), Norway (10.05), and United Kingdom (10.00) were from 10 to 16.89. Thus, United States' HEPGDP is the highest among the 39 countries. Moreover, these eight countries correspond to Point A groups (SPBC 1, survival probability 91–185) in Fig. 2.15.1.

Additionally, the HEPGDP of Netherlands (9.97), Portugal (9.41), Australia (9.28), New Zealand (9.21), Republic of Korea (7.56), Israel (7.52), Chile (9.14), Finland (9.04), Spain (8.98), Italy (8.67), Iceland (8.47), Slovenia (8.30), and Greece (7.72) are from 7.52 to 9.97 categories. Therefore, their Point B groups fall under the SPBC 2 (survival probability 86–128) classes.

Lastly, the HEPGDP of Ireland (6.93), Croatia (6.83), Hungary (6.70), Estonia (6.69), Slovakia (6.69), Luxembourg (5.29), Lithuania (6.57), Poland (6.33), Latvia (6.19), Belarus (5.64), and Russian Federation (5.32) are from 5.29 to 6.93 categories. These countries fall under the categories of Point C groups (SPBC 3, survival probability 31–96).

Thus, we confirm that HEPGDP is critical in raising SPBC (82 to 100) from Point C and B to Point A countries.

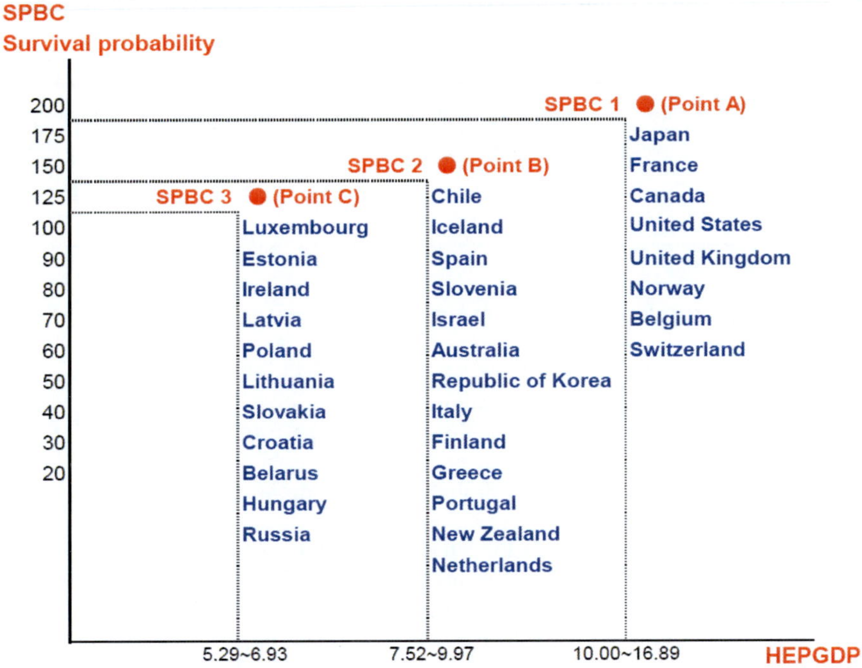

Fig. 2.15.1 SPBC (82) associated with HEGDP

In addition, this book of 2021 shows the correlation coefficient for SPBC (82) and HEPGDP in 39 countries (r = 0.544). Table 2.3 presents research proving that SPBC (82) is associated with HEPGDP. This means that if it is an increased HEPGDP, SPBC (82) will also increase. Therefore, we know if healthcare expenditure in GDP increases, the survival probability of centenarians will increase.

Table 2.3. Correlation coefficient for SPBC (82) and HEPGDP (N = 39)

Variables		Correlations coefficient	p-value
SPBC (82 to 100)	HEPGDP	0.544	0.000

2.2.5 Fixed telephone and mobile phone subscribers (FTMPS)

Does the percentage of telephone subscribers affect the probability that an 82-year-old will live to be 100 years of age? The telephone is important in everyday life and critical in emergencies such as fires, natural disasters, and health issues. Therefore, subscribing to a telephone service is one of the main factors in the survival probability of living to 100 years of age.

Fig. 2.16 presents a graph of the survival probability and LE at 82, based on FTMPS. Thus, the survival probability increases from 60 to 70 years, while the LE extends from 80 to 90 years.

In this case, this is based on the premise that individuals aged 80 and older can use the telephone to communicate with their family members and notify them of any health concerns and emergencies, regardless of whether they live alone or with others. Therefore, the telephone, to some extent, can increase the survival probability of such individuals.

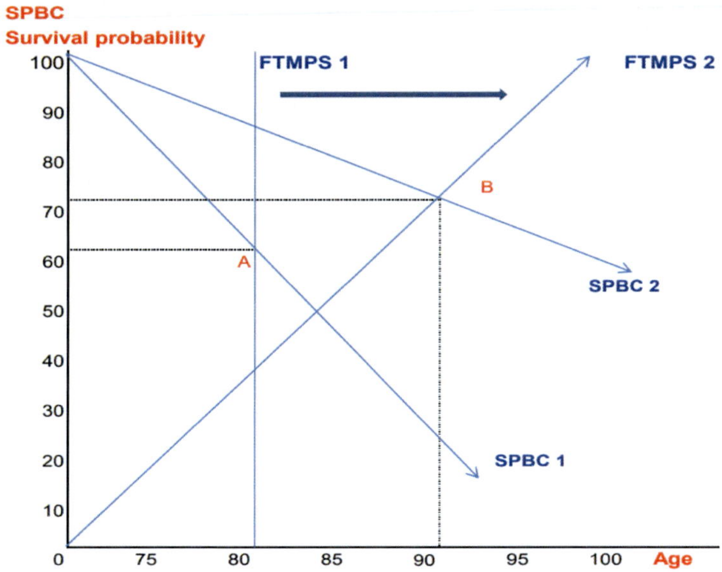

Fig. 2.16. Increase in SPBC and FTMPS

Fig. 2.17 includes a graph on the survival probability and LE from 82 to 100 years due to the development of global technology and the participation of local citizens. In [1] of this figure, the cost of electricity generation technology is as follows.

In the initial stage (Point A) of technological development, the investment cost is low, and the number of telephone subscribers is relatively small.

However, depending on the development method of the telephone technology, the investment cost of the intermediate stage (Point B) gradually increases. In other words, it assumes that only consumers who can purchase expensive mobile phones use such technology.

The final stage (Point C) is when the prices of the mobile phones are lower than those in the intermediate stage by accumulating technology and reducing investment and production costs.

As a result, the number of mobile phone subscribers can increase to Point D, where individuals used one mobile phone per person in their 80s and 90s.

In other words, if a social environment is created in which individuals can purchase mobile phones at a low cost, then the population of those in their 80s and 90s who purchase mobile phones will naturally increase, thus extending their healthy lifespan.

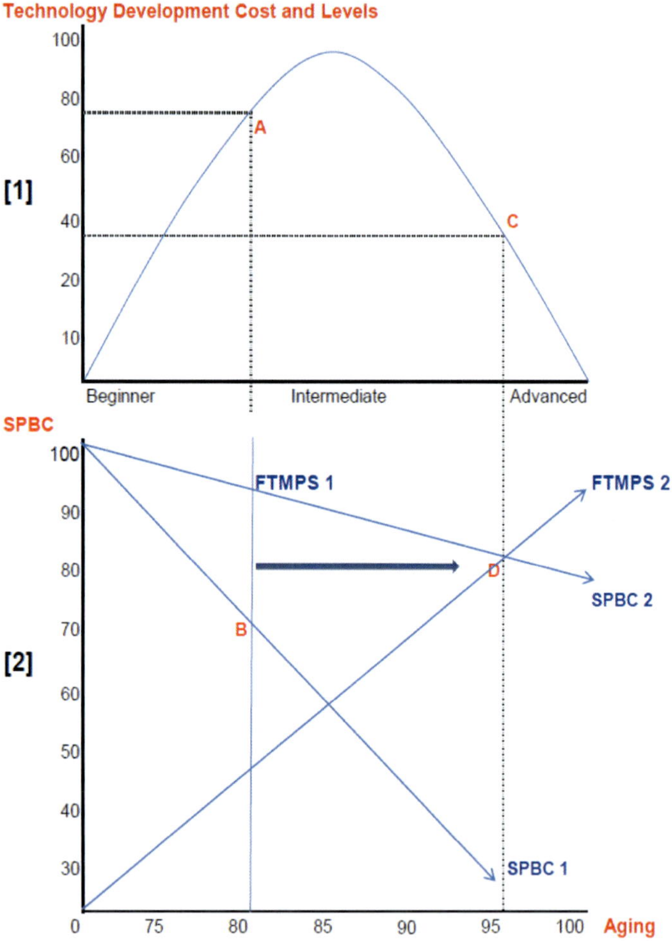

Fig. 2.17. Life extension and development of FTMPS

It is important to note that increasing the telephone subscription and usage rates can improve the quality of life of individuals since they can regularly communicate with neighbors, friends, and family. As a result, such communication can help individuals establish and maintain relationships, which, in turn, can have a positive impact on their mental health. In this regard, the telephone is an SEF that supports the survival probability of living to 100 years of age.

Previous studies have also demonstrated a high correlation between FTMPS and SPBC (70). In developed countries, significant investments in telecommunications have been shown to improve the quality of life of individuals (Kim, 2013).

For instance, various aspects, such as regular telephone counseling and maintaining social relationships with friends and family, can positively impact mental health (Ailshire et al., 2011). In addition, telemedicine services (provided free of charge) can play an essential role in improving the health status of the elderly (Wang, 2011). In sum, FTMPS is a significant independent contributor to SPBC (70) (Kim & Kim, 2014).

In related research, the social factors of FTMPS, which indirectly reflect the standard of living, are related to health by accessing high-quality, health-related information (Kim & Kim, 2014). Furthermore, the increase in FTMPS can lead to an increase in SPBC (70), suggesting that it is an essential contributing factor for healthy aging and the production of 100-year-olds.

In a previous study (Kim & Kim, 2014), Poland's FTMPS score was the lowest among the 32 countries surveyed, while Sweden had the highest score. As FTMPS was the highest significant factor in raising SPBC (70), it was the highest correlation in Table 2.4 (Kim & Kim, 2014).

In Fig. 2.18, FTMPS is also shown to be an essential factor of healthy aging. These results suggest a high correlation between FTMPS and the survival probability of living to 100 years of age (Kim & Kim, 2014).

Table 2.4 Correlation coefficient for SPBC (70) and SEFs (N = 32)

Variable		Correlations coefficient	p-value
SPBC (70 to 100)	FTMPS	0.611	0.0001
	HEPGDP	0.583	0.0001
	GNI	0.555	0.0001
	BSS	0.382	0.0311

Jong In Kim & Gukbin Kim. Factors affecting the survival probability of becoming a centenarian for those aged 70, based on the Human Mortality Database: income, health expenditure, telephone, and sanitation. *BMC Geriatrics* 2014; 14:113.

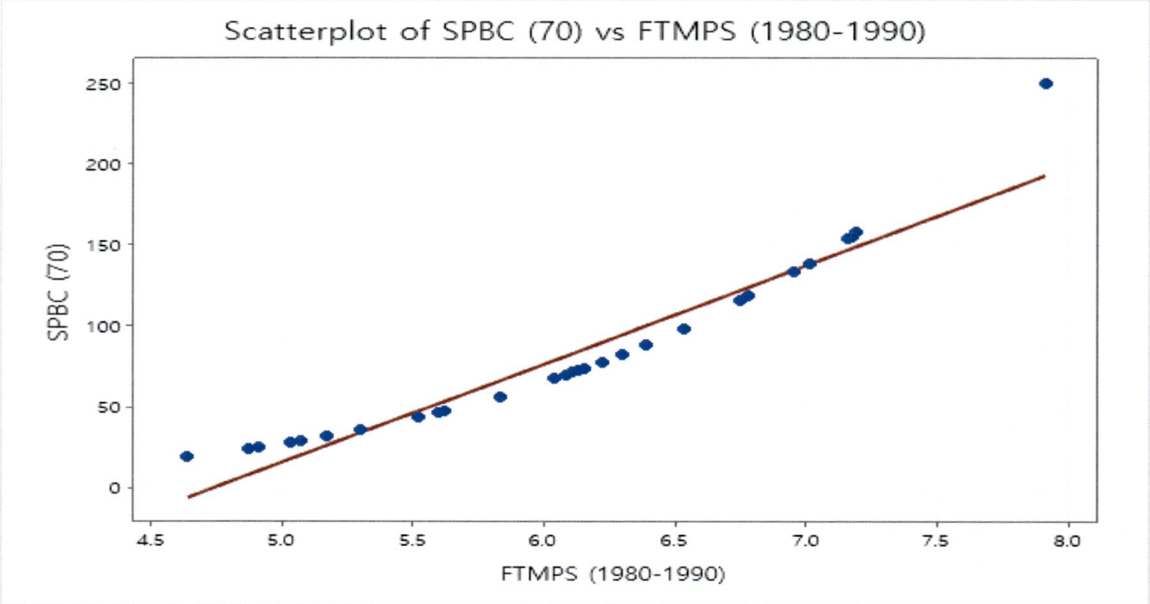

Fig. 2.18. SPBC (70) associated with FTMPS

Jong In Kim & Gukbin Kim. Factors affecting the survival probability of becoming a centenarian for those aged 70, based on the Human Mortality Database: income, health expenditure, telephone, and sanitation. *BMC Geriatrics* 2014; 14:113.

Fig. 2.18.1 shows the FTMPS by country. In a previous study (Kim & Kim, 2014), FTMPS also affected SPBC (70) in 32 countries surveyed. In other words, this confirms that the SEFs of FTMPS are essential in the production of SPBC.

In SPBC (82 to 100) of this book, the FTMPS of France (60), South Korea (53), and Japan (50) are from 50 to 60. Frances' FTMPS is the highest among the 39 countries. These three countries correspond to Point A groups (SPBC 1, survival probability 101–185) in Fig. 2.18.1.

In addition, the FTMPS of Iceland (44), Spain (42), Greece (49), the United Kingdom (48), Luxembourg (47), and Switzerland (42) are from 49 to 42 people. These countries' Point B groups fall under the (SPBC 2, survival probability 91–122) categories.

Conversely, the FTMPS of the Russian Federation (22), Poland (20), Bulgaria (18), Latvia (18), Lithuania (17), Ukraine (17), the Czech Republic (15), and the Slovak Republic (14) were under 22. The Slovak Republic had the lowest FTMPS. These countries fall under the Point C groups (SPBC 3, survival probability 21–62) categories.

Thus, we confirm that FTMPS is critical in raising SPBC (82 to100) from Point C and B to Point A countries.

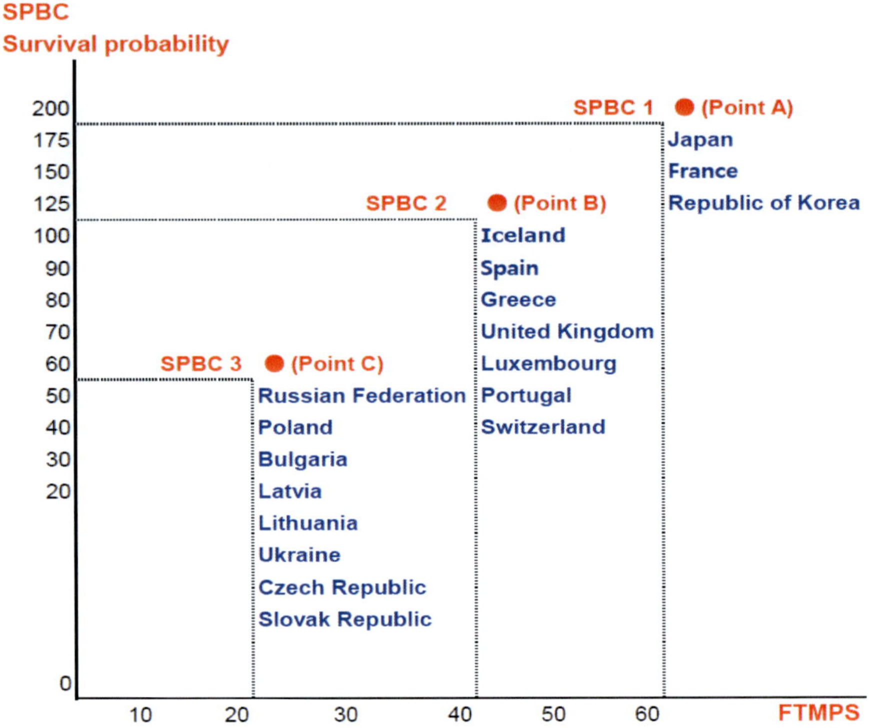

Fig. 2.18.1 SPBC (82) associated with FTMPS

In addition, this book of 2021 shows the correlation coefficient for SPBC (82) and FTMPS in 39 countries (r = 0.493). Table 2.5 presents research proving that SPBC (82) is associated with FTMPS. This means that if FTMPS is increased, SPBC (82) will also increase. Therefore, we know if the telephone and mobile phone increase, the survival probability of centenarians will increase.

Table 2.5. Correlation coefficient for SPBC (82) and FTMPS (N = 39)

Variables		Correlations coefficient	p-value
SPBC (82 to 100)	FTMPS	0.493	0.001

2.2.6 Basic sanitation services (BSS)

Environmental pollution (e.g., air/water pollution) is another risk factor for a healthy lifespan. For example, water-borne infectious diseases can occur due to the community's lack of BSS. In addition, hazardous minerals or tap water can cause various diseases. Thus, the community must have an adequate water supply facility to provide safe drinking water to the public.

The adverse effects derived from the concentration of population in large cities and the harmful environmental pollutants emitted from factories (due to large-scale industrialization) are becoming health risks. If these aspects are not controlled or updated, reaching 100 years of age will be extremely difficult. Hence, national political leaders should prioritize their country's hygiene issues.

Fig. 2.19 presents the two types of leadership according to the hygiene situation, which are as follows:

(A) Public sanitation-oriented leadership (PSL): Focus on environmental hygiene, such as water and sewage, implemented by the national and local communities.

(B) Personal hygiene-oriented leadership (PHL): Focus on food and mental hygiene.

First, in Fig. 2.19, the country's economic level is divided into developed, developing, and underdeveloped. If it is a developed country, then "Good" is selected, whereas if it is a developing or underdeveloped country, then "Bad" is selected.

Second, "High" is selected if CLSS is sufficient, whereas "Low" is selected if it is insufficient.

Third, "Strong" is selected if PLI is sufficient, whereas "Weak" is selected if PLI is insufficient. Specifically, it is "Bad" if the national economic level is an underdeveloped country, "Low" if CLSS is insufficient, and "Weak" if PLI is insufficient.

Hence, the leadership style for this situation should be PSL. Conversely, if the economic situation is bad and CLSS and PLI are not high (strong) or low (weak), the leadership style should be PHL. This is because the economic background conditions are insufficient.

Country economic level	Good				Bad			
CLSS	High		Low		High		Low	
PLI	Strong	Weak	Strong	Weak	Strong	Weak	Strong	Weak
Hygiene leadership types	PSL	PSL	PSL	PHL	PHL	PHL	PHL	PSL

CLSS: Country-local society support
PLI: Personal life improvement
PSL: Public sanitation-oriented leadership
PHL: Personal hygiene-oriented leadership

Fig. 2.19. Hygiene-oriented leadership types associated with BSS

Fig. 2.20 shows the survival probability and LE of individuals 60 to 100 years of age in regard to community and individual sanitation facilities. As a result, the survival probability increases from 70 to 80 years, while the healthy lifespan extends from 60 to 80 years. This is based on the premise that inadequate environmental sanitation facilities can shorten the human lifespan.

In particular, installing water and sewage facilities and improving toilets in the local community can directly/indirectly affect the health level of the community and individuals. In large cities, especially in developed countries, sanitation management mainly consists of building sanitation, quarantine, and cleaning agencies.

However, with an LE of 63 years in Uganda, the government has implemented community-led clean hygiene management due to the severe lack of sanitation facilities. Without improvements in such facilities and personal hygiene management, the dream of reaching 100 years of age cannot be achieved. Conversely, if it effectively implements a comprehensive sanitation program focusing on personal hygiene management, the country's LE can increase to 80 years or more.

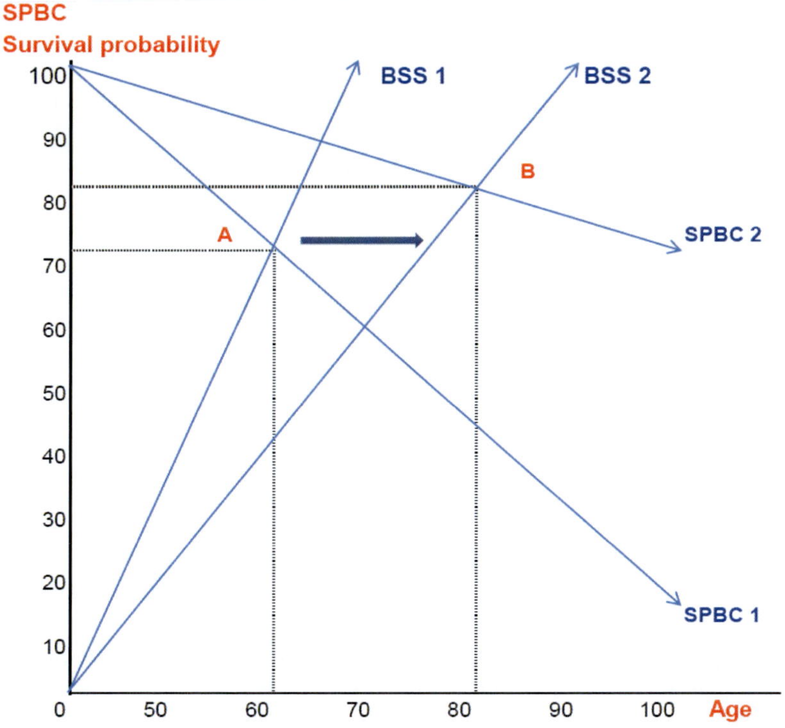

Fig. 2.20. Increase in SPBC and BSS

Fig. 2.21 shows the BSS by country. In a previous study (Kim & Kim, 2014), BSS also affected SPBC (70) in the 32 countries surveyed. In other words, this confirms that the social factors of BSS are essential in the production of 100-year-olds. Additionally, Russia's BSS (76%) was the lowest among the 32 countries (Kim & Kim, 2014). This corresponds to SPBC 1, and Latvia (82%) is SPBC 2 in Fig. 2.21. Conversely, Japan, Canada, Switzerland, and the United Kingdom (100%) had the highest BSS. These countries fall under the SPBC 3 categories. This confirms that BSS is a critical factor in raising SPBC (70) in SPBC 2 and SPBC 3 countries.

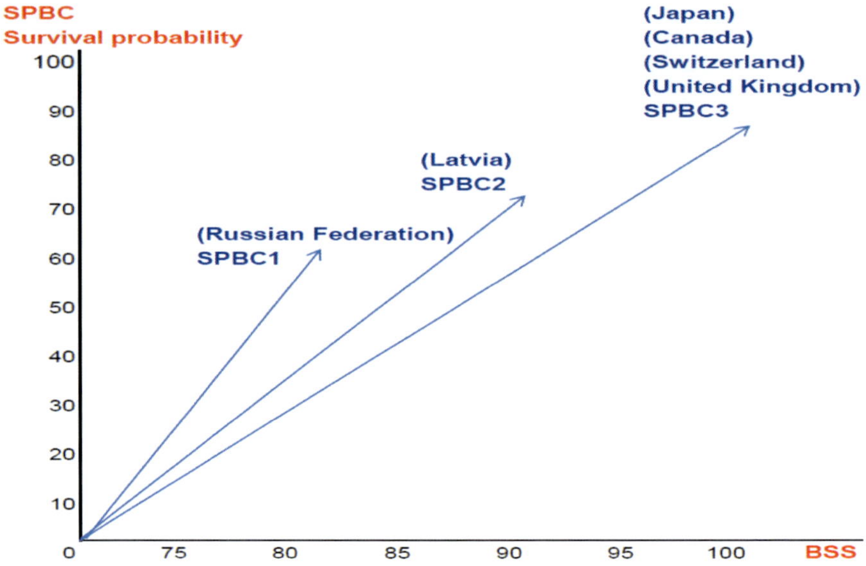

Fig. 2.21. Difference in SPBC (70) and BSS

Mortality due to BSS is also a well-known public health and sanitation issue. For instance, the incidence index of typhus in Russia is attributed to poor sanitation and is considered a health indicator for general sanitation conditions. If this indicator is ignored, the consequences can be catastrophic (Tarasevich et al., 1998). In other words, Russia, a SPBC 1 country, has the lowest BSS for the probability of survival until the age of 100. This reflects the lack of government investment in health and sanitation infrastructure.

In a previous study (Kim & Kim, 2014), BSS indirectly affected the probability of survival to 100 years of age. Thus, the higher the BSS among 100-year-olds, the greater the health promotion as a preventive measure against infectious diseases and sanitation (Tumwebaze et al., 2013; Kim & Kim, 2014). At the same time, if the BSS is adequate, it can help maintain the environmental hygiene necessary to survive at age 70 and live to 100. In Fig. 2.22, the correlation between the predictor variables of SPBC (70) and BSS is positive, independent of the survival probability of becoming 100 years old (Kim & Kim, 2014). This confirms that it is a contributing factor.

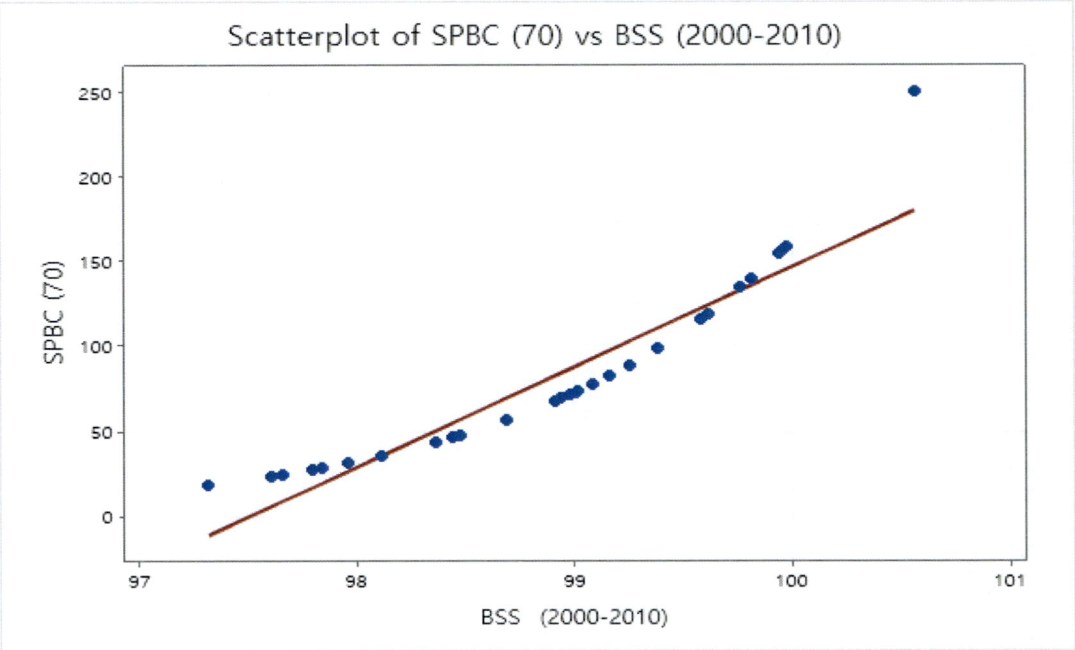

Fig. 2.22. SPBC (70) associated with BSS

Jong In Kim & Gukbin Kim. Factors affecting the survival probability of becoming a centenarian for those aged 70, based on the Human Mortality Database: income, health expenditure, telephone, and sanitation. *BMC Geriatrics* 2014; 14:113.

Fig. 2.22.1 shows BSS by country. In a previous study (Kim & Kim, 2014), BSS also affected SPBC (70) in 32 countries surveyed. In other words, this confirms that the SEFs of BSS are essential in the production of SPBC.

In SPBC (82 to 100) of this book, the BSS (2016) of Japan, Chile, Spain, the United States, Israel, Australia, and the Republic of Korea were 100%. These countries' BSS is the highest among the 39 countries. These seven countries correspond to Point A groups (SPBC 1, survival probability 101–185) in Fig. 2.22.1.

In addition, the BSS of France, Canada, Iceland, Slovenia, Italy, the United Kingdom, and Greece are 99%. These countries' Point B groups fall under the SPBC 2 (survival probability 91–158) categories.

Lastly, the BSS of Luxembourg, Norway, Netherlands, Poland, Slovakia, Belarus, and Hungary are 98%. These countries fall under the categories of Point C groups (SPBC 3, survival probability 45–96).

Thus, we confirm that BSS is critical in raising SPBC (82) from SPBC 1 (Point A) to SPBC 2 (Point B) countries.

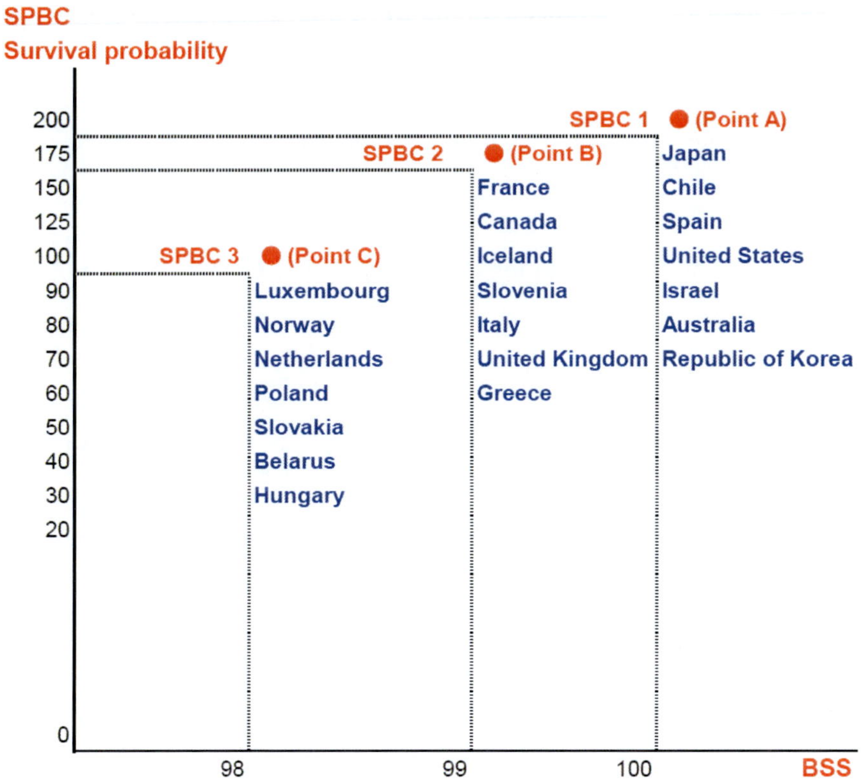

Fig. 2.22.1 SPBC (82) associated with BSS

In addition, this book of 2021 shows the correlation coefficient for SPBC (82) and BSS in 39 countries (r = 0.554). Table 2.6 presents research proving that SPBC (82) is associated with BSS. This means that if BSS is increased, SPBC (82) will also increase. Therefore, we can establish that an increase in sanitation equipment can increase the survival probability of centenarians.

Table 2.6. Correlation coefficient for SPBC (82) and BSS (N = 39)

Variables		Correlations coefficient	p-value
SPBC (82 to 100)	BSS	0.554	0.000

2.2.7 Gender inequality index (GII)

The concept of gender equality requires that men and women equally enjoy socially valuable goods, opportunities, and rewards. Fig. 2.23 shows that the rights for gender equality are equally distributed.

Specifically, the male-dominant authority (MDA) is Point A, which decreases to the right and increases to the left. In other words, the MDA is a social structure in which males have the most significant authority, compared to females. Due to gender inequality, the female survival probability (FSP) is 80%.

In addition, the female-dominant authority (FDA) is Point B, which increases from the left to right. In other words, the FDA is a social structure in which females have the most significant authority, compared to males. Due to gender inequality, the male survival probability (MSP) is also 80%.

Finally, Point C is a social structure that equally distributes male and female rights. Moreover, the gender equality index point is where opportunities and rewards for males and females are equal. In this case, the MSP and FSP are 95%, respectively.

In other words, the probability of survival is higher in a gender-equal society than in a gender-unequal society. It is important to note that since the advancement of gender equality is highly related to the human lifespan, a gender-equal society must be established to extend the survival probability of reaching 100 years of age.

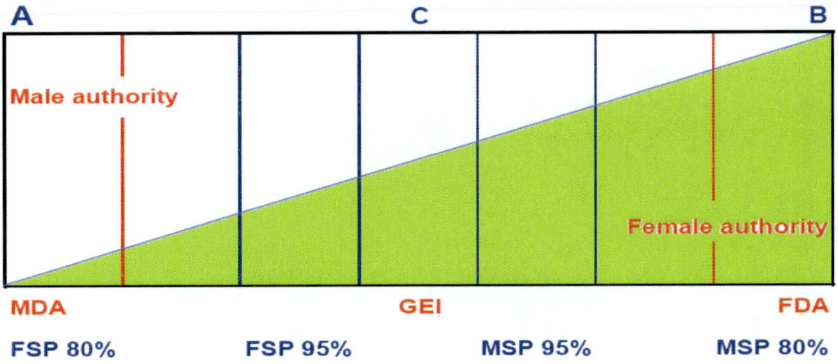

MDA: Male dominant authority

FDA: Female dominant authority

GEI: Gender equality index

MSP: Male survival probability

FSP: Female survival probability

Fig. 2.23. Male and female authority and equality

Fig.2.24 presents the GII and its association with SPBC. For example, if the GII decreases from 0.15 to 0.09, it moves from GII 1 to GII 2.

Meanwhile, the point where the 0.15 vertical curve of GII 1 meets SPBC 1 is the 100-year-old survival probability. Here, the survival probability of Point A is 20%.

Additionally, the 0.09 vertical curve of GII 2 moves from GII 1 and has a 60% chance of survival as the point of contact with SPBC 1 (Point C). In other words, it is the result of increasing the survival probability to 40% by easing the country's gender discrimination index.

For instance, if males and females possess all rights equally, then there will be a decrease in gender discrimination by moving upwards from Point A to Point C. However, if males exclusively own all rights, then there will be an increase in gender discrimination by moving downwards from Point C to Point A.

In conclusion, this means gender equality can improve humanity's chances of survival probability. Humanity is evolving to the point where the rights of males and females are equal and balanced. Therefore, we must be a gender-equal society with a high probability of surviving to 100 years of age.

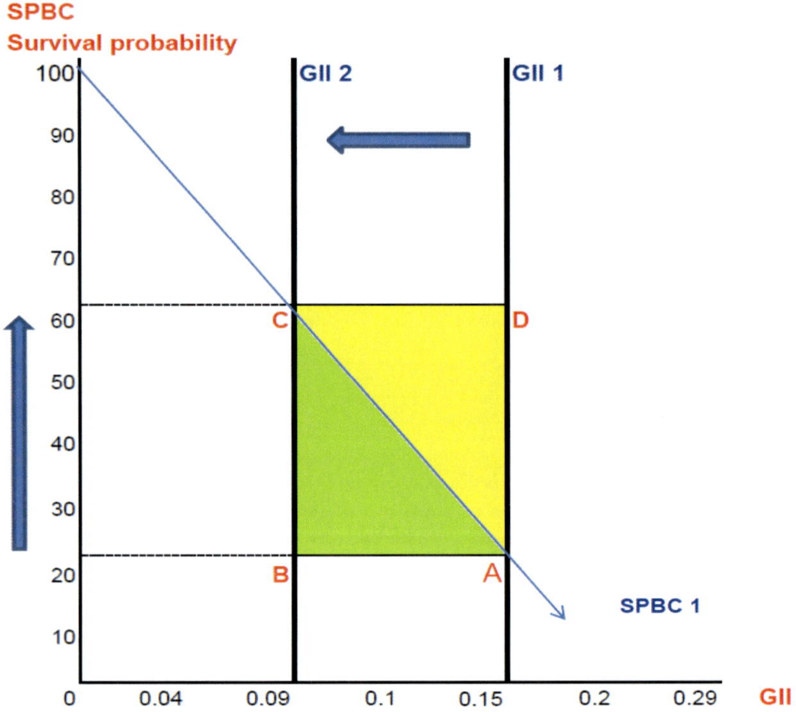

Fig. 2.24. SPBC associated with GII

Fig. 2.24.1 shows GII by country. In a previous study (Kim & Kim, 2017), GII also affected SPBC (65–69) in the 34 European countries surveyed. In other words, this confirms that the SEFs of GII are essential in the survival of individuals to 100 years old.

In SPBC (82 to 100) of this book, the GII (2018) of Switzerland (0.037), Norway (0.044), Belgium (0.045), Finland (0.050), France (0.051), Iceland (0.057), Rep. of Korea (0.058), Slovenia (0.069), and Italy (0.069) were from 0.037 to 0.069. Switzerland's GII is the highest among the 39 countries. These seven countries correspond to Point A groups (SPBC 1, survival probability 91–153) in Fig. 2.24.1.

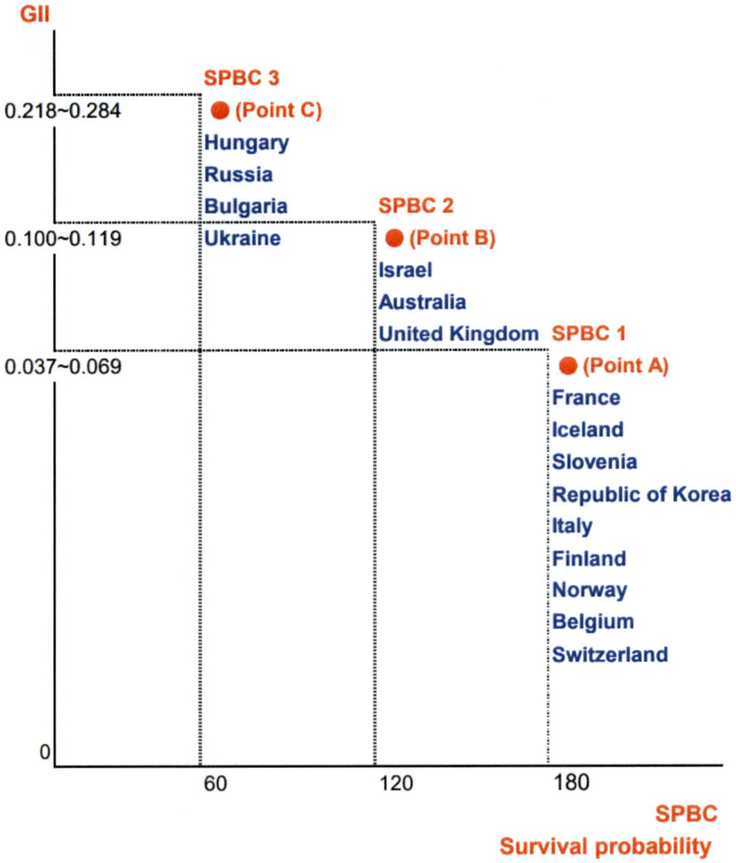

Fig. 2.24.1 SPBC (82) associated with GII

Additionally, the GII of Israel (0.100), Australia (0.103), and the United Kingdom (0.119) are from 0.100 to 0.119. Therefore, their Point B groups fall under the SPBC 2 (survival probability 97–108) categories.

Lastly, the GII of Bulgaria (approximately 0.218), Russian Federation (0.255), Hungary (0.258), and Ukraine (0.284) are from 0.218 to 0.284. These countries fall under the categories of Point C groups (SPBC 3, survival probability 21–45).

Thus, we confirm that GII is critical in raising SPBC (82 to 100) from Point C and B to Point A countries.

Fig. 2.25 shows the SPBC (82) associated with GII. As described earlier, gender discrimination is a significant global factor influencing the probability of survival from 82 to 100 years of age because the lower the gender discrimination, the higher the survival probability at 82 to 100 years of age (Table 2.3).

Furthermore, in this regard, if there is gender discrimination in the national social structure, then women may suffer from mental stress, thus affecting their healthy lifespan. Specifically, such stress can result in depression and anxiety, which can have a negative impact on the quality of life and the survival probability of reaching 100 years of age. However, if the social environment is gender-equal, then the situation is different. In this case, recognizing women as social leaders indicates an advanced society that most likely also includes a well-equipped healthcare system. Such a system can improve women's health and quality of life, thus increasing their LE to 100 years of age.

In addition, although economic activities have traditionally centered on men, if women want to participate, such activities should be based on gender equality. With women's gender equality, their participation in economic activities can increase household income.

As for labor participation, if a regular source of household income is created, then a healthy lifestyle can occur. However, if such participation is complex, and there is a lack of regular income, this can impair mental/physical health and lead to irregular lifestyles. Additionally, since equal participation in labor or economic activities between men and women is directly related to income, active encouragement is required.

Thus, with lower GII as SEFs, the economic activity of women increases, which directly leads to higher household income. In the absence of gender discrimination, increases in women's social advancement and the equal participation of men and women in labor can lead to a rise in income. Meanwhile, an increase in revenue would naturally lead to an interest in healthcare, which will increase the probability of reaching the age of 100 through health promotion (Fig. 2.25).

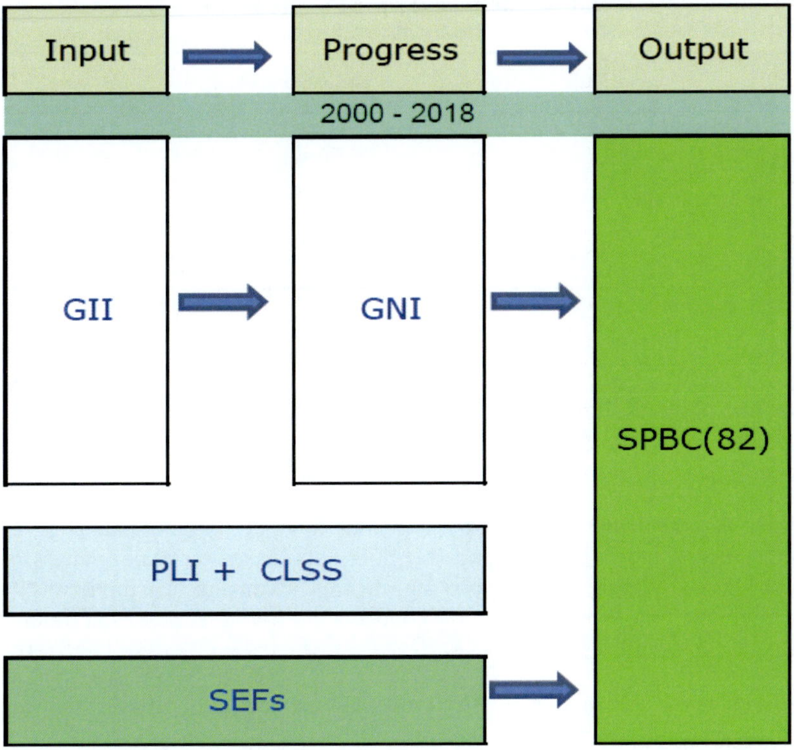

Fig.2.25. SPBC associated with GII

In contrast, the author's previous study on European countries (Kim & Kim, 2017) along with this book of worldwide countries reveals that individuals who do not face gender discrimination have a greater chance of surviving till the age of 100 (Table 2.3).

Table 2.3 presents an assessment of SPBC (82). GII and GNI have a relationship of more than 47% in the SEFs; thus, they are significant factors in SPBC (82). Thus, at least for humanity's survival probability, if one wants to become a centenarian at 82, it is essential to curtail significant factors, such as gender inequality in society. Therefore, we must observe these two factors that have a decisive influence on humanity's fundamental survival probability.

Table 2.7. Correlation coefficient for SPBC (82) and GII (N = 39)

Variables		Correlations coefficient	p-value
SPBC (82 to 100)	GII	-0.471	0.003
	GNI	0.487	0.002

2.2.8 Urban population (UP)

At this point, the following question is raised: What are the pros and cons of living in a large city? Based on Fig. 2.26, the next discusses them in detail.

First, the most fundamental aspects include food, clothing, and housing. In this regard, the location and facilities of one's residence must be considered. Perhaps the most significant advantage of modern city dwellers is the convenience of comfortable living spaces and related facilities.

The second advantage is proximity to government offices, medical facilities, and schools.

The third advantage is market access for groceries and daily necessities. If the purchase needs for these necessities are satisfied, then the next step is residential safety. In this regard, it would be advantageous to live in a large city with a pleasant residential environment free from fire risk, theft, and air pollution.

If individuals live in these urban environments, then it is assumed that it would increase LE. However, if an emergency occurs and it takes more than 60 minutes to reach the general hospital, it is not necessarily beneficial. For example, some emergencies, such as cerebral hemorrhage, must be treated within 30 minutes. In this regard, the populations in large cities are more likely to receive regular and emergency healthcare than those living in rural areas.

Conversely, living in a large city includes some disadvantages. First, since the population is dense and concentrated, there is a higher chance of accidents, fires, theft, and environmental pollution. However, as described earlier, the advantages outweigh the risks, especially regarding the survival probability of living to 100 years of age.

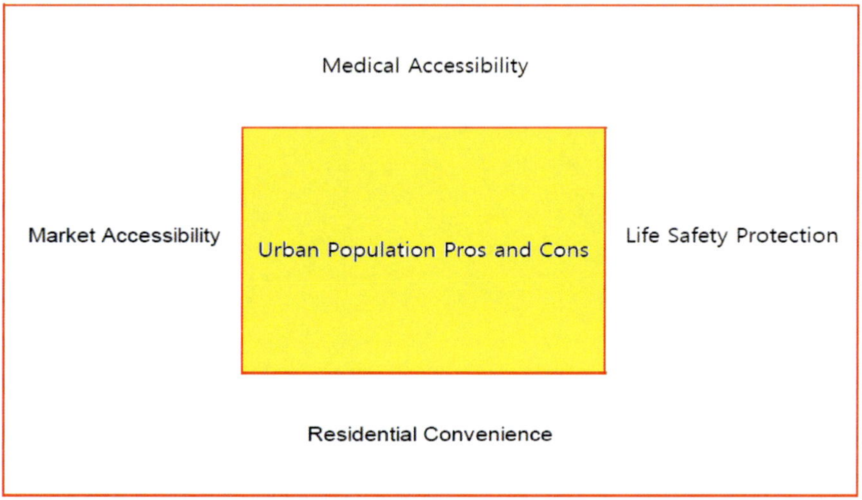

Fig. 2.26. Urban population (UP) pros and cons

Fig. 2.27 shows that when the proportion of the UP in large cities increases from UP1 to UP2, it extends the lifespan from 82 to 92 years. At the same time, SPBC increases from 60% to 70%. This indicates that an increase in UP will prolong the lifespan of the national population and incrementally affect the survival probability. Examples are as follows. In Iceland, the proportion of 82-year-old women reaching 100 years of age in 2018 was 123 (per 10,000 people; see Additional File 1).

Meanwhile, Iceland's UP was 94%, the second-highest among the 39 countries surveyed. However, in Slovakia, the UP was the lowest at 54%, with the number of 82-year-old women reaching 100 years was 62.

In this case, Iceland's production of 100-year-olds was approximately 1.7 times the urbanization rate of the population. This is under the assumption that the SEFs affecting numerous lifespans are constant. Thus, the country's UP should be increased as much as possible.

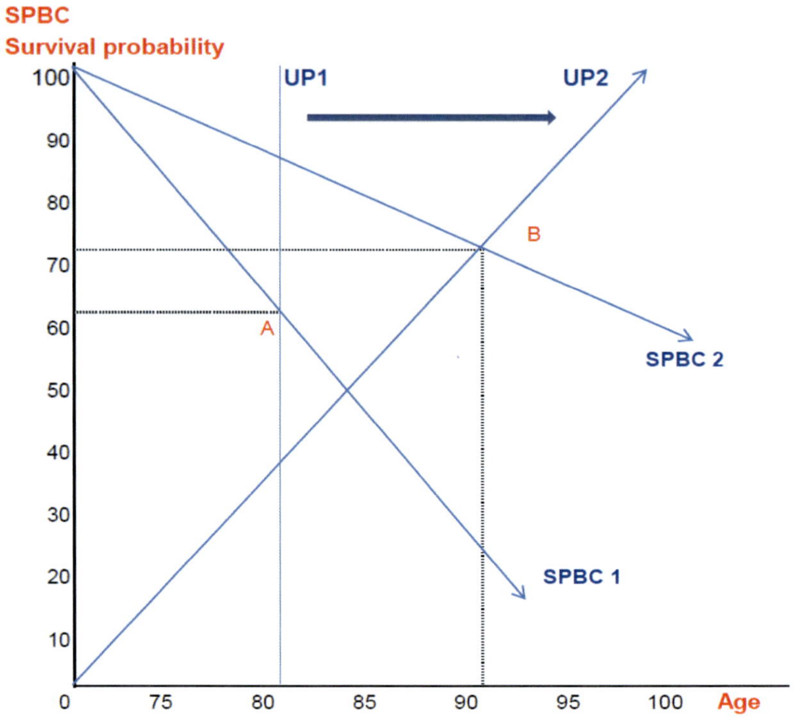

Fig. 2.27. Increase in SPBC and UP

Fig. 2.27.1 shows UP by country. In a previous study (Kim & Kim, 2016), GII also affected SPBC (65–69) in the country surveyed, that is, South Korea. In other words, this confirms that the SEFs of UP are essential to the survival of individuals to 100 years old.

In SPBC (82 to 100) of this book, the UP (2018) of Belgium (98), Iceland (94), Israel (93), Japan (92), and Luxembourg (91) were from 91 to 98. Belgium's UP is the highest among the 39 countries. These five countries correspond to Point A groups (SPBC 1, survival probability 93–185) in Fig. 2.27.1.

Additionally, the UP of Denmark (88), Sweden (88), Chile (88), New Zealand (87), Australia (86), Finland (85), United Kingdom (84), Norway (83), the United States (82), Canada (81), Republic of Korea (81), France

(81), and Spain (81) are from 81 to 88. Therefore, these countries' Point B groups fall under the SPBC 2 (survival probability 87–153) categories.

Lastly, the UP of Switzerland (74), Hungary (72), Russia (75), the Czechia (74), Germany (77), and Bulgaria (75) are from 72 to 77. These countries fall under the Point C groups (SPBC 3, survival probability 30–91) categories.

Thus, we confirm that UP is critical in raising SPBC (82 to 100) from Point C and B to Point A countries.

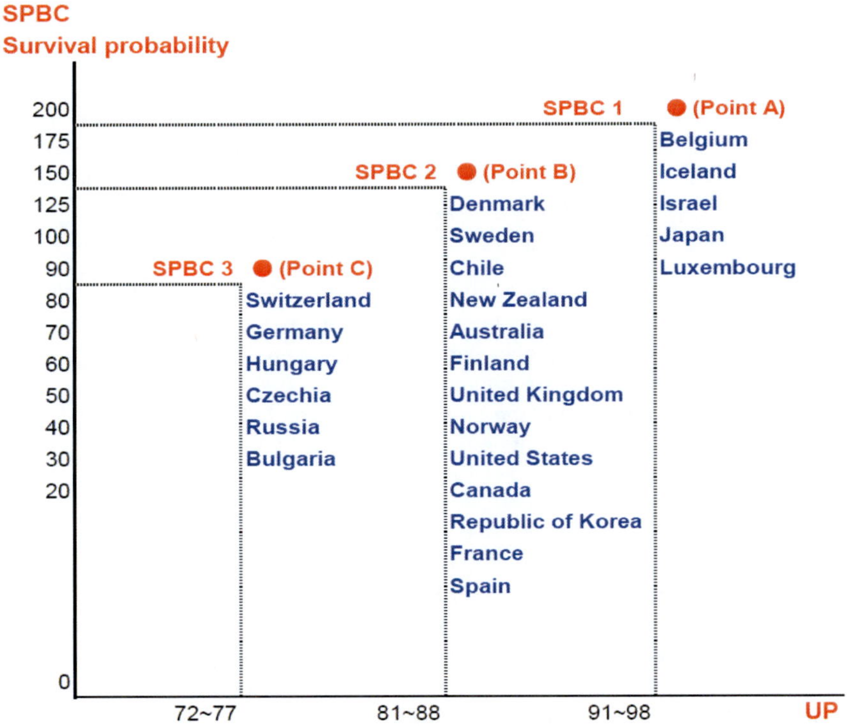

Fig. 2.27.1 SPBC (82) associated with UP

In addition, this book shows the correlation coefficient for SPBC (82) and UP in 39 countries as of 2021 (r = 0.481). Table 2.8 presents research proving that SPBC (82) is associated with UP. This means that if it is an increased UP, SPBC (82) also increases. Therefore, if the UP increases, the survival probability of centenarians will increase.

Table 2.8. Correlation coefficient for SPBC (82) and UP (N= 39)

Variables		Correlations coefficient	p-value
SPBC (82 to 100)	UP	0.481	0.002

2.2.9 Individuals using the Internet (IUI)

In today's society, the majority of individuals spend a significant amount of time on the Internet. In this regard, if such individuals are interested in obtaining medical information for health promotion, then it is possible that their health levels can increase. As a case study, it appears that the correlation between the IUI and the SPBC (82) in the 39 countries described earlier is very high ($r = 0.535$, $p = 0.001$).

This indicates that reliable health-related information has been collected and utilized for health promotion. We can use such data in various ways, such as answering questions about disease symptoms before visiting a doctor and resolving fears about specific illnesses. In other words, the collection of such information on the Internet can help promote the health of individuals and communities.

Fig. 2.28 presents a flow chart of the health practices and changes through IUI. The first step is determining whether there is a compelling reason or motivation to use the Internet. The second step is to check the medical information on the Internet before visiting a medical institution or doctor. The final step is to bring about changes in health behaviors by visiting doctors, thereby achieving the best health management. In this regard, if we prevent diseases in advance and practice effective health management, it is possible to achieve HLE. Moreover, IUI is SEFs that increase SPBC (82).

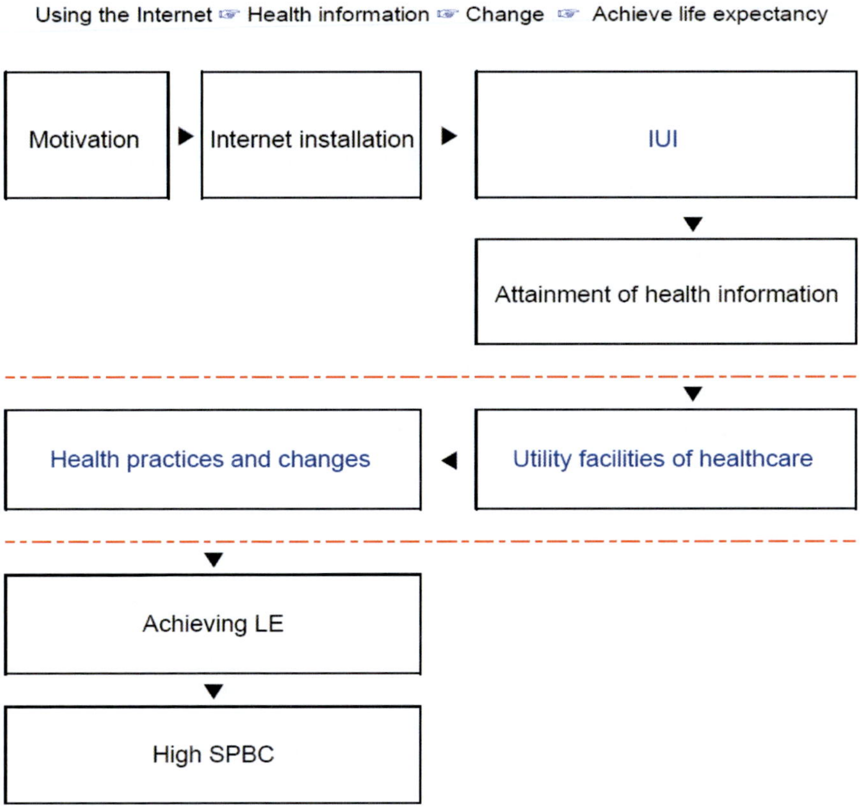

Fig. 2.28. Health practices and changes through IUI

Fig. 2.29 shows that when IUI increases from IUI 1 to IUI 2, the lifespan extends from 82 to 92 years of age. In the case in which the SPBC simultaneously increases from 70% to 80%, this indicates that if the proportion of IUI increases, the LE of the entire national population will increase. Examples are as follows. In South Korea, the proportion of 82-year-old women reaching 100 years of age in 2017 was 121 (per 10,000 people; see Additional File 1).

Meanwhile, the IUI in South Korea was 95%, the fifth-highest among the 39 countries surveyed. However, Bulgaria had the third-lowest IUI, at 63%. In addition, the country had the second-lowest number of 82-year-old women reaching 100 years of age, with 35.

In this case, the production of 100-year-olds in South Korea is approximately 1.5 times that of the IUI population. This is based on the premise that all social and ecological requirements affecting human lifespan are constant. Hence, the country's IUI ratio should be increased.

In a national society lacking informatization, information, and communication policies that allow citizens to access necessary medical information on the Internet should take precedence. In addition, it is important to prepare policies that can regulate false health- and medical-related information on the Internet. Since such information is directly related to human lifespan, accessing reliable and high-quality medical information is the primary key.

Furthermore, suppose that health and medical information is equally shared by humanity in the future and recognized as a major SEF for promoting human health and prolonging LE. In this case, the SPBC is very high.

Fig. 2.29.1 shows IUI by country. A previous study (Kim & Kim, 2016) studied how IUI affected healthy LE in the 178 surveyed countries. Thus, confirming that the SEFs of IUI may be essential to the production of SPBC.

In SPBC (82 to 100) of this book, the IUI (% of population, 2017) of Iceland (98), Luxembourg (97), Norway (96), Republic of Korea (95), Canada (93), Japan (92), and the United Kingdom (90) were from 92 to 98. Iceland's IUI is the highest among the 39 countries. These seven countries correspond to Point A groups (SPBC 1, survival probability 94–185) in Fig. 2.29.1.

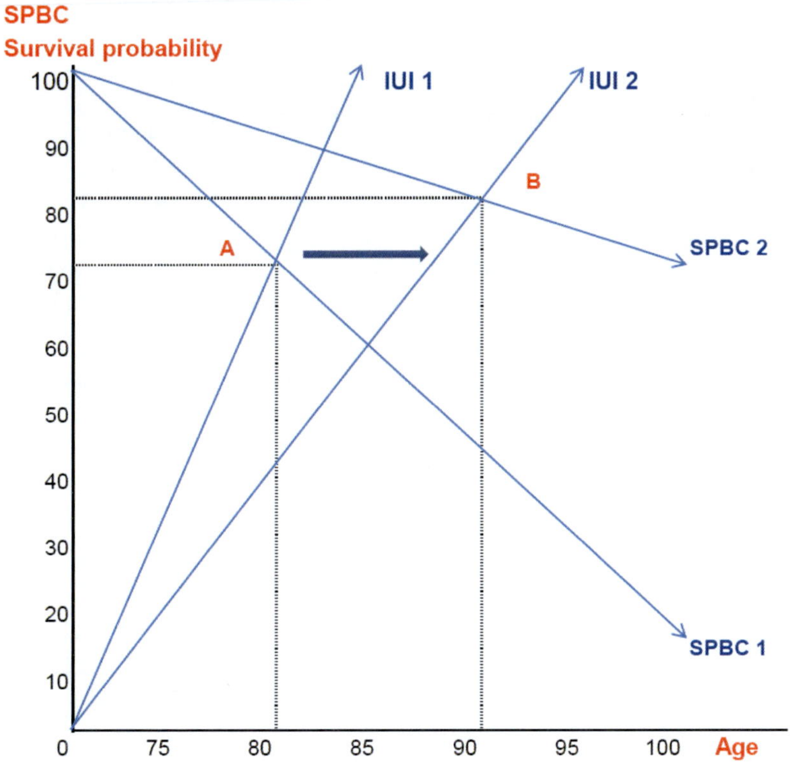

Fig. 2.29. Increase in SPBC and IUI

Further, the UP of France (81), Chile (82), Spain (85), United States (87), Israel (82), Australia (87), and Belgium (88) are from 81 to 88. Therefore, their Point B groups fall under the SPBC 2 (survival probability 93–153) categories.

Lastly, the IUI of Slovenia (79), Czech Republic (79), Lithuania (78), Hungary (77), Russian Federation (76), Poland (76), and Belarus (74) are from 72 to 77. These countries fall under the Point C groups (SPBC 3, survival probability 31–110) categories.

Thus, we confirm that IUI is critical in raising SPBC (82 to 100) from Point C and B to Point A countries.

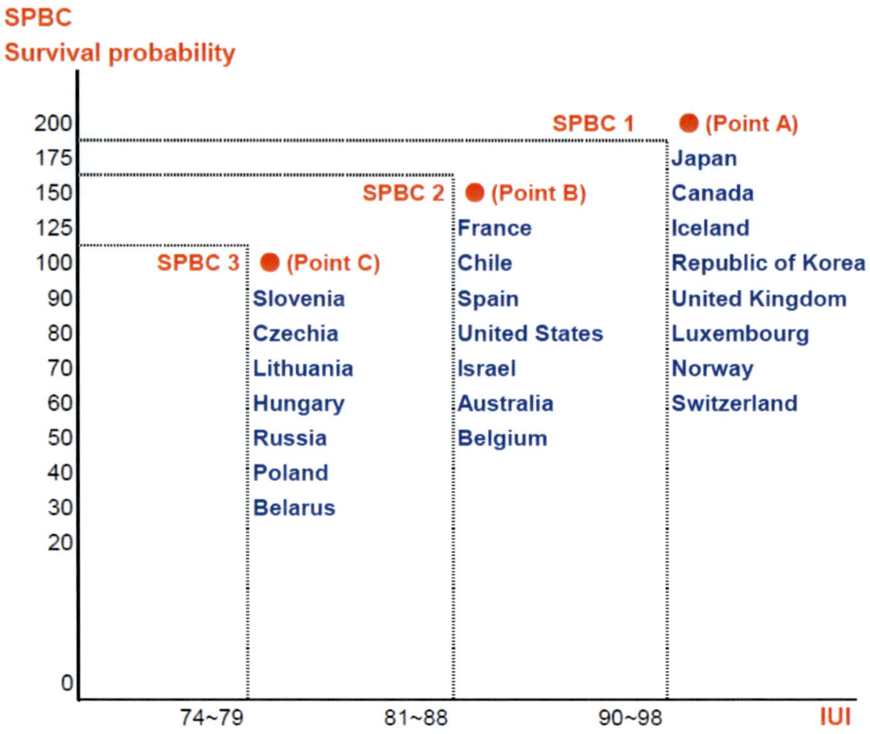

Fig. 2.29.1 SPBC (82) associated with IUI

In addition, this book of 2021 shows the correlation coefficient for SPBC (82) and IUI in 39 countries (r = 0.535). Table 2.9 presents research proving that SPBC (82) is associated with IUI. This means that if it is an increased IUI, SPBC (82) will also increase. Therefore, we can see that if the number of Internet users increases, the survival probability of centenarians will increase.

Table 2.9. Correlation coefficient for SPBC (82) and IUI (N = 39)

Variables		Correlations coefficient	p-value
SPBC (82 to 100)	IUI	0.535	0.000

2.2.10 Safely managed drinking water (SMDW)

As shown in Fig. 2.30, the water individuals drink every day should be free from pollution and considered high-quality drinking water. In addition, to maintain healthy standards and lifestyles, we should consider the following aspects:

· Manage safe drinking water
· Consume high-quality drinking water
· Cope with insufficient drinking water by consuming commercially available, high-quality bottled water
· The majority of the population drinks beneficial water to promote health.
· Contributing to safe drinking water will improve individuals' health.

As a case study, the correlation between SMDW and SPBC (82) in the 39 countries described earlier indicates that it is very high ($r = 0.482$, $p = 0.002$). This suggests that drinking water for residents can be easy to obtain with safe drinking water management. In fact, approximately 50% of residents consume safe, high-quality drinking water without restrictions. Moreover, drinking safe drinking water can prevent water-borne diseases and increase individuals' LE.

Fig 2.30 shows the process of SMDW in impoverished countries. The first step is to ask governments to resolve their own polluted drinking water issue. Then, of course, the private sector can receive foreign aid in terms of humanitarian support. However, the second step is for the countries to openly request foreign aid to solve the water supply problem for the entire nation. The third step is for the governments to obtain foreign support for a continuous supply of drinking water. The final step is to ask the governments to prioritize the water supply and related facilities for the most urgent sectors. When these steps are complete, adequate water supply facilities and safe drinking water for these countries will be achieved.

In general, if the health level improves with adequate water supply facilities and safe drinking water, it will bring about beneficial health behavior changes. Additionally, water-borne diseases will be prevented, thus increasing LE. In sum, SMDW will help increase SPBC (82).

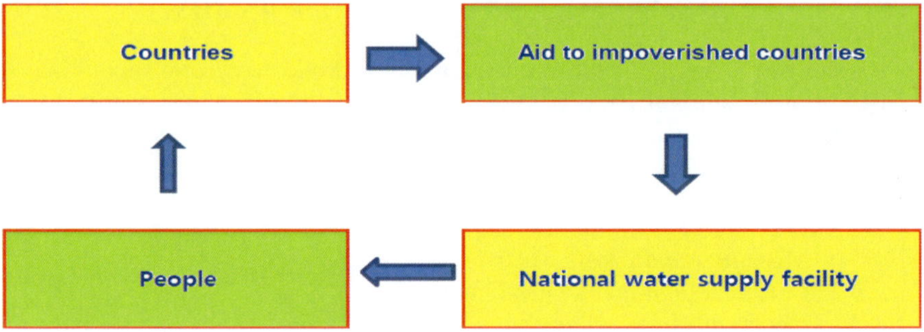

Fig. 2.30. Process of SMDW in impoverished countries

Fig. 2.31 shows that when the SMDW ratio increases from SMDW 1 to SMDW 2, the human lifespan is extended from 82 to 92 years of age, and the LE in the same age group increases. Meanwhile, the SPBC increases by 20%, from 50% to 70%. This indicates that if the proportion of safe drinking water users increases, the LE and survival probability will increase. Examples are as follows. In 2017, the proportion of 82-year-old women reaching 100 years of age in the United Kingdom was 120 (per 10,000 people; see Additional File 1).

Of the 39 countries surveyed, only 11 had an SMDW rate of 100%, one of which was the United Kingdom. However, Russia had the lowest SMDW at 76%, and the second-lowest number of 82-year-old women reaching 100 years was 34.

In this case, the production of 100-year-olds in the United Kingdom is approximately 1.3 times that of the SMDW population. This is also based on the premise that all social and ecological requirements affecting the human lifespan are constant. Thus, the SMDW should be increased.

Finally, national governments should improve water supply facilities and make drinking water accessible to as many people as possible. In this regard, institutional devices should be put in place so that water supply facilities and drinking water can be provided securely and practically, which, in turn, can increase LE and the survival probability of reaching 100 years of age.

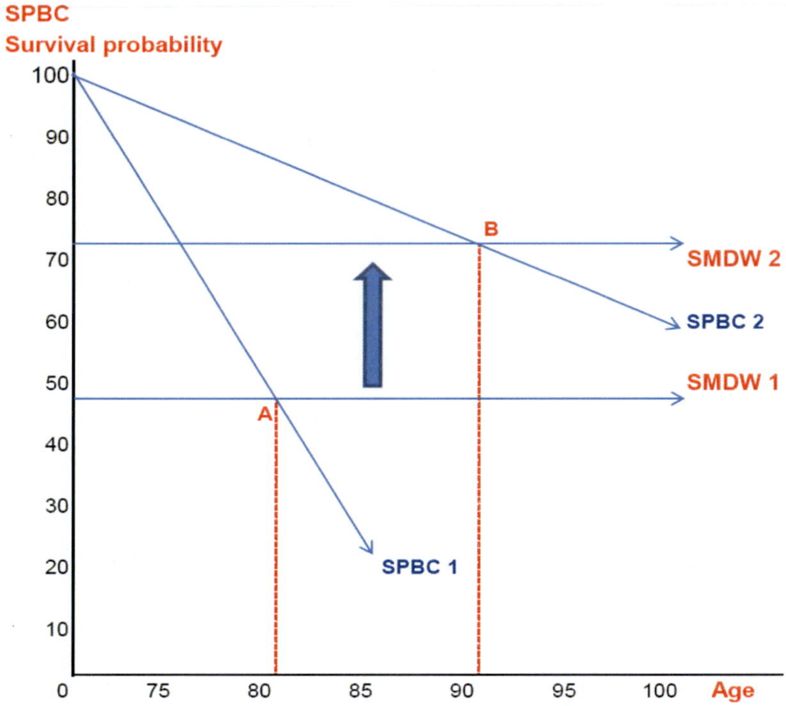

Fig. 2.31. Increase in SPBC and SMDW

Fig. 2.31.1 shows SMDW by country. In a previous study (Kim & Kim, 2016), SMDW also affected SPBC (65–69) in South Korea as surveyed. In other words, this confirms that the SEFs of SMDW are essential in the production of SPBC.

In SPBC (82 to 100) of this book, the SMDW services (% of population, 2017) of Canada (99), Chile (99), Iceland (100), United States (99), Israel (99), Finland (100), Greece (100), the United Kingdom (100), and Luxembourg (100) were from 99 to 100. Iceland, Finland, Greece, the United Kingdom, and Luxembourg's SMDW are the highest among the 39 countries. These nine countries correspond to Point A groups (SPBC 1, survival probability 96–149) in Fig. 2.31.1.

In addition, the SMDW of Spain, Slovenia, Australia, the Republic of Korea, and Norway are all 98%. Therefore, these countries' Point B groups fall under the SPBC 2 (survival probability 94–117) categories.

Lastly, the SMDW of Portugal (95), Switzerland (95), Denmark (97), Ireland (97), and Latvia (95) are from 95 to 97. These countries fall under the Point C groups (survival probability SPBC 3, 62–92) categories.

Thus, we confirm that SMDW is critical in raising SPBC (82 to 100) from Point C and B to Point A countries.

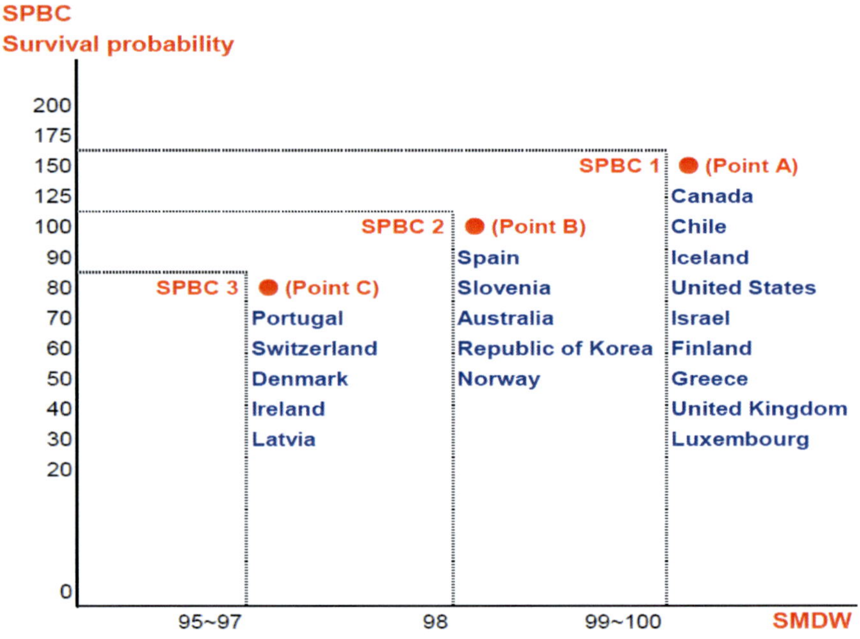

Fig. 2.31.1 SPBC (82) associated with SMDW

In addition, this book of 2021 shows the correlation coefficient for SPBC (82) and SMDW in 39 countries (r = 0.482). Table 2.10 presents research proving that SPBC (82) is associated with SMDW. This means that if SMDW increases, SPBC (82) will also increase. Therefore, if the safe water drinking service increases, the survival probability of centenarians will increase.

Table 2.10. Correlation coefficient for SPBC (82) and SMDW (N = 39)

Variables		Correlations coefficient	p-value
SPBC (82 to 100)	SMDW	0.482	0.002

2.2.11 Services value-added per worker (SVPW)

As the final SEFs, this chapter describes the SVPW, which is defined as the measure of labor productivity value-added per unit of input. In this case, value-added denotes the net output of a sector after adding all of the outputs and subtracting the intermediate inputs. The data is in constant 2010 U.S. dollars (The World Bank, 2021).

Fig. 2.32 presents the SVPW and the inputs of labor and capital. In this regard, capital refers to all inputs of raw materials and equipment, including land. When labor is input, the productivity per unit of labor increases. However, labor productivity cannot indefinitely increase productive power. This indicates that a threshold is reached at some point, after which it decreases. The law of diminishing marginal product is applied here because human labor also has a limit.

Labor productivity is also an index indicating how many goods and services are produced when a certain amount of labor is input for a specific period. Labor productivity is calculated by dividing output by labor input, while the added value (excluding the capital of raw materials and intermediate goods) is converted into monetary value. In addition, labor productivity leads to an increase/decrease in productivity according to skill level. Specifically, if workers have the same capabilities, then productivity can be increased by expanding state-of-the-art production facilities or introducing new technologies. It can also increase the added value of labor productivity. Hence, labor productivity depends on the technical ability of the workers and the input capital of high-quality facilities.

Meanwhile, the value of national labor productivity is closely related to economic growth and the standard of living. In this regard, as labor productivity increases, the GDP and standard of living increase, thereby improving the health and welfare of the citizens. In other words, as the value-added productivity per worker increases, the government's ability to pay for healthcare expenses is retained. It is also an opportunity to increase the LE and the probability of survival to 100 years of age. Thus, it is important to increase the added value of labor productivity per unit through, for example, the robotization of advanced production facilities and the informatization of state-of-the-art facilities. Ultimately, it will have a positive impact on human health, global welfare, and LE.

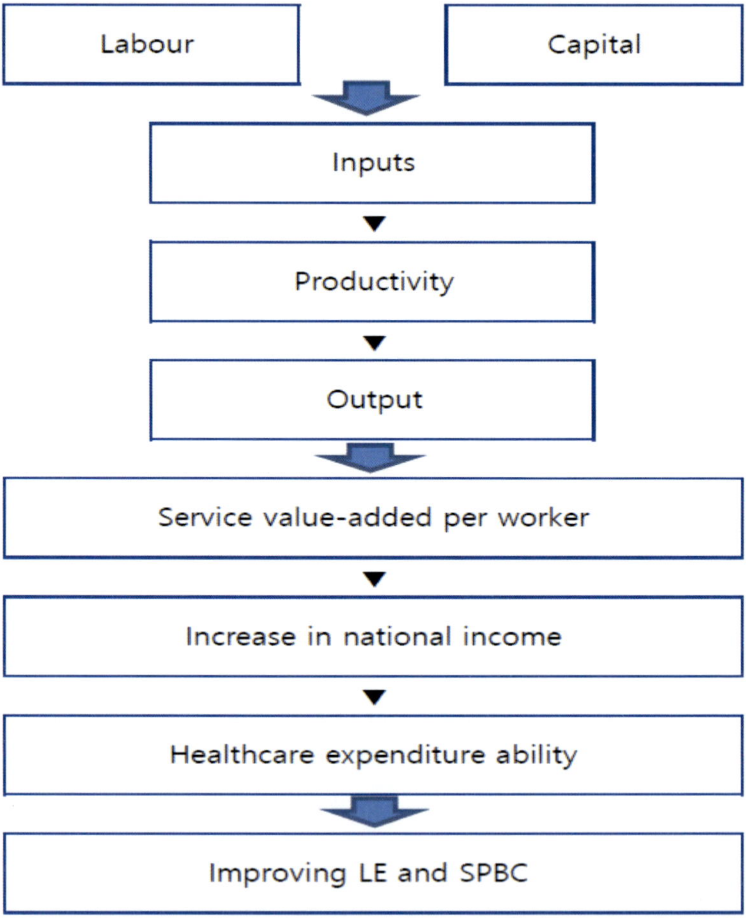

Fig. 2.32. Improving LE and SVPW

Fig. 2.33 shows that when the monetary value increases from SVPW 1 to SVPW 2, SPBC increases through SVPW, while LE is extended from 82 to 92 years of age. In addition, if the LE of the same age group increases, the SPBC increases by 10%, from 50% to 60%. This indicates that if labor productivity increases, then the entire population's LE is extended. Examples are as follows. In 2017, the proportion of 82-year-old women reaching 100 years of age in the United States was 143 (per 10,000 people) (see Additional File 1).

Meanwhile, the SVPW for the United States was $108,240, ranking it sixth out of the 39 countries surveyed. However, Ukraine had the lowest SVPW at $7,164, while the number of 82-year-old women reaching 100 was the lowest at 23.

In this case, the production of centenarians in the United States is approximately 15 times the value of SVPW. Again, the results are based on the premise that all SEFs affecting the human lifespan are constant. Thus, it is important to increase the monetary value of SVPW. For this purpose, the countries must develop a health and welfare policy that can increase labor productivity, while improving the standard of living for all people.

Finally, since the added value of labor productivity is directly related to human lifespan, the primary key is to strengthen the health and welfare of the working population by increasing productivity and income as much as possible. Specifically, an increase in SVPW can lead to more income for the working population, which will ultimately improve their health and well-being and increase the survival probability of living to 100 years of age.

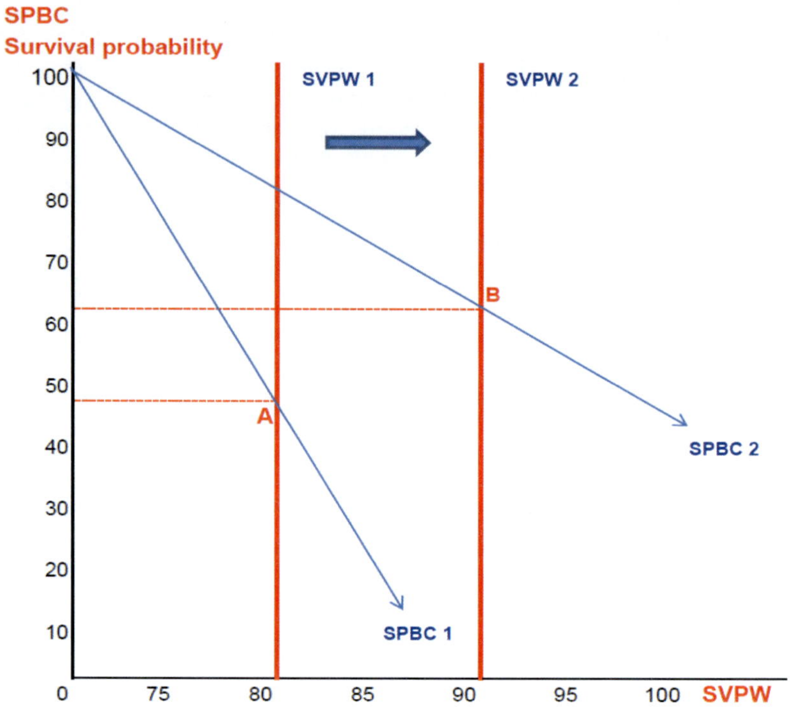

Fig. 2.33. Increase in SPBC and SVPW

Fig. 2.33.1 shows SVPW by country. In a previous study (Kim & Kim, 2018), SVPW also affected inequality in LE in 108 countries surveyed. In other words, this confirms that the SEFs of SVPW may be essential in the production of SPBC.

In SPBC (82 to 100) of this book, the SVPW (constant 2010 US$), 2018~2019 of Luxembourg (202,578), Switzerland (129,264), Norway (127,467), United States (108,240), France (100,572), and Australia (100,466) were 100,466 from to 202,578. Luxembourg's SVPW is the highest among the 39 countries. These six countries correspond to Point A groups (SPBC 1, survival probability 91–153) in Fig. 2.33.1.

In addition, the SVPW of Iceland (71,663), Spain (71,513), United Kingdom (78,629), and Germany (80,803) are from 71,513 to 80,803 categories. Therefore, their Point B groups fall under the SPBC 2 (survival probability 78–122) categories.

Lastly, the SVPW of Portugal (49,128), Estonia (36,120), Latvia (31,825), Poland (36,460), Lithuania (33,329), Slovak Republic (39,628), Croatia (36,434), and Hungary (34,589) are from 31,825 to 49,128. These countries fall under the Point C groups (SPBC 3, survival probability 45–92) categories.

Thus, we confirm that SVPW is critical in raising SPBC (82 to 100) from Point C and B to Point A countries.

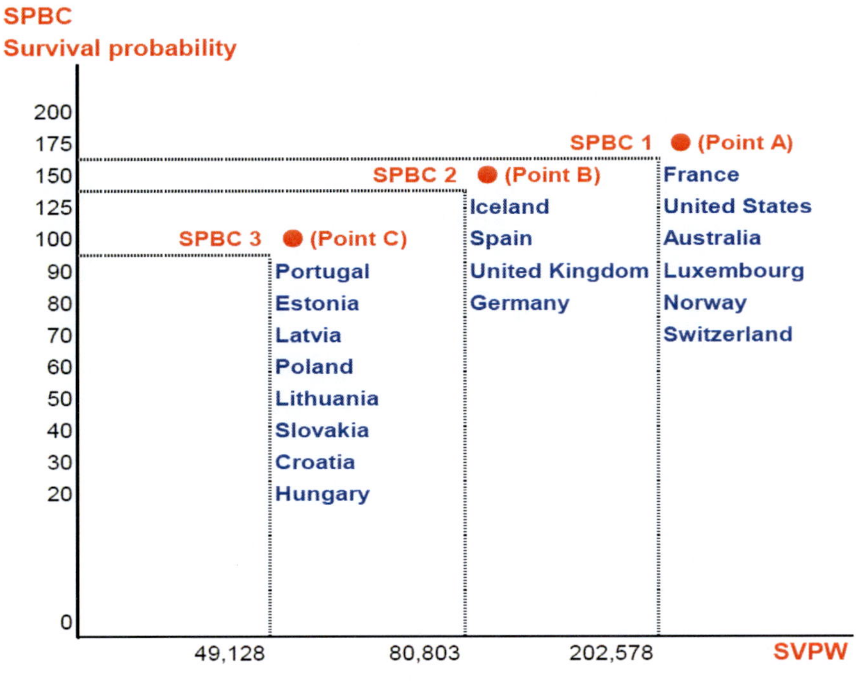

Fig. 2.33.1 SPBC (82) associated with SVPW

In addition, this book of 2021 shows the correlation coefficient for SPBC (82) and SMDW in 39 countries (r = 0.491). Table 2.12 presents research proving that SPBC (82) is associated with SVPW. This means that if SVPW increases, SPBC (82) will also increase. Therefore, if the added value of labor productivity increases, the survival probability of centenarians will increase.

Table 2.12. Correlation coefficient for SPBC (82) and SVPW (N = 39)

Variables		Correlations coefficient	p-value
SPBC (82 to 100)	SVPW	0.491	0.002

References

Ailshire JA, Crimmins EM. Psychosocial factors associated with longevity in the United States: Age differences between the old and oldest-old in the health and retirement Study. *J Aging Res* 2011; 2011: 530534. PMCID: PMC3199053.

Ailshire JA, Beltrán-Sánchez H, Crimmins EM. Becoming centenarians: disease and functioning trajectories of older US adults as they survive to 100. *The Journals of Gerontology Series A: Biological Sciences and Medical Sciences. 2015;* 70(2): 193–201.

Cairncross S, Hunt C, Boisson S, Bostoen K, Curtis V, Fung IC, Schmidt WP. Water, sanitation and hygiene for the prevention of diarrhoea. *Int J Epidemiol* 2010; 39 Suppl 1:i193–205.

Candore G, Balistreri CR, Listi F, Grimaldi MP, Vasto S, Colonna-Romano G, Franceschi C, Lio D, Caselli G, Caruso C. Immunogenetics, gender, and longevity. *Annals of the New York Academy of Sciences. 2006;* 1089: 516–537.

Duflo E. Women's empowerment and economic development. *Journal of Economic Literature.2012;* 50(4): 1051–1079.

Fenge LA, Hean S, Worswick L, Wilkinson C, Fearnley S, Ersser, S. The impact of the economic recession on well-being and quality of life of older people. *Health & Social Care in the Community. 2012;* 20(6): 617–624.

Fernández-Sáez, J, Ruiz-Cantero MT, Guijarro-Garví M, Carrasco-Portiño M, Roca-Pérez V, Chilet-Rosell E, Álvarez-Dardet C. Looking twice at the gender equity index for public health impact. *BMC Public Health. 2013;* 13(1): 659.

Gavrilov LA, Gavrilova NS. Demographic consequences of defeating aging. *Rejuvenation Research. 2010;* 13(2–3): 329–334.

Guthmann JP, Bonnet M, Ahoua L, Dantoine F, Balkan S, van Herp M, Tamrat A, Legros D, Brown V, Checchi F. Death rates from malaria epidemics, Burundi and Ethiopia. *Emerg Infect Dis* 2007; 13(1): 140–143.

Hájek O, Grebeníček P, Popesko B, Hrabinová Š. Czech Republic vs. EU-27: Economic level, health care and population health. C*entral European Journal of Public Health.* 2012; 20(3), 167.

Hall AK, Bernhardt JM, Dodd V, Vollrath MW. The digital health divide: evaluating online health information access and use among older adults. *Health Education & Behavior. 2014;* 42(2): 202–209.

Hsu HC. Impact of morbidity and life events on successful aging. *Asia Pac J Public Health.* 2011; 23(4): 458–469.

Inglehart R, Norris P, Welzel C. Gender equality and democracy. Comparative Sociology. 2002; 1(3): 321–345.

Johnson TE, de Castro E, de Castro SH, Cypser J, Henderson S, Tedesco P. Relationship between increased longevity and stress resistance as assessed through gerontogene mutations in Caenorhabditis elegans. *Experimental Gerontology. 2001;* 36(10): 1609–1617.

Kabeer N. Gender equality and women's empowerment: A critical analysis of the third millennium development goal 1. *Gender & Development. 2005;* 13(1): 13–24.

Kaplan WA. Can the ubiquitous power of mobile phones be used to improve health outcomes in developing countries? *Global Health.* 2006; 2: 9.

Kim JI. Social factors associated with centenarian rate (CR) in 32 OECD countries. *BMC International Health and Human Rights.* 2013; 13(1), 16.

Kim JI, Kim G. Country-level socioeconomic indicators associated with survival probability of becoming a centenarian among older European adults: gender inequality, male labor force participation, and proportions of women in parliaments. *Journal of Biosocial Science.* 2017a; 49(2) 239–250.

Kim JI. Association between social factors of health ageing and longevity: determinants of the longevity index (LI) in OECD countries. *Ageing International*. 2014c; 39(2): 97–105.

Kim JI, Kim G. Factors affecting the survival probability of becoming a centenarian for those aged 70, based on the human mortality database: income, health expenditure, telephone, and sanitation. BMC Geriatrics. 2014a; 14(1): 113.

Kim JI, Kim G. Labor force participation and secondary education of gender inequality index (GII) associated with healthy life expectancy (HLE) at birth. *International journal for equity in health. 2014b;* 13(1): 1–8.

Kim JI, Kim G. Effects on inequality in life expectancy from a social ecology perspective. BMC Public Health. 2018; 18, 243.
Kim JI, Kim G. Country-level socioeconomic indicators associated with healthy life expectancy: income, urbanization, schooling, and internet users: 2000–2012. *Social Indicators Research. 2016a;* (129), 391–402: DOI:10.1007/s11205-015-1107-2
Kim JI, Kim G. Social Structural influences on healthy aging: Community-level socioeconomic conditions and survival probability of becoming a centenarian for those aged 65 to 69 in South Korea. *The International Journal of Aging and Human Development.* 2015; 81(4): 241–259.
Kim JI, Kim G. & Choi Y. Effects of air pollution on children from a socioecological perspective. BMC Pediatrics. 2019; 19, 442.
Kim JI, Kim G. Socio-ecological perspective of older age life expectancy: income, gender inequality, and financial crisis in Europe. Globalization and Health. 2017b; 13, 58.
Kim JI. Hospital Management, Gyechuk Culture Publishing Co. 2016.
Kim JI. Health Administration, Gyechuk Culture Publishing Co. 2016.
Krook ML. Women's representation in parliament: A qualitative comparative analysis. *Political Studies. 2010;* 58(5): 886–908.
Lenzen M. Decomposition analysis and the mean-rate-of-change index. *Applied Energy. 2006;* 83(3): 185–198.
Lin HJ, Sung TI, Chen CY, Guo HR. Arsenic levels in drinking water and mortality of liver cancer in Taiwan. *J Hazard Mater*. 2013; 262: 1132–1138.
Mackenbach JP, Looman CW. Life expectancy and national income in Europe, 1900–2008: an update of Preston's analysis. *International Journal of Epidemiology. 2013;* 42(4): 1100–1110.
Mackenbach JP, Stirbu I, Roskam AJR, Schaap MM, Menvielle G, Leinsalu M, Kunst AE. Socioeconomic inequalities in health in 22 European countries. *New England Journal of Medicine*. 2008; 358(23): 2468–2481.
Magnolfi SU, Petruzzi E, Pinzani P, Malentacchi F, Pazzagli M, Antonini FM. Longevity index (LI%) and centenarity index (CI%): new indicators to evaluate the characteristics of aging process in the Italian population. *Archives of Gerontology and Geriatrics. 2007;* 44(3): 271–276.
Mao Z, Zhao L, Pu L, Wang M, Zhang Q, He DZ. How well can centenarians hear? *PLOS ONE. 2013;* 8(6): e65565.
Maslow AH. A theory of human motivation. Psychological Review.1943; 50: 370–396.

Mossakowska M, Barcikowska M, Broczek K, Grodzicki T, Klich-Raczka A, Kupisz-Urbanska M, Zyczkowska J. Polish Centenarians Programme–multidisciplinary studies of successful ageing aims, methods, and preliminary results. *Experimental Gerontology. 2008;* 43(3): 238–244.

Mossakowska M, Broczek K, Wieczorowska-Tobis K, Klich-Rączka A, Jonas M, Pawlik-Pachucka, E, Puzianowska-Kuznicka M. Cognitive performance and functional status are the major factors predicting survival of centenarians in Poland. *The Journals of Gerontology A Biological Sciences and Medical Sciences. 2014;* 69(10): 1269–1275.

Rahi M. Human development report 2010. Changes in parameters and perspectives. *Indian J Public Health.2011;* 55(4): 272–275.

Ringard Å, Sagan A, Sperre Saunes I, Lindahl AK. Norway: health system review. *Health Syst Transit. 2013;* 15(8): 1–162.

Robine JM, Paccaud F. Nonagenarians and centenarians in Switzerland, 1860–2001: a demographic analysis. *Journal of Epidemiology and Community Health. 2005;* 59(1): 31–37.

Robine JM, Herrmann FR, Arai Y, Willcox DC, Gondo Y, Hirose N, Saito, Y. Exploring the impact of climate on human longevity. *Experimental Gerontology.2012;* 47(9): 660–671.

Rodriguez-Laso A, Zunzunegui MV, Otero A. The effect of social relationships on survival in elderly residents of a Southern European community: a cohort study. *BMC Geriatrics. 2001;* 7(1): 19.

Rosero-Bixby L. The exceptionally high life expectancy of Costa Rican nonagenarians. *Demography* 2008; 45(3): 673–691.

Rowe JW, Kahn RL. Human aging: Usual and successful. Science. 1987; 237(4811): 143–149.

Ruedin D. The representation of women in national parliaments: A cross-national comparison. *European Sociological Review. 2012;* 28(1): 96–109.

Sachuk NN. Population longevity study: sources and indices. *J Gerontol* 1970; 25(3): 262–264.

Schirle T. Why have the labor force participation rates of older men increased since the mid-1990s? *Journal of Labor Economics. 2008;* 26(4): 549–594.

Steptoe A, O'Donnell K, Marmot M, Wardle J. Positive affect and psychosocial processes related to health. *British Journal of Psychology. 2008;* 99(2): 211–227.

Steyer A, Torkar KG, Gutiérrez-Aguirre I, Poljšak-Prijatelj M. High prevalence of enteric viruses in untreated individual drinking water

sources and surface water in Slovenia. *Int J Hyg Environ Health* 2011; 214(5): 392–398.
Tarasevich I, Rydkina E, Raoult D. Outbreak of epidemic typhus in Russia. *Lancet.* 1998; 352(9134): 1151.
Theou O, Brothers TD, Rockwood MR, Haardt D, Mitnitski A, Rockwood K. Exploring the relationship between national economic indicators and relative fitness and frailty in middle-aged and older Europeans. *Age and Ageing. 2013;* 42(5): 614–619.
Tumwebaze IK, Orach CG, Niwagaba C, Luthi C, Mosler HJ. Sanitation facilities in Kampala slums, Uganda: users' satisfaction and determinant factors. *Int J Environ Health Res.* 2013; 23(3): 191–204.
United Nations (UN). UN data, a world of information, Dataset. Available at http://data.un.org, Accessed on June 02, 2014.
United Nations Development Programme (UNDP): open data. Available at https://data.undp.org, Accessed on June 02, 2014.
United Nations (UN). World population prospects, the 2010 Revision. http://esa.un.org/unpd/wpp/Excel-Data/population.htm, , andAccessed on August 15, 2014a.
United Nations (UN). UN data, a world of information, Dataset. http://data.un.org/DataMartInfo.aspx#PopDiv, Accessed on August 15, 2014b.
Human Development Report. http://hdr.undp.org/en/data. Accessed on Jun 16, 2015b.
University of California, Berkeley (USA), and Max Planck Institute for Demographic Research (Germany). *Human mortality database.* Available at www.mortality.org, Accessed on June 02, 2014.
Väinö Kannisto. On the survival of centenarians and the span of life. *Population Studies: A Journal of Demography* 1988; 42(3): 389–406.
Viña J, Borrás C, Gambini J, Sastre J, Pallardó FV: Why females live longer than males? Importance of the upregulation of longevity-associated genes by oestrogenic compounds. *FEBS Lett* 2005; 579(12): 2541–2545.
Wang F. Economic evaluations of the effects of longevity on telemedicine and conventional healthcare provision. *Telemed J E Health* 2011; 17(6): 431–4.
WHO, UNICEF. https://www.thesourcemagazine.org/billions-still-lack-safe-drinking-water-says-new-report/. Accessed July 22, 2021.
WHO. Library Cataloguing-in-Publication Data, Safely managed drinking water-thematic report on drinking water 2017.
Wikipedia. Burundi. ttps://en.wikipedia.org/wiki/Burundi#cite_note-:8-133, Accessed July 18, 2021.

World Bank (WB). Services, value added per worker. Derived using World Bank national accounts data and OECD National Accounts data files and employment data from International Labour Organization, ILOSTAT database.
https://data.worldbank.org/indicator/NV.SRV.EMPL.KD
Accessed July 16, 2021.

World Bank (WB). GNI per capita, Atlas method, (current US$). World Bank national accounts data.
https://data.worldbank.org/indicator/NY.GNP.PCAP.CD?view=chart.
Accessed 16 July 2021a.

World Bank (WB). Incidence of tuberculosis (per 100,000 people). World Health Organization, global tuberculosis report.
https://data.worldbank.org/indicator/SH.TBS.INCD?view=chart.
Accessed July 16, 2021b.

World Bank. (WB). Labor force participation rate, male (% of male population ages 15–64) (modeled ILO estimate),
http://data.worldbank.org/indicator/SL.TLF.ACTI.MA.ZS.
Accessed December 16, 2015a.

World Bank. (WB). Proportion of seats held by women in national parliaments (%),
http://data.worldbank.org/indicator/SG.GEN.PARL.ZS.
Accessed December 16, 2015b.

World Health Organization. (WHO). Definition of an older or elderly person. http://www.who.int/healthinfo/survey/ageingdefnolder/en/.
Accessed on December 16, 2015.

Wright JA, Yang H, Rivett U, Gundry SW. Public perception of drinking water safety in South Africa 2002–2009: a repeated cross-sectional study. *BMC Public Health.* 2012; 12(1): 556.

Wu JY1, Leung WY, Chang S, Lee B, Zee B, Tong PC, Chan JC. Effectiveness of telephone counselling by a pharmacist in reducing mortality in patients receiving polypharmacy: randomised controlled trial. *BMJ.* 2006; 333(7567): 522.

Xie G, Laskowitz DT, Turner EL, Egger JR, Shi P, Ren F, Wu Y. Baseline health-related quality of life and 10-year all-cause mortality among 1739 Chinese adults. *PLOS ONE.2014;* 9(7):e101527.

Zeng Y, Gu D. Reliability of age reporting among the Chinese oldest-old in the CLHLS datasets. In: Zeng Y, Poston D, Vlosky DA, Gu D, editors. Healthy longevity in China: Demographic Methods and Population Analysis. The Netherlands. Springer. 2008; 61–78.

PART 3

FACTORS OF LIFE EXPECTANCY (LE)

Part 3 introduces the four sections of LE that influence SPBC: (1) old age LE (OLE), (2) remaining years of LE (RLE), (3) inequality in LE (ILE), and (4) healthy life expectancy (HLE). Overall, there are 14 LE related factors.

CHAPTER 3

LIFE EXPECTANCY (LE) FACTORS IN BECOMING A CENTENARIAN

This chapter confirms the SEFs related to LE. Within the LE group, 14 variables, including nine indicators of SPBC, are defined as main variables. In addition, correlations among the 14 variables and the association between LE and SEFs are discussed.

3.1 LE and SEFs

There are SEFs to consider reaching 100 years of age, including inequality in LE (ILE), remaining years of LE (RLE), old age LE (OLE), and healthy LE (HLE). In addition, the probability of reaching the age of 100 is high when these factors are overcome. Thus, it is necessary to examine these factors and establish an effective strategy for achieving this milestone.

First, the SEFs of LE are shown in Table 3.1. Using the World Bank and WHO Database, we selected 14 statistically significant variables. In Chapter 2, we discussed the correlations between the nine variables in the survival probability of reaching 82 years of age. Of course, these variables were included as those affecting LE. However, out of the 14 variables in this chapter, it also includes five variables: old age pension recipient (OPR), secondary education (SE), the Gini index (GI), government health expenditure (GHE), and depth of credit information (DCI), affect LE (Fig.3.1). Thus, 14 variables of SEFs affect LE, and 9 of 14 SEFs affect the survival probability of becoming centenarians (SPBC) (Fig. 3.1).

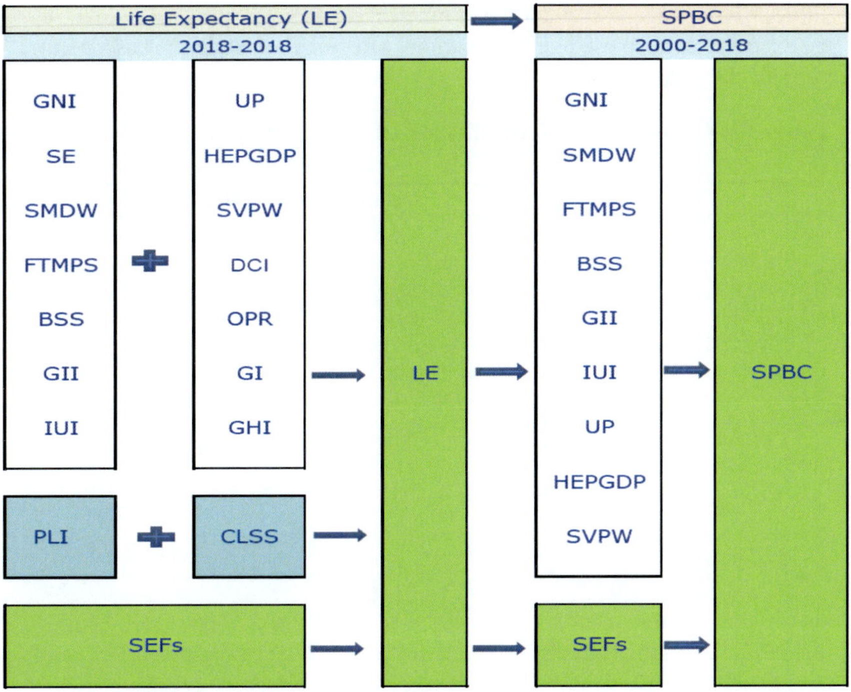

Fig.3.1. Relationship between LE and SEFs

The main characteristics of these variables are as follows. First, GI and Gender Inequality Index (GII) have a negative (−) sign regarding LE. In addition, GI is a reverse phenomenon for personal income, since LE increases when individual income disparities are relatively small. In addition, gender discrimination is similar. In other words, having a negative (−) sign means gender equality. Thus, the two variables with a negative sign can positively affect PLI and CLSS in the social development of SEFs and increase LE.

Among these variables, more than 80% of the correlation factors are SMDW, GII, BSS, and IUI. Their meanings are as follows. First, SMDW means that drinking water is an essential food item that anyone can easily access when necessary. As for GII, it correlates with more than 88% of the factors, meaning that gender equality has the most significant influence on LE. Second, high IUI has an 86% correlation. The last, the BSS is making a significant contribution to protecting human life (Table 3.1). As shown in

Table 3.1, we macroscopically examined the SEFs affecting LE. Next, let us examine how these verified factors affect LE includes a case study published by the author.

Table 3.1. Correlations coefficient for LE and SEFs

Variables		Correlations coefficient	p-value
LE	GNI	0.647	0.000
	OPR	0.621	0.000
	SE	0.706	0.000
	SMDW	0.821	0.000
	FTMPS	0.727	0.000
	BSS	0.853	0.000
	GI	-0.352	0.000
	UP	0.636	0.000
	GII	-0.861	0.000
	IUI	0.859	0.000
	GHE	0.708	0.000
	HEGDP	0.317	0.000
	SVPW	0.668	0.000
	DCI	0.279	0.005

3.1.1 LE and GNI

Fig.3.1.1 shows the GNI and LE by country. In a previous study (Kim & Kim, 2016, 2018), GNI also affected Older Age LE (OLE) and Healthy Life Expectancy (HLE) in 34 and 170 countries surveyed, respectively. In other words, this confirms that the SEFs of GNI are essential in the production of LE.

In LE (2018) of this book, the GNI per capita, Atlas method (current US$), 2019 of Switzerland (85,500), Iceland (72,850), Norway (82,500), Luxembourg (73,910), Ireland (64,000), Bermuda (117,730), Denmark (63,950), and Qatar (61,180) were between 61,180 and 117,730. Bermuda's GNI was the highest among the 175 countries. These countries correspond to Point A (LE 1, from age 80 to 84) in Fig. 3.1.1.

Additionally, the GNI of Maldives (9,680), Turkey (9,690), Montenegro (9,060), Brazil (9,130), Mexico (9,480), Bulgaria (9,570), and Grenada (9,840) are between 9,130 and 9,840 categories. Therefore, these countries'

Point B groups fall under the LE 2 (from age 72 to 79) classes.

Lastly, Madagascar (520), Sudan (590), Liberia (580), Congo, Dem. Rep. (530), Mozambique (490), Sierra Leone (540), Afghanistan (530), the Central African Republic (520), Malawi (380), and Burundi (280) accounted for less than 600. Burundi had the lowest GNI. These countries' Point C groups fall under the LE 3 (from age 53 to 67) classes.

Thus, we confirm that GNI is critical in raising LE (2018) from LE 2 (Point B) and LE 3 (Point C) to LE 1 (Point A) countries.

The difference in GNI for Switzerland (85,500) and Burundi (280) was 305 fold, while the LE difference between Switzerland (84) and Burundi (61) was 23 years. Therefore, the LE gap between these countries is judged to be mainly due to GNI. The remaining 13 variables are also related to economic factors. Drinking water supply, telephone, basic sanitation, Internet use, urbanization, national health expenditure as a percentage of GDP, education level, wealth gap, gender discrimination, national credit index, and labor productivity index are all related. Therefore, if we want to promote LE to Point B from Point A, we must first determine the priorities for each factor in SEFs. Advanced countries need to provide medical support to humanity and aid underdeveloped countries, such as essential drinking water and sanitation facilities.

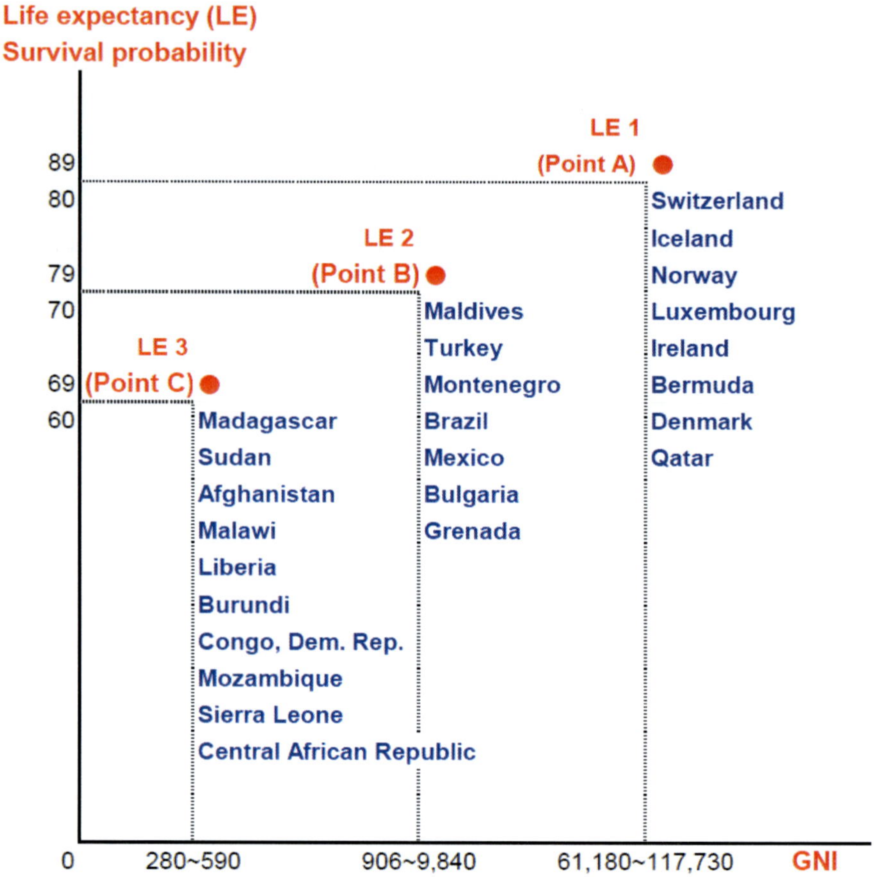

Fig. 3.1.1 LE associated with GNI

In addition, this 2021 book shows the correlation coefficient for LE (2018) and GNI in 175 countries (r = 0.647). Table 3.1.1 illustrates that LE is associated with GNI. This means that if GNI increases, LE will also rise. Therefore, if the national income level increases, LE and the survival probability will increase.

Table 3.1.1 Correlations coefficient variables for the LE and GNI

Variables		Correlations coefficient	p-value
LE	GNI	0.647	0.000

3.1.2 LE and SMDW

Fig. 3.1.2 shows the SMDW and LE by country. In a previous study (Kim & Kim, 2015, 2016), SMDW also affected Remaining Years of Healthy Life Expectancy (RHLE) in older age in 148 countries and SPBC (65–69) in some countries surveyed. In other words, this confirms that the SEFs of SMDW are essential in the production of LE.

In LE (2018) of this book, the safely managed drinking water (SMDW) 2017 for Singapore, Iceland, Sweden, Malta, New Zealand, Netherlands, Greece, Finland, Belgium, United Kingdom, Cyprus, and Germany were 100%, placing their SMDW as being the highest among the 88 countries. They correspond to Point A (LE 1, from age 81 to 83) in Fig. 3.1.2.

Additionally, the SMDW of Bosnia and Herzegovina (89), Romania (82), Oman (90), Croatia (90), Hungary (90), Kazakhstan (90), Armenia (86), Georgia (80), and Grenada (87) are from 80 to 90 categories, indicating that their Point B groups fall under the LE 2 (from age 72 to 78) classes.

Lastly, the Congo Republic (45), Nepal (27), Mongolia (24), Cambodia (26), Pakistan (35), Ethiopia (11), Ghana (36), Uganda (7), Nigeria (20), Côte d'Ivoire (37), and Sierra Leone (10) were less than 38%. Sierra Leone had the lowest SMDW. Therefore, these countries' Point C groups fall under the LE 3 (from age 54 to 67) categories.

Thus, we confirm that SMDW is critical in raising LE (2018) from LE 3 (Point C) and LE 2 (Point B) to LE 1 (Point A) countries.

The difference in SMDW for Singapore (100) and Uganda (7) was 14 times, and the LE difference for Singapore (83) and Uganda (63) was 20 years. The LE gap between these countries is judged to be mainly caused by SMDW and GNI. These variables are related to economic factors.

The higher national income countries also have a higher safe drinking water supply rate because when a country's income is high, people are more interested in health-related drinking water issues, and the priority is to increase the safe water supply rate. If it is difficult for a low-income country to supply water due to its self-strength, it should quickly be given help from advanced countries. We aim for humanity's coexistence. The earth should be without water shortages because we should become a society where all humans can live longer than the current average LE.

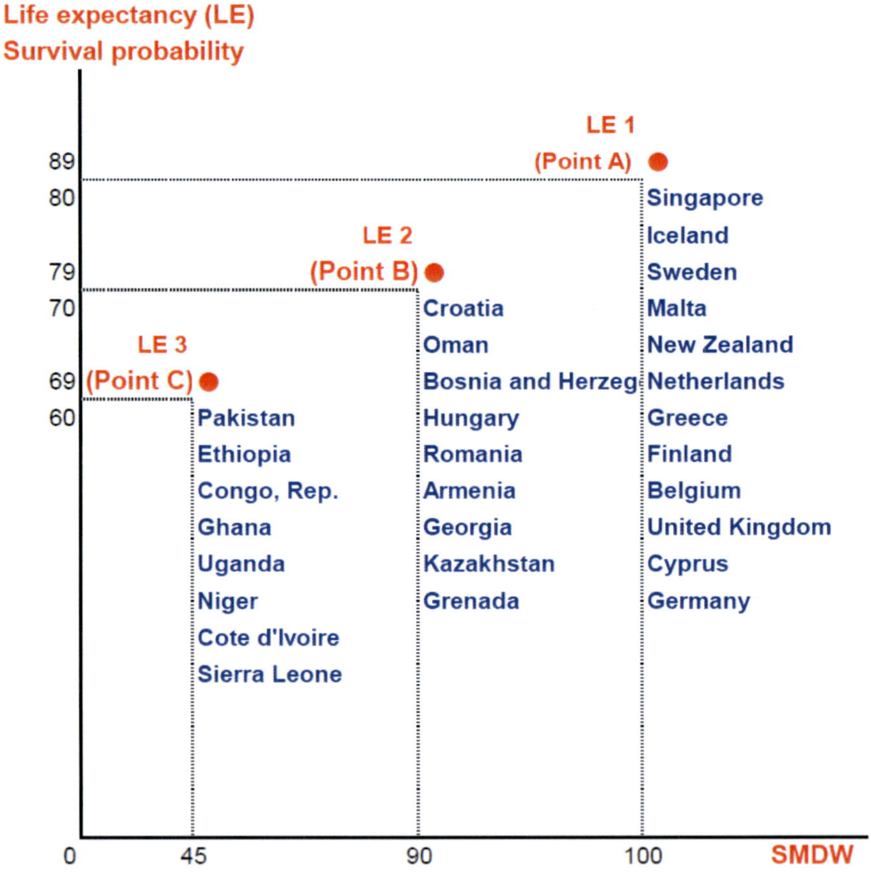

Fig. 3.1.2 LE associated with SMDW

In addition, this 2021 book shows the correlation coefficient for LE (2018) and SMDW in 148 countries (r = 0.821). Table 3.1.2 presents results research proving that LE is associated with SMDW. This means that if SMDW increases, LE will also increase. Therefore, if the national SMDW level increases, LE and the survival probability will increase.

Table 3.1.2 Correlations coefficient variables for the LE and SMDW

Variables		Correlations coefficient	p-value
LE	SMDW	0.821	0.000

3.1.3 LE and BSS

Fig. 3.1.3 shows BSS and LE by country. In a previous study (Kim & Kim, 2014), BSS also affected SPBC (70) in 32 countries surveyed. In other words, this confirms that the SEFs of BSS are essential in the production of LE.

In LE (2018) of this book, the people using at least basic sanitation services (BSS) (% of the population) 2017 of Japan, Switzerland, Spain, Singapore, Israel, Australia, Republic of Korea, Malta, New Zealand, Austria, Bermuda, Portugal, Denmark, Qatar, and Chile were 100%, making their BSS the highest among the 166 countries. This country corresponds to Point A, LE 1 (from age 80 to 84) in Fig. 3.1.3.

Additionally, the BSS of Colombia (89), Antigua and Barbuda (88), Ecuador (87), Algeria (88), Morocco (88), Guyana (86), Bulgaria (86), Belize (88), Jamaica (87), Paraguay (89), El Salvador (87), and Brazil (87) are from 86 to 89 categories. Therefore, these countries' Point B groups fall under the LE 2 (from age 70 to 77) classes.

Conversely, the BSS of Nepal (59), Mongolia (58), Cambodia (57), India (57), Timor-Leste (52), Rwanda (65), Senegal (51), Pakistan (58), Myanmar (65), and Djibouti (62) were from 51 to 65 categories. These countries fall under the LE 3 (from age 67 to 70) groups.

Lastly, the countries that are lagging in BSS are as follows. Guinea (22), Congo Democratic Republic (20), Guinea-Bissau (20), the Congo Republic (20), Burkina Faso (19), Uganda (18), Ghana (18), Liberia (17), Benin (16), Togo (16), Sierra Leone (15), Papua New Guinea (14), Niger (13), and Chad (9) were less than 20%. Chad had the lowest BSS. These countries fall under the LE 4 (from age 54 to 64) categories.

Thus, we confirm that BSS is critical in raising LE (2018) from LE 4 (Point D) and LE 3 (Point C) and LE 2 (Point B) to LE 1 (Point A) countries.

The difference in BSS for Japan (100) and Chad (9) was about 11 times, and the difference in LE for Japan (84) and Chad (54) was 30 years. The LE gap between these countries is mainly due to BSS, SMDW, and GNI. These variables are related to economic and lifestyle factors.

Although the national income level is low, sanitation is a problem that we can solve if people's will to live and public health are carefully considered. Therefore, if we first think about what we can do for public health and sanitation in each country, we will solve the sanitation problem of that country. Water and wastewater treatment is the most fundamental problem in public health. Only by solving this can the LE of underdeveloped countries be raised.

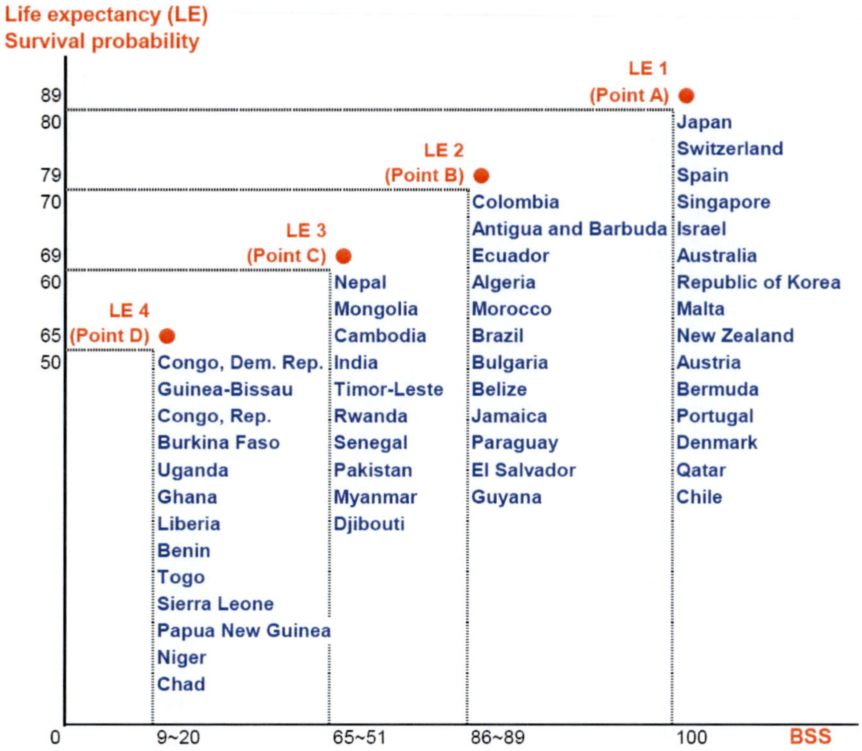

Fig. 3.1.3 LE associated with BSS

In addition, this 2021 book shows the correlation coefficient for LE (2018) and BSS in 166 countries (r = 0.853). Table 3.1.3 illustrates that LE is associated with BSS. This means that if BSS increases, LE will also rise; therefore, if the people using at least BSS level increases, LE and the survival probability will increase.

Table 3.1.3 Correlations coefficient variables for the LE and BSS

Variables		Correlations coefficient	p-value
LE	BSS	0.853	0.000

3.1.4 LE and GII

Fig. 3.1.4 shows GII and LE by country. In a previous study (Kim & Kim, 2017a, 2017b), BSS also affected SPBC (65-69) and LE at age 60 years in 34 countries surveyed. In other words, this confirms that the SEFs of GII are essential in the production of LE.

In LE (2018) of this book, the Gender Inequality Index (GII, 2018) of Switzerland (0.037), Denmark (0.040), Sweden (0.040), Netherlands (0.041), Norway (0.044), Belgium (0.045), Finland (0.050), France (0.051), Iceland (0.057), Republic of Korea (0.058), Singapore (0.065), Slovenia (0.069), Italy (0.069), Austria (0.073), Spain (0.074), and Luxembourg (0.078) were from 0.078 to 0.037 categories. These countries' GII is high groups, and Switzerland is the highest among the 154 countries. These countries correspond to Point A, LE 1 (from age 81 to 84) in Fig. 3.1.4.

In addition, the GII of Bulgaria (0.218), Saudi Arabia (0.224), Republic of Moldova (0.228), Brunei Darussalam (0.234), Albania (0.234), Russian Federation (0.255), Barbados (0.256), Hungary (0.258), and Armenia (0.259) are from 0.218 to 0.259 categories. Therefore, their Point B groups fall under the LE 2 (from age 72 to 79) classes.

Conversely, the GII of India (0.501), Ethiopia (0.508), Burundi (0.520), Senegal (0.523), Zimbabwe (0.525), Uganda (0.531), Gabon (0.534), and Tanzania (0.539) are from 0.501 to 0.539 categories. Therefore, these countries' Point C groups fall under the LE 3 (from age 65 to 69) classes.

Lastly, Haiti (0.620), Mauritania (0.620), Gambia (0.620), Sierra Leone (0.644), Niger (0.647), Liberia (0.651), Democratic Republic the of Congo (0.655), Côte d'Ivoire (0.657), Mali (0.676), Central African Republic (0.682), Chad (0.701), and Papua New Guinea (0.740) had a GII of more than 0.62. Papua New Guinea had the highest GII. These countries fall under the LE 4 (from age 54 to 65) categories.

Thus, we confirm that BSS is critical in raising LE (2018) from LE 4 (Point D) and LE 3 (Point C) and LE 2 (Point B) to LE 1 (Point A) countries.

The difference in GII for Switzerland (0.037) and Papua New Guinea (0.740) was about 20 times, and the difference in LE for Switzerland (84) and Chad (64) was 20 years. The LE gap between these countries is mainly due to GII, BSS, SMDW, and GNI. These variables are related to economic, lifestyle, and socio-cultural factors.

Despite low national income levels in a country, gender discrimination is a problem we can solve if we carefully consider gender equality and coexistence. Therefore, if we first think about what we can do for public lifestyle and gender equality in each country, we can solve the gender inequality problem of that country. Gender equality and socio-cultural lifestyle is the most fundamental problem in life health. The LE of underdeveloped countries can be raised only by solving this.

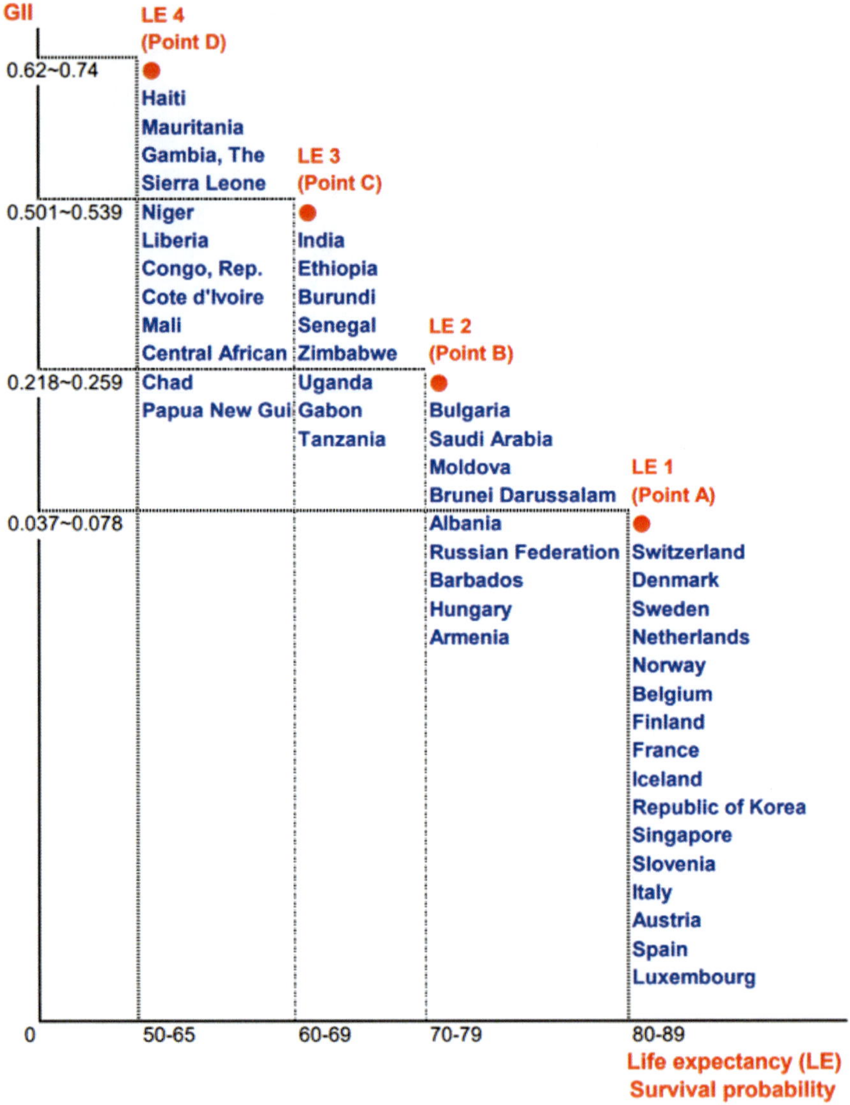

Fig. 3.1.4 LE associated with GII

In addition, this 2021 book shows the correlation coefficient for LE (2018) and GII in 154 countries (r = −0.861). Table 3.1.4 proves that LE is associated with GII. This means that if GII decreases, LE will rise as well. Therefore, if the GII decreases, LE and the survival probability will increase.

Table 3.1.4 Correlations coefficient variables for the LE and GII

Variables		Correlations coefficient	p-value
LE	GII	-0.861	0.000

3.1.5 LE and IUI

Fig. 3.1.5 shows IUI and LE by country. In a previous study (Kim & Kim, 2016), IUI also affected Healthy Life Expectancy (HLE) in 178 countries surveyed. In other words, this confirms that the SEFs of IUI are essential in the production of LE.

In LE (2018) of this book, the Individuals using the Internet (% of the population) 2017 of Iceland (98), Norway (96), Republic of Korea (95), Luxembourg (97), Bermuda (98), Denmark (97), Qatar (97), Netherlands (93), Sweden (93), Canada (93), Japan (92), New Zealand (91), United Kingdom (90), and Switzerland (90) are from 90 to 98 categories. Iceland's IUI was the highest among the 160 countries. This corresponds to Point A, LE 1 (from age 80 to 84) in Fig. 3.1.5.

In addition, the IUI of Oman (80), Malaysia (80), Latvia (80), Azerbaijan (79), Czech Republic (79), Lebanon (78), Lithuania (78), Trinidad and Tobago (77), Hungary (77), Kazakhstan (76), Moldova (76), Russian Federation (76), Poland (76), and North Macedonia (75) are from 76 to 80 categories. Therefore, these countries' Point B groups fall under the LE 2 (from age 72 to 79) classes.

Conversely, the IUI of South Africa (56), Djibouti (56), Gabon (50), Fiji (50), Botswana (41), Ghana (38), Namibia (37), India (32), and Sudan (31) are from 31 to 56 categories. Therefore, these countries' Point C groups fall under the LE 3 (from age 63 to 69) groups.

Lastly, Cameroon (23), Lesotho (30), Mali (13), Equatorial Guinea (26), Nigeria (7), Sierra Leone (13), Guinea-Bissau (4), Nigeria (7), and Chad (6) were less than 30%. Burundi had the lowest IUI. These countries fall under the LE 4 (from age 54 to 59) categories.

Thus, we confirm that IUI is critical in raising LE (2018) from LE 4 (Point D) and LE 3 (Point C) and LE 2 (Point B) to LE 1 (Point A) countries.

The difference in IUI for Iceland (98) and Guinea-Bissau (4) was about 25 times, and the difference in LE for Iceland (83) and Guinea-Bissau (58) was 25 years. The LE gap between these countries is mainly due to IUI, GII, BSS, SMDW, and GNI. These variables affect LE related to economic level, lifestyle, information and communication development, and socio-cultural factors.

Activating the Internet and infrastructure for information and communication in the national industry is essential. In countries with insufficient information and communication infrastructure, people's Internet use is inevitably low. Therefore, it is necessary to prepare alternatives to revitalize information and communication technologies in underdeveloped countries such that they can spread faster than economic development. We must devise measures to extend the information and communication capabilities of developed countries to the most underdeveloped countries.

Thus, all humanity will be able to share information at high speed, and the world can become one. We hope that even in underdeveloped countries, information that can increase LE will be quickly disseminated so that users can familiarize themselves with and practice the internalization of helpful health information, thereby laying the foundation for a healthy life.

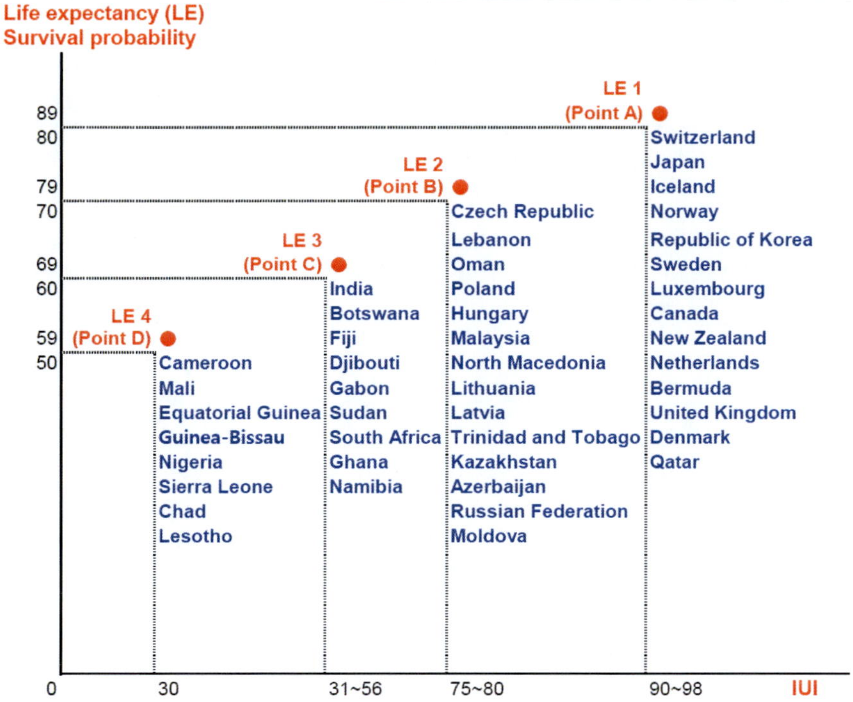

Fig. 3.1.5 LE associated with IUI

In addition, this 2021 book shows the correlation coefficient for LE (2018) and IUI in 160 countries (r = 0.859). Table 3.1.5 displays that LE is associated with IUI. This means that if IUI increases, LE will also increase. Therefore, if the IUI level increases, LE and the survival probability will increase.

Table 3.1.5 Correlations coefficient variables for the LE and IUI

Variables		Correlations coefficient	p-value
LE	IUI	0.859	0.000

3.1.6 LE and FTMPS

Fig. 3.1.6 shows FTPS and LE by country. In a previous study (Kim, 2013; Kim & Kim, 2014), FTMTS affected the centenarian rate (50–54) in the 32 OECD countries and involved SPBC (70) in 32 countries surveyed. In other words, this confirms that the SEFs of FTMPS are essential in the production of LE.

In LE (2018) of this book, for example of fixed telephone subscriptions (per 100 people, 2017) of France (60), Japan (50), Switzerland (42), Spain (42), Iceland (44), Republic of Korea (53), Malta (55), Luxembourg (47), Greece (49), Austria (42), Portugal (47), United Kingdom (48), Germany (54) are FTMPS categories from 54 to 60. These countries' FTPS was high groups among the 160 countries. These countries correspond to Point A, LE 1 (from age 81 to 84) in Fig. 3.1.6.

In addition, the FTMPS of Croatia (34), Uruguay (33), Serbia (30), Mauritius (33), Hungary (32), Antigua and Barbuda (25), Grenada (29), Moldova (28), Estonia (27), Antigua and Barbuda (25), and the Bahamas (30) are from 25 to 34 categories. Therefore, their Point B groups fall under the LE 2 (from age 72 to 78) classes.

Lastly, the FTMPS of Fiji (9), South Africa (8), Namibia (8), Djibouti (4), Botswana (6), Comoros (2), Senegal (2), Papua New Guinea (2), Zimbabwe (2), and India (2) were less than 10. These countries fall under the LE 3 (from age 61 to 69) categories.

Thus, we confirm that FTMPS is critical in raising LE (2018) from LE 3 (Point C) and LE 2 (Point B) to LE 1 (Point A) countries.

The difference in FTMPS for France (60) and Comoros (2) was about 30 times, and the difference in LE for France (83) and Comoros (64) and Zimbabwe (61) was each 19 and 22 years. Results study so far in this book, the LE gap between these countries is mainly due to FTMPS, IUI, GII, BSS, SMDW, and GNI. These variables affect LE related to economic level, lifestyle, information and communication development, and socio-cultural factors.

Telephones are essential in human life. Now, the phone has evolved into a mobile phone that is easy to carry. Telephone communication is primary. It is a medium of communication with family, relatives, and friends. It has become a valuable means of communication to speak and listen to news through contact with people and convey opinions. Communication over the phone can help smooth human relationships and relieve mental stress, helping mental health.

However, telephone penetration rate may still be low depending on the country's economic level. Since the telephone is an essential means of communication for humans, the telephone penetration rate should be increased in the same way as each country's Internet business. It is a crucial factor in achieving the average human LE in underdeveloped countries.

Therefore, developed countries can extend the basic lifespan of humanity by helping less developed countries expand their information and communication business.

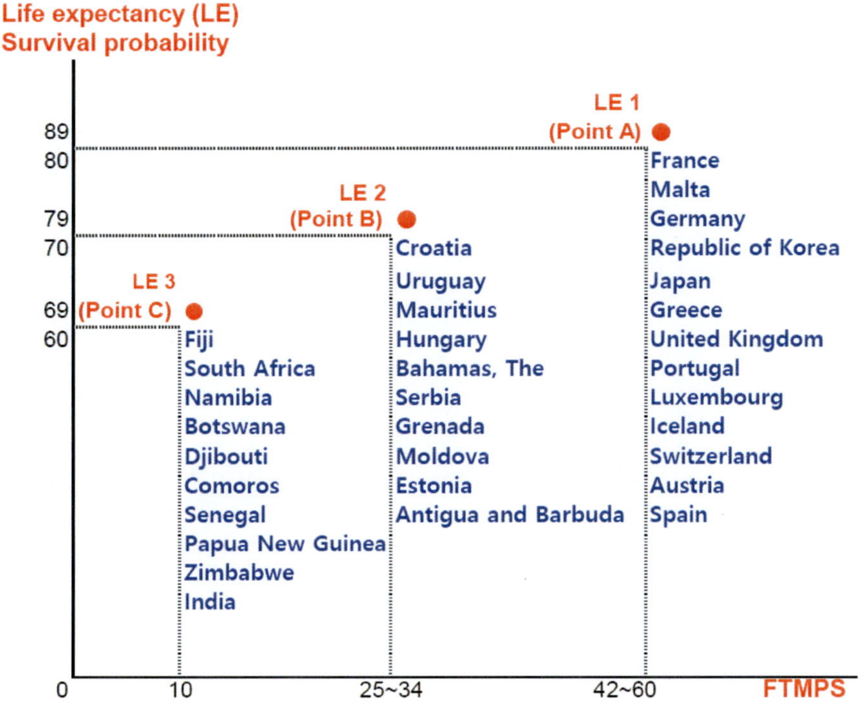

Fig. 3.1.6 LE associated with FTMPS

In addition, this 2021 book shows the correlation coefficient for LE (2018) and FTMPS in 160 countries (r = 0.727). Table 3.1.6 proves that LE is associated with FTMPS. This means that if it is an increased FTMPS, LE will also increase. Therefore, if the national fixed telephone subscriptions level increases, LE and the survival probability will increase.

Table 3.1.6 Correlations coefficient variables for the LE and FTMPS

Variables		Correlations coefficient	p-value
LE	FTMPS	0.727	0.000

3.1.7 LE and GHE

Fig. 3.1.7 shows GHE and LE by country. In a previous study (Kim, 2013; Kim & Kim, 2014), GHE affected the centenarian rate (50–54) in the 32 OECD countries and also involved SPBC (70) in 32 countries surveyed. In other words, this confirms that the SEFs of GHE are essential in LE production.

In LE (2018) of this book, domestic general GHE (% of current health expenditure) of Norway (85), Sweden (85), Luxembourg (85), Japan (84), Denmark (84), and Iceland (82) are from 82 to 85 categories. These countries' GHE is a high class in the 167 countries. These countries correspond to Point A, LE 1 (from age 81 to 84) in Fig. 3.1.7.

In addition, the GHE of Estonia (74), Uruguay (73), Poland (71), Poland (71), Turkey (77), Colombia (72), Thailand (76), Belarus (70), Samoa (72), and Bolivia (71) are from 70 to 77 categories. Therefore, their Point B groups fall under the LE 2 (from age 71 to 78) classes.

Conversely, the GHE of Djibouti (50), Kenya (42), Gabon (59), Tanzania (43), South Africa (54), Namibia (46), Angola (42) are from 42 to 59 categories. Therefore, these countries' Point C groups fall under the LE 3 (from 61 to 67) categories.

Lastly, the GHE of Cameroon (6), Equatorial Guinea (20), Guinea-Bissau (9), Nigeria (15), Sierra Leone (10), Chad (17), and Central African Republic (6) were less than 20. Cameroon and the Central African

Republic had the lowest GHE. These countries fall under the LE 4 (from age 53 to 59) categories.

Thus, we confirm that GHE is critical in raising LE (2018) from LE 4 (Point D) and LE 3 (Point C) and LE 2 (Point B) to LE1 (Point A) countries.

The difference in GHE for Norway (85) and Cameroon (6) was about 14 times, and the difference in LE for Norway (83) and Cameroon (59) was 24 years. Results study so far in this book, the LE gap between these countries is mainly due to GHE, FTMPS, IUI, GII, BSS, SMDW, and GNI. These variables affected LE by indicators related to economic level, lifestyle, information and communication development, GHE, and socio-cultural factors.

The proportion of government healthcare expenditure is determined by the economic situation of the country and the health level of the people. However, even if the economy is a high-level one, the proportion of health and medical expenses is not always high. It is determined by the degree of interest in the health of the people of that country and the will of the political leaders for the health of the people. Therefore, the government's expenditure on health care depends on whether the country's economic reality has the financial capacity to spend on public health. However, it is possible to determine the people's health level based on its priority in national affairs. Let us suppose the state is managed by making the health level of the country its top priority. In that case, the national LE of the country will exceed the average LE of the people of the world.

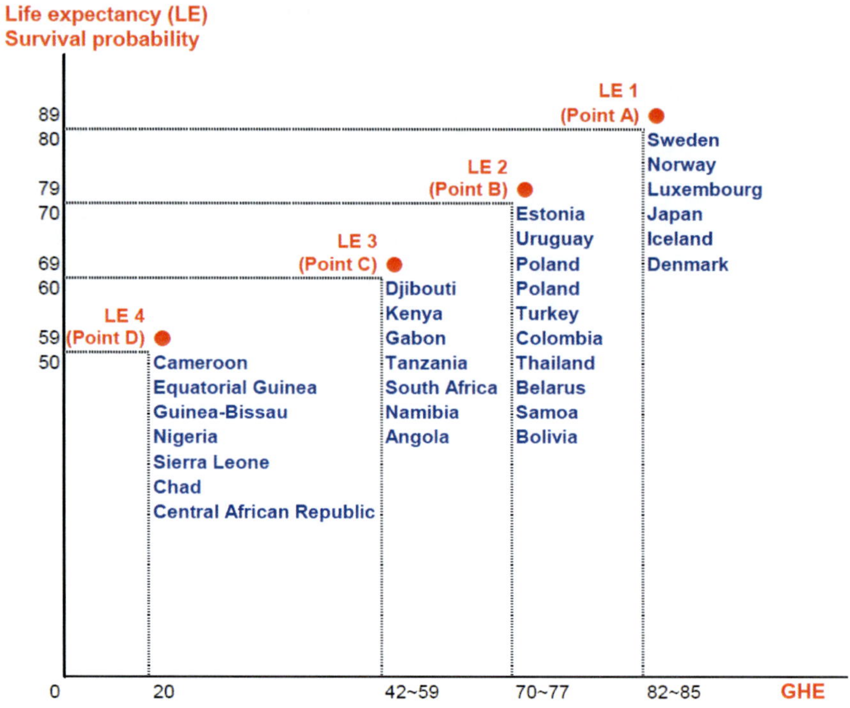

Fig. 3.1.7 LE associated with GHE

Additionally, this 2021 book shows the correlation coefficient for LE (2018) and GHE in 167 countries (r = 0.708). Table 3.1.7 presents results research proving that LE is associated with GHE. This means that if GHE increases, LE will also rise; therefore, if the domestic general government of health expenditure level increases, LE and the survival probability will increase.

Table 3.1.7 Correlations coefficient variables for the LE and GHE

Variables		Correlations coefficient	p-value
LE	GHE	0.708	0.000

3.1.8 LE and UP

Fig. 3.1.8 shows UP and LE by country. In a previous study (Kim & Kim, 2016), UP affected the Healthy Life Expectancy (HLE) in the 178 countries surveyed. In other words, this confirms that the SEFs of UP are essential for LE production.

In LE (2018) of this book, the urban population (% of the total population) of Bermuda (100), Singapore (100), Qatar (99), Belgium (98), Malta (95), Iceland (94), Puerto Rico (94), Israel (93), Netherlands (92), Japan (92), and Luxembourg (91) are from 91 to 100 categories. These countries' UP is a high class in the 162 countries. These countries correspond to Point A, LE 1 (from age 80 to 84) in Fig. 3.1.8.

Additionally, the UP of Bahrain (89), Curacao (89), Brazil (87), United Arab Emirates (87), Oman (85), Saudi Arabia (84), United States (82), Dominican Republic (82), Mexico (80), and Libya (80) are from 80 to 89 categories. Therefore, these countries' Point B groups fall under the LE 2 (from age 73 to 79) classes.

Conversely, the UP of Gambia (62), Djibouti (78), Botswana (70), Congo, Rep. (67), South Africa (67), and Angola (66) are from 62 to 78 categories. These countries fall under the LE 3 (from age 61 to 69) categories.

Thus, we confirm that UP is critical in raising LE (2018) from LE 3 (Point C) and LE 2 (Point B) to LE 1 (Point A) countries.

The difference in UP for Singapore (100) and Gambia (62) was about 1.6 times, and the difference in LE for Singapore (83) and Gambia (62) was 21 years. Results study so far in this book, the LE gap between these countries is mainly due to UP, GHE, FTMPS, IUI, GII, BSS, SMDW, and GNI. These variables affected LE by indicators related to economic level, lifestyle, information and communication development, GHE, urban population, and socio-cultural factors.

The proportion of urban population can be determined by the country's economy, geographical conditions, and lifestyle. Urbanization of countries with geographical conditions can increase national economic benefits by forming tourist cities and attracting international audiences. In other words, if we can improve the national income level through international tourism, we can raise the national economy urbanization. Thus, national tourism leads to an increase in income. In addition, it can be used to invest in health care through urbanization. This can improve the health of the state's citizens by its investing in medical facilities and health projects to promote the health of the people.

In addition, we live in cities rather than in rural areas because of the convenience of life and the high accessibility of medical institutions. Proximity to the market and management of water and sewage facilities can improve the city's standard of living and maintain quality of life. Finally, the most crucial thing in city life is excellent medical facilities in close proximity to the residence. In the case of the elderly, this is an incredible advantage to prolonging a healthy lifespan.

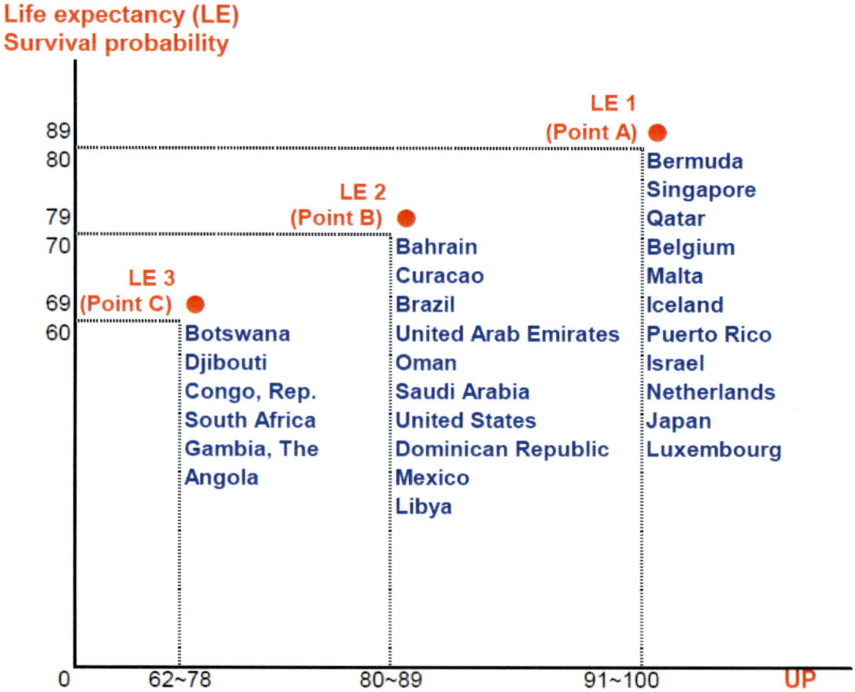

Fig. 3.1.8 LE associated with UP

In addition, this 2021 book shows the correlation coefficient for LE (2018) and UP in 162 countries (r = 0.636). Table 3.1.8 illustrates that LE is associated with UP. This means that if UP increases, LE will also increase.

Therefore, if the national urban population increases, LE and the survival probability will increase.

Table 3.1.8 Correlations coefficient variables for the LE and UP

Variables		Correlations coefficient	p-value
LE	UP	0.636	0.000

3.1.9 LE and SE

Fig. 3.1.9 shows SE and LE by country. In a previous study (Kim & Kim, 2014, 2016, 2018), SE affected the Healthy Life Expectancy (HLE), Inequality in Life Expectancy (ILE), and Remaining Years of Healthy Life Expectancy (RHLE) in all countries surveyed. In other words, this confirms that the SEFs of SE are essential in LE production.

In LE (2018) of this book, the population with at least SE (% ages 25 and older) of Austria, Canada, Finland, Iceland, and Luxembourg are 100% categories. These countries' SE was the highest in the 157 countries. These countries correspond to Point A, LE 1 (from age 82 to 83) in Fig. 3.1.9.

In addition, the SE of United States (96), Croatia (95.7), Lithuania (95.6), Bulgaria (95.4), Azerbaijan (95.6), and Russian Federation (95.9) are about 96 categories. Therefore, their Point B groups fall under the LE 2 (from age 73 to 79) classes.

Conversely, the SE of India (39.2), Pakistan (37.2), Kenya (35.2), Lao People's Democratic Republic (40.4), Congo, Democratic Republic (50.7), Uganda (32.1), Gambia (36.8), Angola (30.2), and Haiti (33.2) were less than about 51. These countries fall under the LE 3 (from age 60 to 69) categories.

Thus, we confirm that SE is critical in raising LE (2018) from LE 3 (Point C) and LE 2 (Point B) to LE 1 (Point A) countries.

The difference in SE for Canada (100) and Angola (30.2) was about 3.3 times, and the difference in LE for Canada (82) and Angola (61) Iceland (83) was 21 years. Results study so far in this book, the LE gap between these countries is mainly due to SE, UP, GHE, FTMPS, IUI, GII, BSS, SMDW, and GNI. These variables affected LE by indicators related to economic level, lifestyle, information and communication development, GHE, urban population, SE, and socio-cultural factors.

Health education can raise the level of national health through health management. Disease prevention education leads to compliance with health rules through preemptive health education. It can increase the effectiveness of prevention education by suppressing the incidence of disease if health rules are well observed. For chronic diseases, it is necessary to maintain a healthy body through health management education in advance. In particular, primary health education on infectious diseases can maximize the response to infectious diseases by blocking the ripple effect of widespread contagious diseases. By blocking external impact on infections in advance, it is possible to protect the public from infectious diseases.

In addition, education is a psychological factor that affects health, and the higher the level of education the higher the interest in health care. The higher the level of education the stronger the brain activity. Brain activation through education can help to prevent brain-related diseases. We can achieve an HLE by reducing the incidence of cardiovascular diseases, such as cerebral infarction and stroke. Therefore, through education, the brain can speed up head rotation and strengthen the brain's activity to lower the probability of dementia in old age.

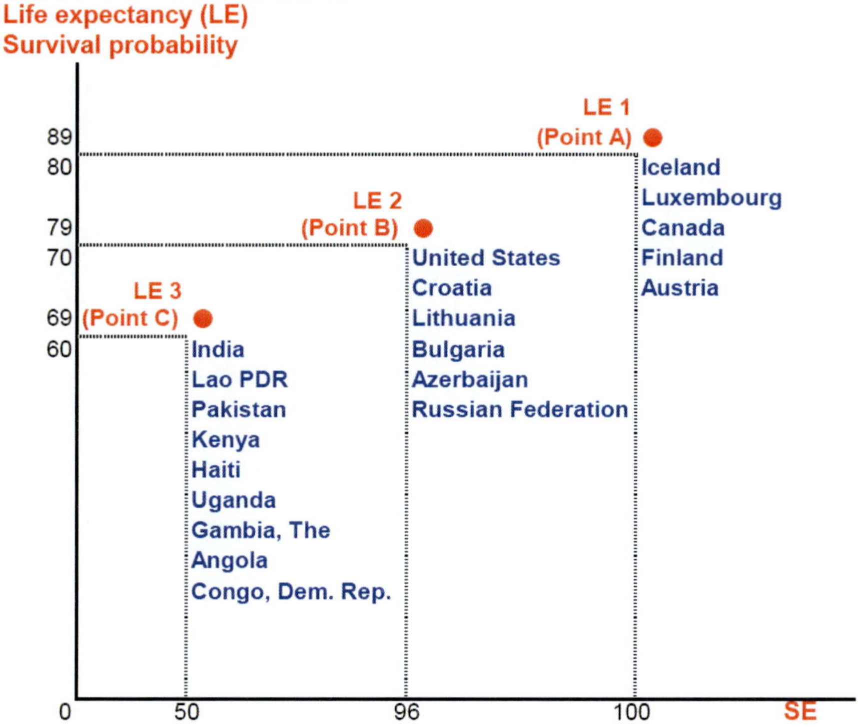

Fig. 3.1.9 LE associated with SE

In addition, this 2021 book shows the correlation coefficient for LE (2018) and SE in 157 countries (r = 0.706). Table 3.1.9 proves that LE is associated with SE. This means that if it is an increased SE, LE will also increase. Therefore, if at least the SE level increases, LE and the survival probability will increase.

Table 3.1.9 Correlations coefficient variables for the LE and SE

Variables		Correlations coefficient	p-value
LE	SE	0.706	0.000

3.1.10 LE and SVPW

Fig. 3.1.10 shows SVPW and LE by country. In a previous study (Kim & Kim, 2018), SVPW affected the Inequality in Life Expectancy (ILE) in 108 countries surveyed. In other words, this confirms that the SEFs of SVPW are essential in LE production.

In LE (2018) of this book, the value of the services added per worker, 2018 (constant 2015 US$) of Luxembourg (207,763), Switzerland (130,515), Norway (126,211), Ireland (116,824), Denmark (107,699), Belgium (99,475), France (98,922), Australia (97,322), Sweden (95,086), and Netherlands (90,346) are from 90,346 to 207,763 categories. Luxembourg's SVPW was the highest in the 151 countries. These countries correspond to Point A, LE 1 (from age 81 to 84) in Fig. 3.1.10.

In addition, the SVPW of Slovak Republic (38,823), Croatia (35,952), Poland (34,623), Estonia (34,396), Hungary (33,487), Bahrain (33,465), Romania (32,981), Lithuania (32,344), Brunei Darussalam (32,230), and Latvia (30,817) are from 30,817 to 38,823 categories. Therefore, these countries' Point B groups fall under the LE 2 (from age 75 to 78) classes.

Conversely, the SVPW of Timor-Leste (3,843), Malawi (3,709), Kenya (3,537), Guinea (3,404), Afghanistan (3,261), Mozambique (3,252), Benin (3,245), Rwanda (3,224), and Togo (3,048) were from 3,048 to 3,843. They fall under the LE 3 (from age 60 to 69) categories.

Thus, we confirm that SVPW is critical in raising LE (2018) from LE 3 (Point C) and LE 2 (Point B) to LE 1 (Point A) countries.

The difference in SVPW for Luxembourg (207,763) and Togo (3,048) was about 68 times, and the difference in LE for Luxembourg (82) and Togo (61) was 21 years. Results study so far in this book, the LE gap between these countries is mainly due to SVPW, UP, SE, GHE, FTMPS, IUI, GII, BSS, SMDW, and GNI. These variables affect LE by indicators related to economic level, lifestyle, information and communication development, GHE, urban population, SE, the value-added per worker, and socio-cultural factors.

The value of the services added per worker is the result of increasing productivity per worker. A high value-added per worker means that countries can improve workers' income. From a holistic point of view, an increase in SVPW leads to an increase in national productivity, which in turn leads to an increase in workers' income. The increase in the state's productivity per worker is work on the premise that the state or capitalists return it to the workers. Even though the added value of workers has increased, if countries cannot pass on a particular part to the workers, it can lead to a decrease in worker morale and subsequent productivity. Therefore, welfare policies that return the added value generated by increasing productivity per worker are necessary.

In addition, the added value that increases worker productivity should be spent on the labor force and provide for workers' income increase. Therefore, it creates an economic margin for workers to spend on welfare and health care. Through this, workers can improve health management and relieve stress caused by work. Ultimately, reinvestment in workers' health and welfare can increase labor productivity by promoting health management. Therefore, we should remember that the improvement of workers' health is directly related to labor productivity. This way, the health management of workers can increase the probability of longevity beyond HLE.

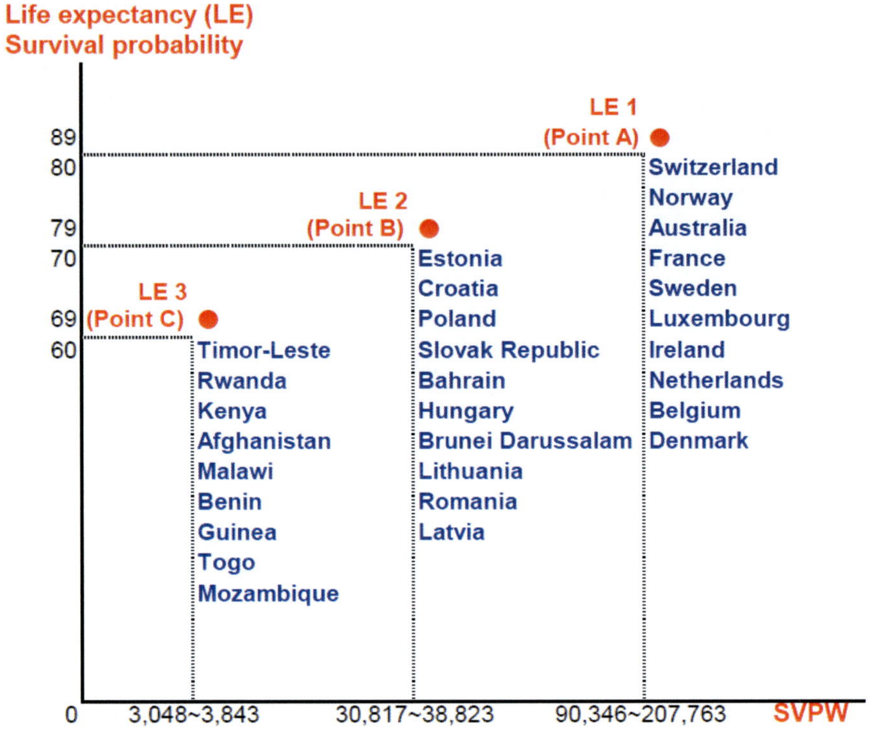

Fig. 3.1.9 LE associated with SVPW

In addition, this 2021 book shows the correlation coefficient for LE (2018) and SVPW in 151 countries (r = 0.668). Table 3.1.10 illustrates that LE is associated with SVPW. This means that if SVPW increases, LE will also increase. Therefore, LE and the survival probability will increase if the value of the services added per worker increases.

Table 3.1.10 Correlations coefficient variables for the LE and SVPW

Variables		Correlations coefficient	p-value
LE	SVPW	0.668	0.000

3.1.11 LE and OPR

Fig. 3.1.11 shows the OPR and LE by country. In a previous study (Kim & Kim, 2018), OPR affected the Inequality in life expectancy (ILE) in the 108 countries that were surveyed, i.e., it confirms that the OPR of SEFs is essential in the production of LE.

In LE (2018) of this book, the old age pension recipients (OPR, % of statutory pension age population) of Japan, Spain, Italy, Israel, France, Republic of Korea, Sweden, Malta, Luxembourg, Ireland, Canada, New Zealand, Finland, Austria, Belgium, Slovenia, Portugal, United Kingdom, Germany, and Chile, had OPR categories as 100%. Their OPR was the highest in the 129 countries. These countries correspond to Point A, LE 1 (from age 80 to 84) in Fig. 3.1.11.

In addition, the SVPW of the Republic of Moldova (75.2), Tonga (73.3), North Macedonia (71.4), Colombia (71.1), Nepal (66.1), Philippines (64), Croatia (57.6), Honduras (56.9), Tunisia (54), Montenegro (52.3), and Ecuador (52) are from 52 to 75 categories. Therefore, their Point B groups fall under the LE 2 (from age 70 to 78) classes.

Conversely, the OPR of India (25.2), Senegal (29.9), Zimbabwe (20.8), Ghana (19), Myanmar (19.3), Ethiopia (15.3), Uganda (24.1), Gambia (17), Togo (19), and Mozambique (17.3) are from about 15 to 30 categories. These countries fall under the LE 3 (from age 60 to 69) classes.

Thus, we confirm that OPR is critical in raising LE (2018) from LE 3 (Point C) and LE 2 (Point B) to LE 1 (Point A) countries.

The difference in OPR for Japan (100) and Ethiopia (15.3) was about 6.5 times, and the difference in LE for Japan (84) and Ethiopia (66) was 18 years. From the results collated in this book, the LE gap between these countries is mainly due to OPR, SVPW, UP, SE, GHE, FTMPS, IUI, GII, BSS, SMDW, and GNI. These variables affect LE by indicators related to economic level, lifestyle, information and communication development, government health expenditure, urban population, education, the value of added per worker, national pension, and socio-cultural factors.

OPRs constitute a significant source of livelihood security and health care. Therefore, the state should implement a pension insurance system. Older people who have a particular job throughout their lives receive monetary compensation, i.e., pension, even after retirement. Seniors receiving pensions will not have much difficulty using hospital clinics. If there is no national pension system for the elderly, there will be difficulties securing old age living expenses and health management. Suppose that we cannot implement a national old age pension system, then the government should implement one. Even basic livelihood security to protect the lives and health of the elderly at a minimum would help the cause greatly.

Additionally, given countries that provide health care, the insured can receive quality health care at a reasonable price. The problem is for people who have lived as day laborers without a job. If the state can build a stable social security system, it will be the country's local social support, which helps maintain a basic life with the National Pension or Living Support. But what needs to be done when a disease occurs in a member of the low-income class? If they fall ill, the state should classify them as healthcare recipients and provide accessible health care. Therefore, institutional arrangements are needed so that all of humanity can enjoy an average lifespan of 74 years or more.

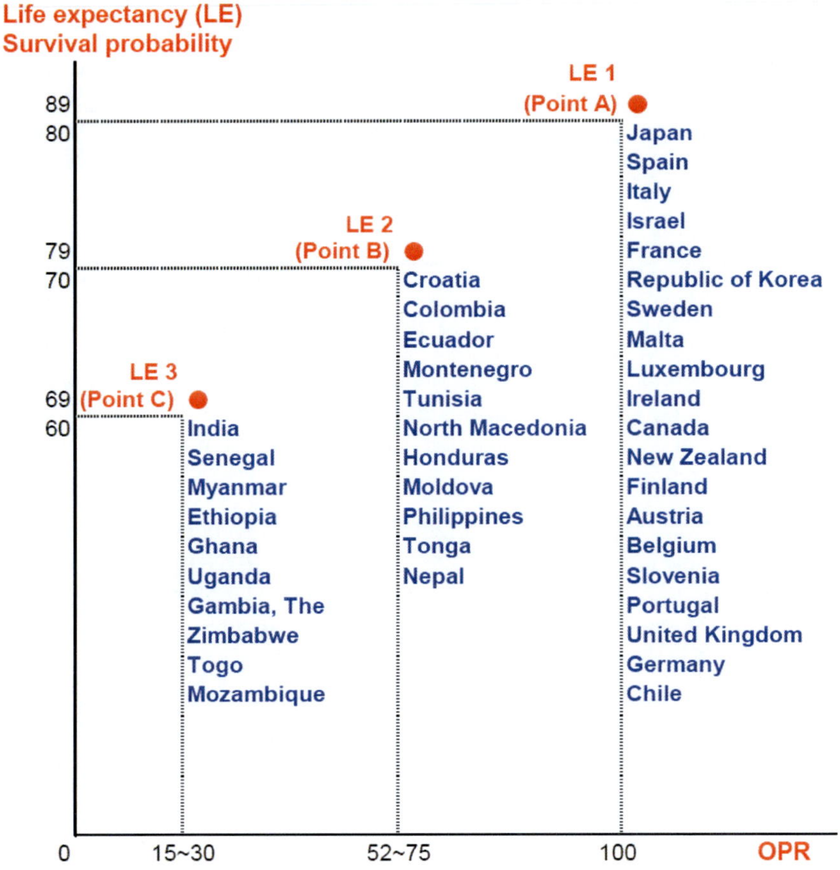

Fig. 3.1.11 LE associated with OPR

In addition, this 2021 book shows the correlation coefficient for LE (2018) and OPR in 129 countries (r = 0.621). Table 3.1.11 proves that LE is associated with OPR. This means that if OPR increases, LE will also rise. Therefore, if the national OPRs increase, LE and the survival probability will increase.

Table 3.1.11 Correlations coefficient variables for the LE and OPR

Variables		Correlations coefficient	p-value
LE	OPR	0.621	0.000

3.1.12 LE and GI

Fig. 3.1.12 shows the GI and LE by country. In a previous study (Kim & Kim, 2018), GI affected the Inequality in life expectancy (ILE) in the 108 countries that were surveyed, confirming that the SEFs of GI are essential in LE production.

In LE (2018) of this book, the GI (2005–2013) of Slovenia (24.9), Sweden (26.1), Iceland (26.3), Norway (26.8), Denmark (26.9), Netherlands (28.9), and Finland (27.8) were from 24.9 to 28.9 categories. Slovenia's GI was the lowest in the 105 countries. These countries correspond to Point A, LE 1 (from age 81 to 83) in Fig. 3.1.12.

Additionally, the GI of Estonia (32.7), Poland (32.8), Bosnia and Herzegovina (33.0), Lithuania (32.6), Azerbaijan (33.0), Bangladesh (32.1), Kyrgyzstan (33.4), Nepal (32.8), and Cambodia (31.8) are from 31.8 to 33.4 categories. Therefore, their Point B groups fall under the LE 2 (from age 70 to 78) classes.

Conversely, the GI of Senegal (40.3), Fiji (42.8), Gabon (42.2), Mauritania (40.5), Malawi (46.2), Ghana (42.8), Uganda (44.6), and Benin (43.5) are from 40.3 to 46.2. These countries fall under the LE 3 (from age 61 to 68) groups.

Thus, we confirm that GI is critical in raising LE (2018) from LE 3 (Point C) and LE 2 (Point B) to LE 1 (Point A) countries.

The difference in GI for Slovenia (24.9) and Malawi (46.2) was about 1.9 times, and the gap in LE for Slovenia (81) and Malawi (64) was 17 years. Results show that the LE gap between these countries is mainly due to GI, OPR, SVPW, UP, SE, GHE, FTMPS, IUI, GII, BSS, SMDW, and GNI. These variables affect LE by indicators related to economic level, lifestyle, information and communication development, public health expenditure, urban population, education, old-age pension, Gini Index, and socio-cultural factors.

GI is an income inequality phenomenon, i.e., a GI of 0 indicates perfect equality, whereas 100 indicate complete inequality. The result is that the GI gap affects LE as well as the inequality in it (Kim & Kim, 2018). Prosperous people do not have to worry about medical bills, only the poor do. As a result, the rich can pursue advanced medical care. Because health care deals with life, the wealthy are willing to pay for health care when it seems pertinent but the poor are less likely to be able to afford it. In this reality, we can see a gap in human LE due to the income gap. Therefore, it is the role of national policymakers to narrow the income gap. Just as there is no difference in human lifespan due to income disparity in medical care, regardless of race, all human beings should receive equal medical aid regardless of income.

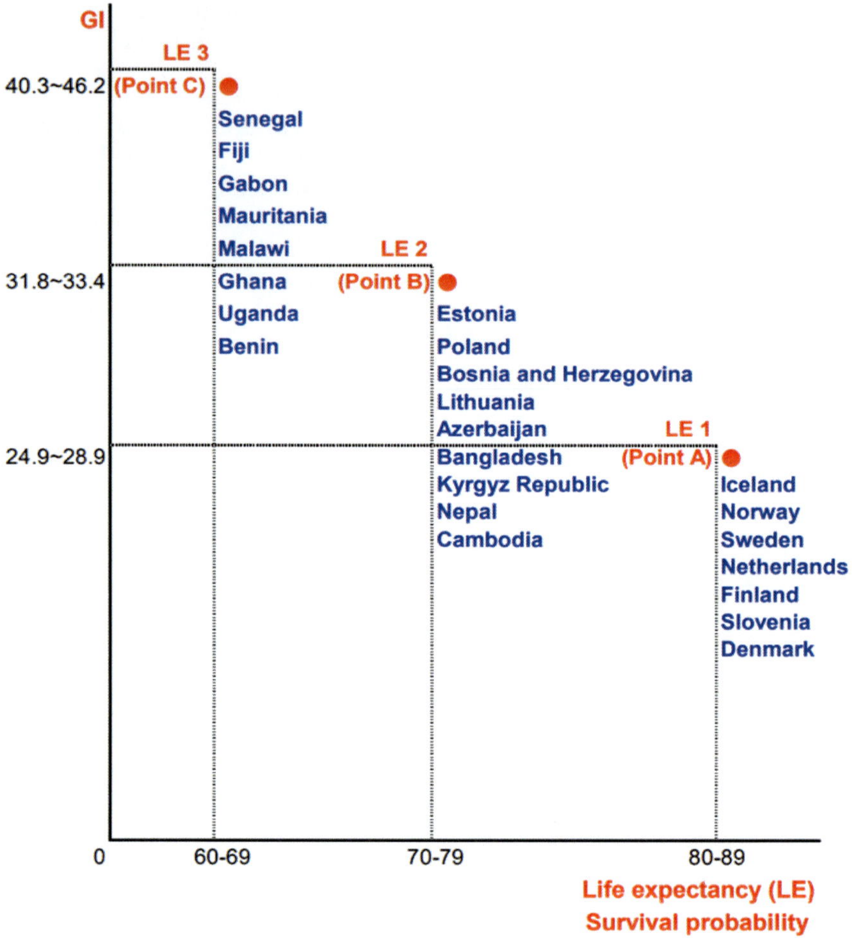

Fig. 3.1.12 LE associated with GI

In addition, this 2021 book shows the correlation coefficient for LE (2018) and GI in 105 countries (r = −0.352). Table 3.1.12 illustrates that LE is associated with GI. This means that if GI decreases, LE will also increase. Therefore, if the national GI level decreases, LE and the survival probability will increase.

Table 3.1.12 Correlations coefficient variables for the LE and GI

Variables		Correlations coefficient	p-value
LE	GI	-0.352	0.000

3.1.13 LE and DCI

Fig. 3.1.13 shows the DCI and LE by country. In a previous study (Kim & Kim, 2017), DCI affected Older Age Life expectancy (OLE) in the 34 European countries that were surveyed, confirming that the SEFs of DCI are essential in the production of LE.

In LE (2018) of this book, the country-level depth of credit index (0 = low to 8 = high) of the Republic of Korea, Canada, New Zealand, United Kingdom, Germany, and the United States is computed at 8. These countries' DCI was the highest among the 128 countries. These countries correspond to Point A, LE 1 (from age 79 to 83) in Fig. 3.1.13.

In addition, the DCI of the Czech Republic, Estonia, Slovak Republic, Colombia, Thailand, Tunisia, Morocco, Serbia, Romania, and Vietnam rank at 7. Therefore, their Point B groups fall under the LE 2 (from age 75 to 79) classes.

Conversely, the DCI of Lao PDR, Madagascar, Ghana, and Zimbabwe were found to be 6. These countries fall under the LE 3 (from age 61 to 68) categories.

Thus, we confirm that DCI is critical in raising LE (2018) from LE 3 (Point C) and LE 2 (Point B) to LE 1 (Point A) countries.

The difference in DCI for the Republic of Korea (8) and Zimbabwe (6) was about 1.3 times, and that in LE for the Republic of Korea (83) and Zimbabwe (61) was 22 years. Results indicate that the LE gap between these countries is mainly due to DCI, GI, OPR, SVPW, UP, SE, GHE, FTMPS, IUI, GII, BSS, SMDW, and GNI. These variables affect LE by indicators related to economic level, lifestyle, information and communication development, public health expenditure, urban population, education, old-age pension, Gini Index, credit index, the value of added per worker, and socio-cultural factors.

The DCI index is economic creditworthiness. It can be based on the country's reliability in paying the money. The index ranges from 0 to 8, with higher values indicating the availability of more credit information (WB, 2021).

Therefore, the creditworthiness of a country is directly related to the economic level of that country as it reflects how well the state is capable of resolving its international debts. Therefore, an excellent national credit rating corresponds to a superior economic level. If the economic level is perfect, the federal financial power is strong and has the financial ability to invest in the public health and welfare sector. Therefore, if national policymakers prioritize their policies, they should prioritize places where they can invest for the welfare and health of their citizens.

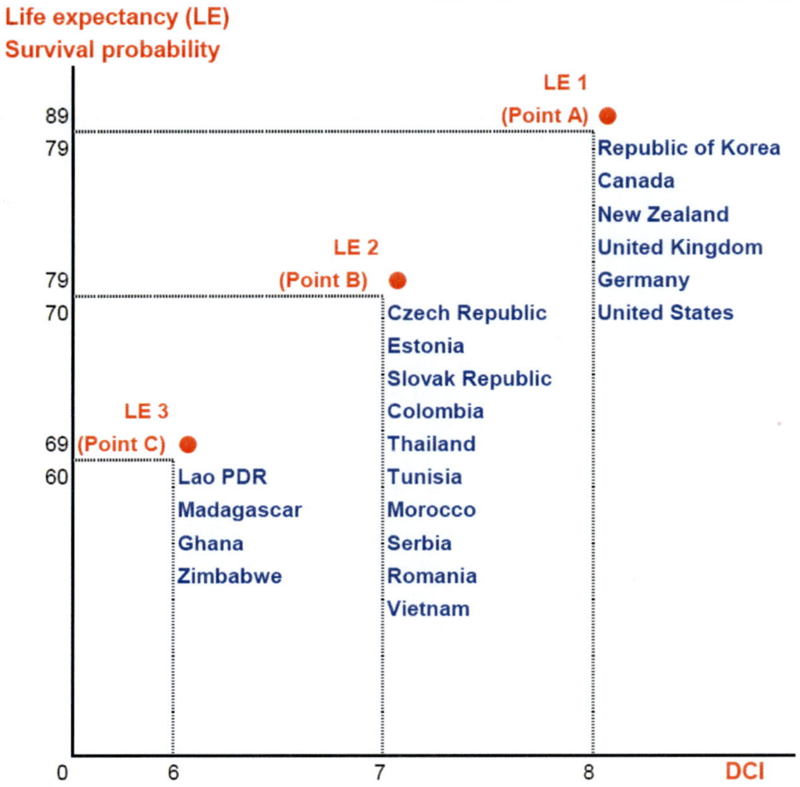

Fig. 3.1.13 LE associated with DCI

In addition, this 2021 book shows the correlation coefficient for LE (2018) and DCI in 128 countries (r = 0.279). Table 3.1.13 proves that LE is associated with DCI. This means that if DCI increases, LE will also rise; therefore, if the country-level depth of credit index increases, LE and the survival probability will increase.

Table 3.1.13 Correlations coefficient variables for the LE and DCI

Variables		Correlations coefficient	p-value
LE	DCI	0.279	0.005

3.1.14 LE and HEPGDP

Fig. 3.1.14 shows the HEPGDP and LE by country. In a previous study (Kim & Kim, 2014), DCI affected the survival probability of becoming a centenarian (SPBC) in the 32 surveyed countries. In other words, this confirms that the SEFs of HEPGDP are essential in the production of LE.

In LE (2018) of this book, the current health expenditure (% of GDP) of United States (16.89), Switzerland (11.88), Germany (11.43), France (11.26), Japan (10.95), Sweden (10.90), Canada (10.79), Austria (10.33), Belgium (10.32), Denmark (10.07), Norway (10.05), and the United Kingdom (10.00), indicate that those HEPGDP categories are from 10 to 17. Thus, United States' HEPGDP was the highest in the 165 countries. These countries correspond to Point A, LE 1 (from age 79 to 84) in Fig. 3.1.14.

Additionally, the HEPGDP of Bosnia and Herzegovina (8.90), Nicaragua (8.56), Serbia (8.54), Montenegro (8.42), Lebanon (8.35), Ecuador (8.14), Suriname (7.97), Jordan (7.79), Ukraine (7.72), the Czech Republic (7.65), and Colombia (7.64) are from 7.64 to 8.90 categories. Therefore, their Point B groups fall under the LE 2 (from age 72 to 79) classes.

Conversely, the HEPGDP of Liberia (6.74), Uganda (6.53), Togo (6.17), Botswana (5.85), and Burkina Faso (5.63) are from 5.36 to 6.74 categories. These countries fall under the LE 3 (from age 61 to 68) classes.

Lastly, Côte d'Ivoire (4.19), Chad (4.10), Nigeria (3.89), Mali (3.88), Cameroon (3.53), and Equatorial Guinea (3.00) correspond to categories between 3.00 and 4.19. These countries fall under the LE 4 (from age 54 to 59) groups.

Thus, we confirm that HEPGDP is critical in raising LE (2018) from LE 3 (Point C) and LE 4 (Point D) and LE 2 (Point B) to LE 1 (Point A) countries.

The difference in HEPGDP for the United States (16.89) and Mali (3.88) was about 4.3 times, and the difference in LE for the United States (79) and Mali (59) was 20 years. Results spotlight that the LE gap between these countries is mainly due to HEPGDP, DCI, GI, OPR, SVPW, UP, SE, GHE, FTMPS, IUI, GII, BSS, SMDW, and GNI. These variables affect LE by indicators related to economic level, lifestyle, information and communication development, public health expenditure, urban population, education, old-age pension, health expenditure of GDP, Gini Index, depth of credit index, and socio-cultural factors.

The level of current health expenditure can be expressed as a percentage of GDP. No matter how high a country's GDP is, if the country's healthcare spending is negligible, the government cannot guarantee the national health level. In other words, HEPGDP can ensure the national health level only when the level of federal current medical expenses can be continuously increased from the current level. National health and medical expenses cannot improve the national health level in a short period by making a significant and timely investment because we can only achieve the level of country health through continuous investment in the mid to long term. If the fitness level deteriorates due to a natural disaster, it is necessary to take immediate action to protect people's lives. However, LE, an indicator of the national health level, is not a short term indicator. Therefore, if the country intends to increase the LE of its citizens, the government is required to set an incremental, mid to long term LE goal, starting now, and expand this index. We are convinced that a country that strengthens the health promotion of its people by establishing a long and short term national health LE will surely achieve be one that exceeds the global average LE.

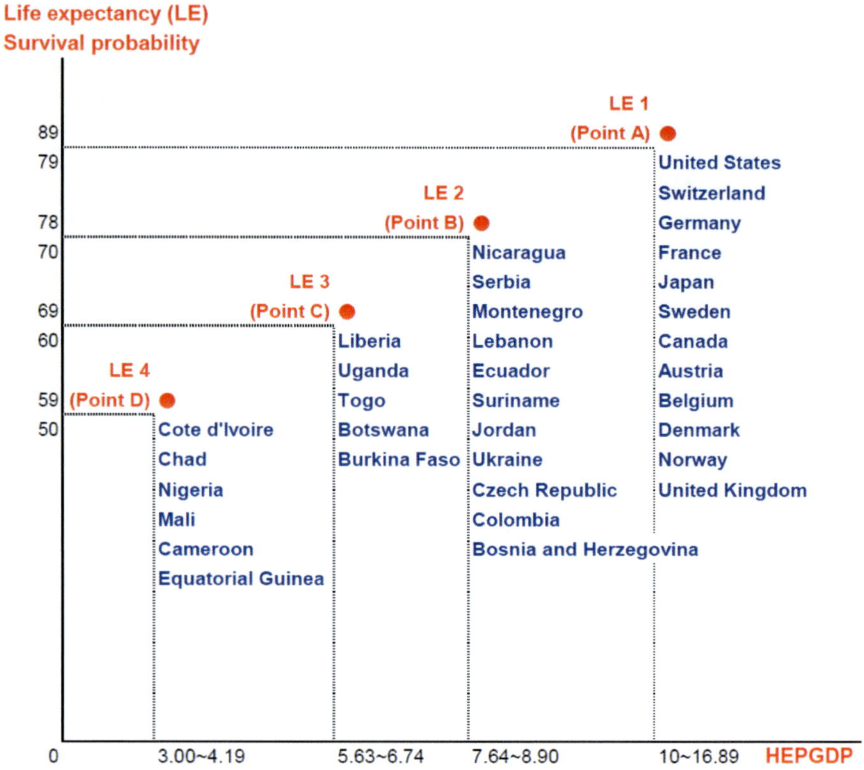

Fig. 3.1.14 LE associated with HEPGDP

In addition, this 2021 book shows the correlation coefficient for LE (2018) and HEPGDP in 165 countries (r = 0.317). Table 3.1.12 proves that LE is associated with HEPGDP. This means that if HEPGDP increased, LE will also rise. Therefore, if the national current health expenditure (% of GDP) level increases, LE and the survival probability will increase.

Table 3.1.14 Correlations coefficient variables for the LE and HEPGDP

Variables		Correlations coefficient	p-value
LE	HEPGDP	0.317	0.000

3.2 LE at age 60

3.2.1 Impact on old age LE (OLE) of SEFs

OLE refers to the LE of individuals from the age of 60. Excluding genetic factors, it differs due to acquired influences. However, if we live in the same area and have similar eating habits and lifestyles, OLE is not expected to enter the discussion. OLE can also arise from the differences in the poor national social environment caused by the per capita income gap.

In addition, gender equality in developed countries can influence OLE. In a national society where there is no gender discrimination, women can expect a stress-free life due to gender equality in all fields such as politics, economy, community, and culture.

Fig. 3.2 confirms this fact. If national income, gender equality, and economic national credibility increase from 20% to 40% in the OLE 2 curve, OLE increases from 60 to 75 years (Point A). However, if these factors increase from 40% to 60% (Point B), the OLE should increase to 90 years. Instead, it decreases to 60 years—the cause found in the SEFs. Specifically, the difference between Points A and C is the result of the GII. For example, in the OLI 1 curve, Point A of the GII is 40%, where Point C is 60%. Hence, since the GII increases by 20%, the OLE decreases to 60 years. The problem is that if the GII is low, then the OLE will increase.

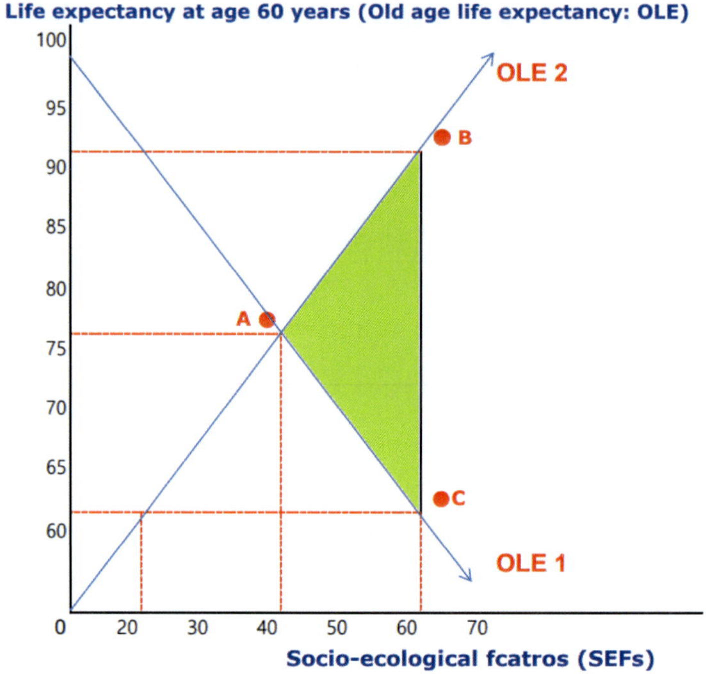

Fig. 3.2. Relationship between OLE and SEFs

(a) GNI

Fig. 3.2.1 shows that an increase in national income increases OLE. For example, if the national income increases from $1,500 to $3,000, OLE will increase from 60 to 85 years (Point B). Hence, income level is also a necessary condition for OLE. In particular, national income is the most critical indicator of individuals' and societies' economic and living standards; when the national income is high, economic activity and the health levels of the elderly increase because income is a means of maintaining health and improving the quality of life. Therefore, it is crucial to raise the income level of the elderly by, for example, creating jobs that can provide such economic support.

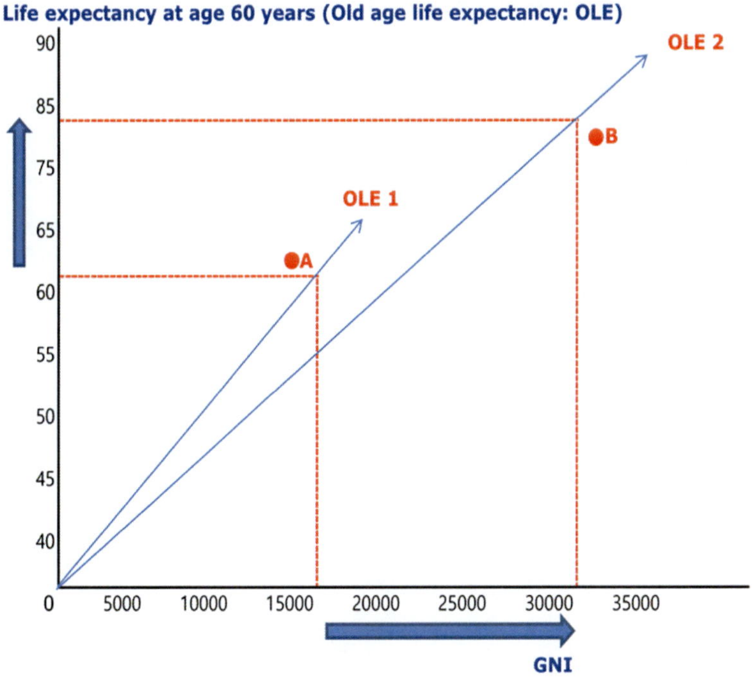

Fig. 3.2.1. Relationship between OLE and the GNI

(b) GII

Fig. 3.2.2 shows that as the GII increases, OLE decreases. For example, if the GII increases from 0.5 to 0.7, OLE decreases to 75 years (Point B), despite a LE of 85 years. Hence, if the GII has an essential meaning in OLE, then future society must focus on the issue of gender equality.

In this regard, LE over the age of 60 is higher for women than for men. Although women have a longer lifespan than men, several factors can affect their health, such as stress due to gender discrimination. In fact, in developed countries without gender discrimination, women's lifespans are increased. But in underdeveloped countries, such discrimination can shorten their lifespans due to the poor social environment and living standards.

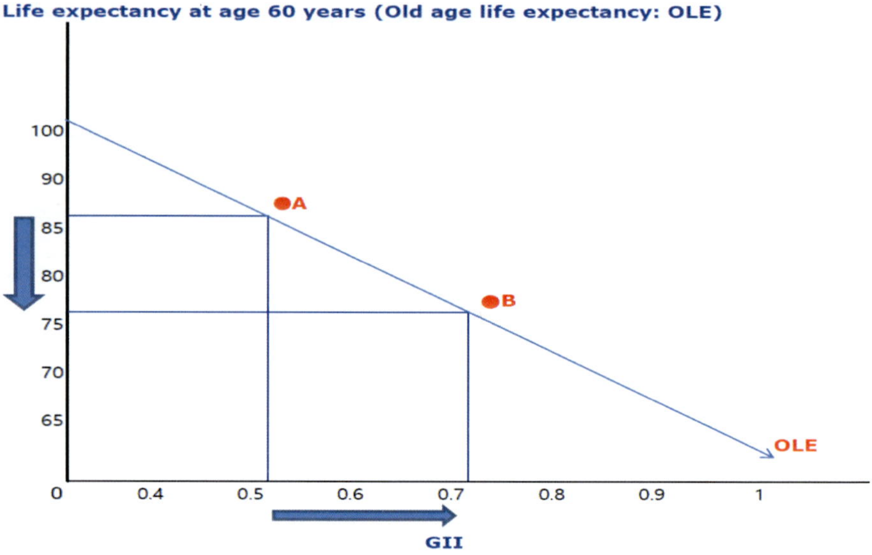

Fig. 3.2.2. Relationship between OLE and the GII

(c) BSS and SMDW

Fig. 3.2.3 shows that as the BSS and SMDW increase, OLE also increases. For example, if the BSS and SMDW increase from 70% to 100%, OLE increases from 60 to 80 years (Point B). Hence, BSS and SMDW are significant variables in OLE. In addition, sanitation services—and safely managed drinking water—are essential factors for increasing OLE. If there are no sanitation services and no SMDW in a village, it cannot protect the inhabitants from infectious diseases. Therefore, sanitation services and SMDW can help save precious lives from contracting contagious diseases.

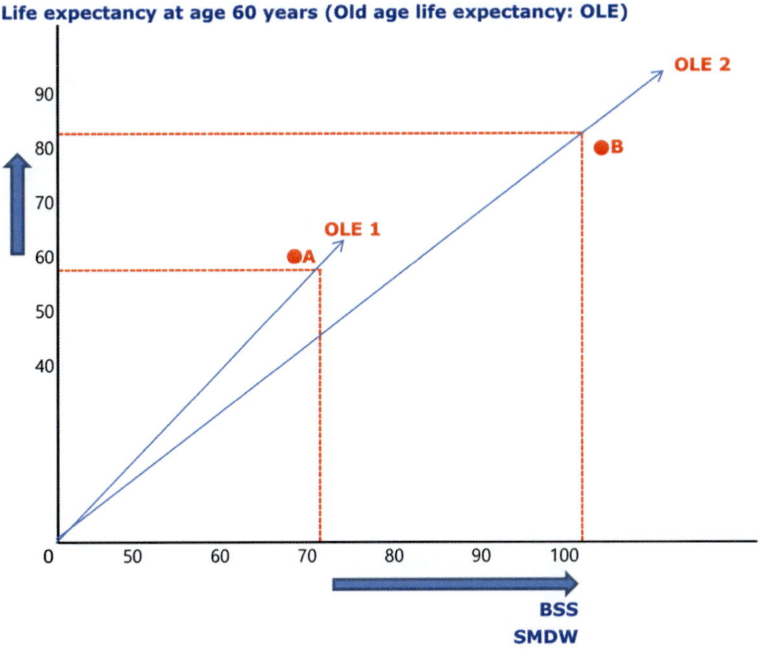

Fig. 3.2.3. Relationship between OLE and the BSS & SMDW

(d) IUI and FTMPS

Fig. 3.2.4 shows that as IUI and FTMPS increase, OLE also increases. For example, if the number of internets and phone users increases from 75% to 90%, the OLE increases from 60 to 80 years (Point B). Thus, IUI and FTMPS are also significant variables in OLE. However, OLE cannot be guaranteed if IUI and FTMPS are ineffective. Therefore, to protect the communication of its citizens and ensure OLE, countries should invest in fundamental communication sectors.

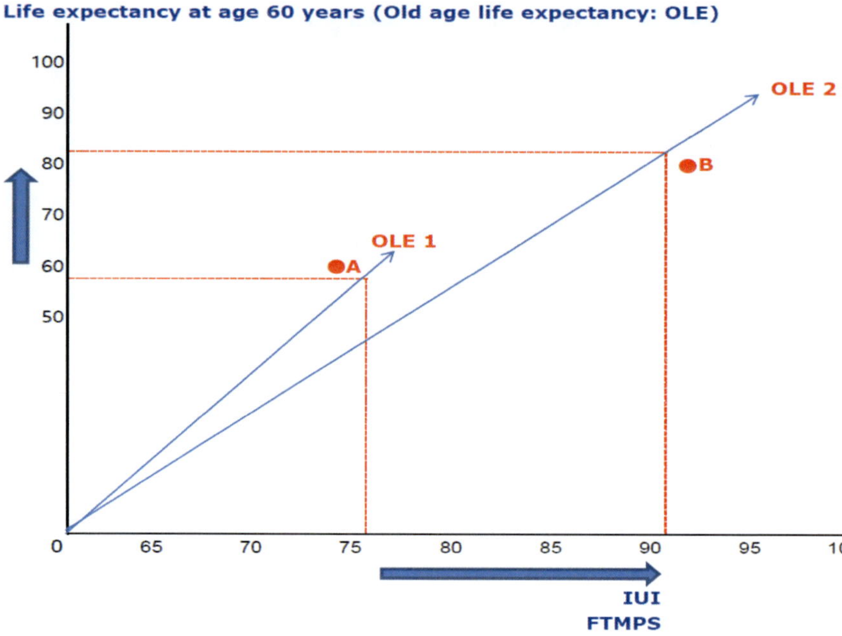

Fig. 3.2.4. Relationship between OLE and the IUI & FTMPS

(e) UP, SVPW and HEPGDP in CLSS

Fig. 3.2.5 indicates that OLE increases as UP, SVPW, and HEPGDP increase. For example, if UP, SVPW, and HEPGDP increase from 75% to 90%, OLE would increase from 60 to 80 years (Point B). Higher SVPW and HEPGDP can pay for medical expenses in case of disease, owing to increased income, and strengthen national health policy. Moreover, UP has the advantage of getting to a general hospital quickly Because of the development of transportation facilities and ambulance facilities in public hospitals in the vicinity. However, OLE cannot be guaranteed if UP, SVPW, and HEPGDP are insufficient in a country's system because of underdeveloped local residence and government medical financial support reduction. Therefore, to protect the health of its citizens and ensure OLE, countries must increase UP, SVPW, and HEPGDP through their economic support.

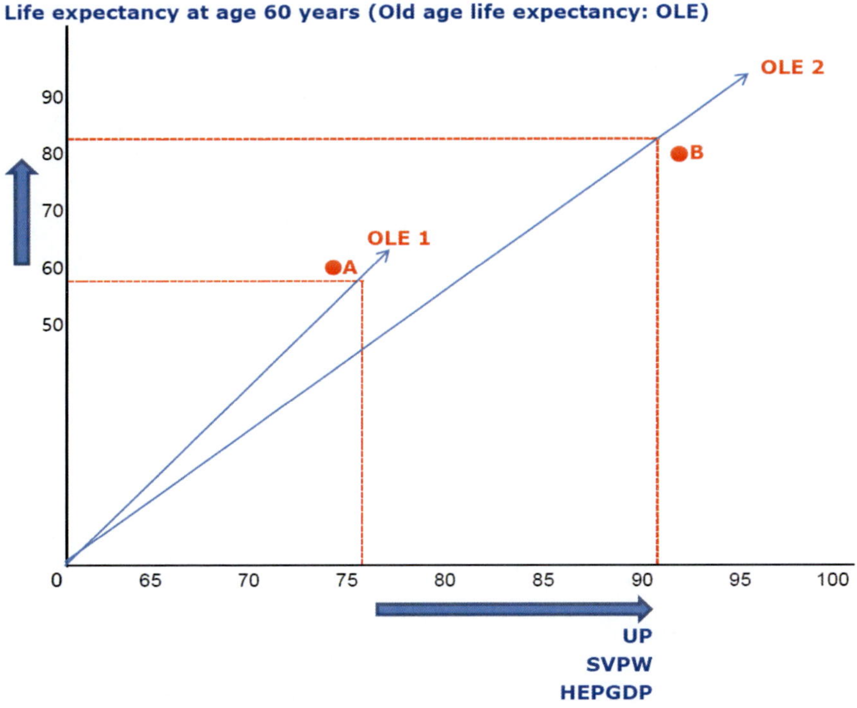

Fig. 3.2.5. Relationship between OLE and the UP & SVPW & HEPGDP

3.2.2 A case study of OLE

Over the past decade, the population in the world has been aging rapidly. The proportion of people aged 65 years and older predict an increase from 14% in 2010 to 25% in 2050 (WHO, 2017). However, although people live longer, the chances of enjoying good health in their old age vary across countries (WHO, 2017). Although previous studies have determined country-level HLE, health expenditure, and income, country-level OLE—associated with the GNI, GII, SVPW, UP, BSS, SMDW, IUI, HEPGDP, and FTMPS—has been overlooked (Mathers et al., 2015; Kim & Kim, 2014a, 2017). Furthermore, from a socio-ecological perspective, no studies have examined OLE according to the GNI, GII, SVPW, UP, BSS, SMDW, IUI, HEPGDP, and FTMPS. These perspectives of OLE require exploration to contribute to research and public policies on the elderly.

The financial crisis in Europe has posed significant threats to health and related systems (Karanikolos et al., 2013). For instance, even though Greece, Spain, and Portugal have adopted strict fiscal austerity, their economies have continued to recede, placing considerable strain on their healthcare systems. Meanwhile, outbreaks of infectious diseases are increasingly common in these countries. Therefore, before making significant cuts in public spending measures, it is essential to compare the lack of evidence for short term fixes that can potentially and adversely affect the health and welfare of the population as a whole (Stuckler et al., 2010; Kim & Kim, 2017b).

Nine SEFs are assumed to be associated with OLE. In addition, to better understand the influence of OLE as an indicator of old age health disparity in 39 countries, it is crucial to determine its contribution to these SEFs.

Moreover, the claim that country-level socio-ecological inequality factors can influence OLE remains untested using national indicators globally (Kim & Kim, 2017b). Therefore, this chapter focuses on the associations between country-level OLE and socio-ecological inequalities such as GNI, GII, SVPW, UP, BSS, SMDW, IUI, HEPGDP, and FTMPS.

While the GNI, GII, SVPW, UP, BSS, SMDW, IUI, HEPGDP, and FTMPS are critical indicators of SEFs, a retrospective analysis of health level factors contributing to GNI, GII, SVPW, UP, BSS, SMDW, IUI, HEPGDP, and FTMPS can identify the critical determinants of OLE within a country. It can also inform policy decisions regarding OLE and SEFs. In this book, 39 countries around the world were investigated.

A conceptual framework for OLE and SEFs

The proposed conceptual framework depicts the SEFs effect on OLE (Fig.3.2.6). In this case, SEFs and hereditary factors may affect or control OLE, although the latter is excluded in this research (Kim & Kim, 2017b). Consequently, SEFs are analyzed in this chapter.

From SEFs perspective, health promotion is determined by multiple influences, including personal, community, and public policy factors (McLeroy et al., 1988; Kim & Kim, 2017b). These factors might be characteristics of the people, the surrounding communities, or the country (NASPA, 2017; Kim & Kim, 2017b). Therefore, this chapter proposes the SEFs model for OLE focusing on the following: (1) GNI, GII, BSS, SMDW, IUI, and FTMPS, from a PLI perspective and (2) UP, SVPW, and HEPGDP, from a CLSS perspective (see Fig.3.2.6).

The PLI level includes GNI because it has the most significant impact on the medical expenditures of the elderly. Since GII includes such inequalities as gender discrimination, it can increase stress levels in the elderly (Kim & Kim, 2017b). Finally, the CLSS has UP and HEPGDP because they can affect the health and welfare of the elderly. Consequently, strategies that promote health policies and improve OLE can be created (see Fig. 3.2.6).

Fig. 3.2.6 shows that in a society without GII, men and women participate equally in the economy, thus improving household income levels (GNI). It also affects SVPW by contributing to the national society's economic development. Therefore, these nine SEFs ultimately positively affect OLE, thereby increasing it.

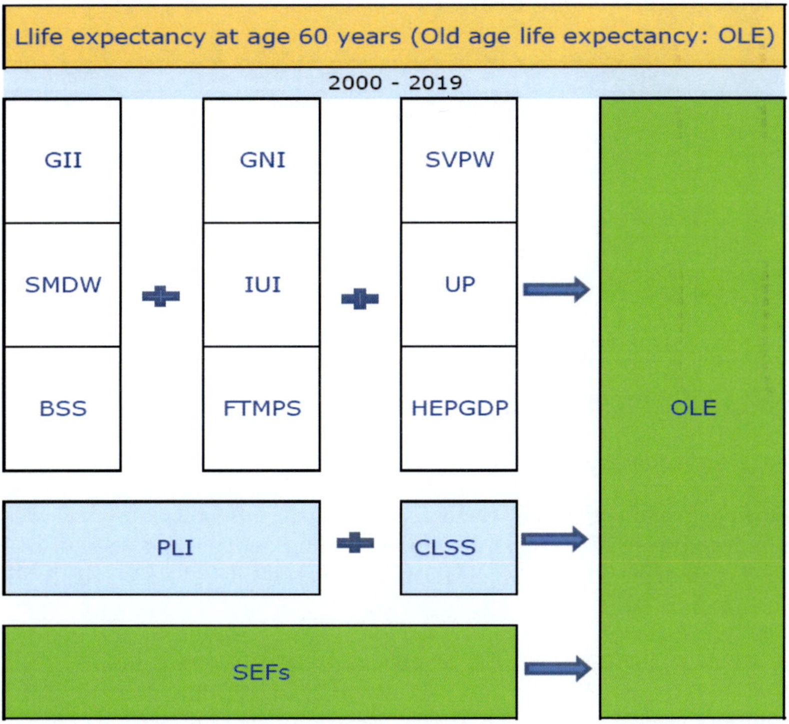

Fig.3.2.6. Relationship between OLE and SEFs

OLE prediction variables

The results of the OLE in the 39 countries surveyed are shown in Table 3.4. Although OLE has positive correlations with GNI ($r = 0.667$, $p = 0.001$), SMDW ($r = 0.484$, $p = 0.002$), BSS ($r = 0.567$, $p = 0.001$), IUI ($r = 0.585$, $p = 0.001$), FTMPS ($r = 0.519$, $p = 0.001$), UP ($r = 0.488$, $p = 0.002$), SVPW ($r = 0.484$, $p = 0.002$), and HEPGDP ($r = 0.533$, $p = 0.001$), it has a negative correlation with the GII ($r = -0.608$, $p = 0.001$).

Meanwhile, the results of the OLE, GII, and DCI in the 34 European countries surveyed are shown in the regression analysis. In this regard, higher GNI and DCI but lower GII were the predictors of OLE ($R^2 = 0.804$, $p < 0.001$) (Kim & Kim, 2017b).

Table 3.4. Correlations coefficient for the OLE (N = 39)

Variables		Correlations Coefficient	P-Value
OLE	GNI	0.667	0.000
	GII	-0.608	0.000
	BSS	0.567	0.000
	SMDW	0.484	0.002
	IUI	0.585	0.000
	FMTS	0.519	0.001
	UP	0.488	0.002
	SVPW	0.484	0.002
	HEPGDP	0.533	0.001

OLE: LE at age 60 years (Old age LE: OLE)

Suggestions for OLE

This chapter investigated whether international differences in OLE were associated with SEFs. According to the findings, countries with high OLE levels had higher GNI, BSS, SMDW, IUI, FTMPS, UP, SVPW, HEPGDP, and a lower GII.

In addition, increases in OLE levels can lead to increases in GNI, BSS, SMDW, IUI, FTMPS, UP, SVPW, and HEPGDP, but a decrease in GII values. Thus, we suggest that SEFs have a significant influence on OLE.

The OLE of Japan, South Korea, Australia, Switzerland, Spain, France, Canada, and Italy were more than the mean of 25 years. However, Russian

Federation, Bulgaria, Belarus, Ukraine, and Pakistan were less than 20 years.

Among the countries surveyed, OLE values were the lowest in countries with low GNI, BSS, SMDW, IUI, FTMPS, UP, SVPW, and HEPGDP. In contrast, OLE values were the highest in countries with high SEFs. Conversely, the GII values were the highest in countries with low national income, while they were the weakest in those with high GNI. Thus, it indicates a country's high SEFs inequality indicators (i.e., GNI, BSS, SMDW, the GII, IUI, FTMPS, UP, SVPW, and HEPGDP) can result in low OLE levels.

The influence of these SEFs on OLE can vary by country. For example, as country-level GNI improves, OLE also increases, due to the association between country-level GII, UP, SVPW, and HEPGDP and health levels. In addition, in countries with a low GNI level, an economic crisis can disproportionately affect vulnerable populations.

Meanwhile, the elderly may be unable to support a healthy lifestyle based on their income. It has decisive implications for health, residential, and social services (O'Sullivan & Ashton et al., 2012; Kim & Kim, 2017b). These aspects increase healthcare requirements and demand for public services, and they can also escalate into health and social crises if unaddressed (Karanikolos et al., 2013; Kim & Kim, 2017b).

The high correlation between OLE and these SEFs becomes instrumental for effective health policies as these variables reflect the government's investment in health infrastructure. Consequently, high OLE levels are likely to contribute to high SEFs but low GII. They also indirectly reflect a country's gender equality because women can become more vulnerable to stress-related illnesses (Kim & Kim, 2017b). In addition, economic change and employment can mitigate the harmful health effects of economic downturns (Kim & Kim, 2017b) because economic indicators reflect healthy living. Thus, the OLE level appears to have a crucial and latent effect on these SEFs. In addition, the nine proposed correlation coefficients for the OLE models indicated that if countries increase their SEFs values, they can obtain increased OLE—but decrease GII. Therefore, successful aging strategies should be developed by considering the influence of these SEFs indicators.

3.3 Remaining years of LE (RLE)

3.3.1 Impact on RLE of SEFs

Assuming that people reach the age of 65 in good health, how much LE remains, and what factors affect this aspect? How do we calculate the RLE of an individual who reaches the age of 65 in good health? It can calculate by subtracting the age of 65 from the LE. In other words, if the national LE is 75 years of age, then we can live another 10 years (on average). However, what SEFs affect an individual's LE in this period?

For instance, Fig. 3.3 shows that if the RLE at age 65 is 10 years, it extends to age 75. In other words, it hypothesizes that the higher the GNI and BSS, the greater the use of SMDW, and the greater the RLE. Thus, as the SEFs increase to 70% (Point A), a lifespan can be achieved up to age 65. In addition, if the SEFs grow to 90% (Point B), a lifespan can be achieved up to age 75. Conversely, if specific SEFs, such as GNI, BSS, and SMDW, continue to decrease, they may stagnate at Point B and eventually reach Point C as RLE drops.

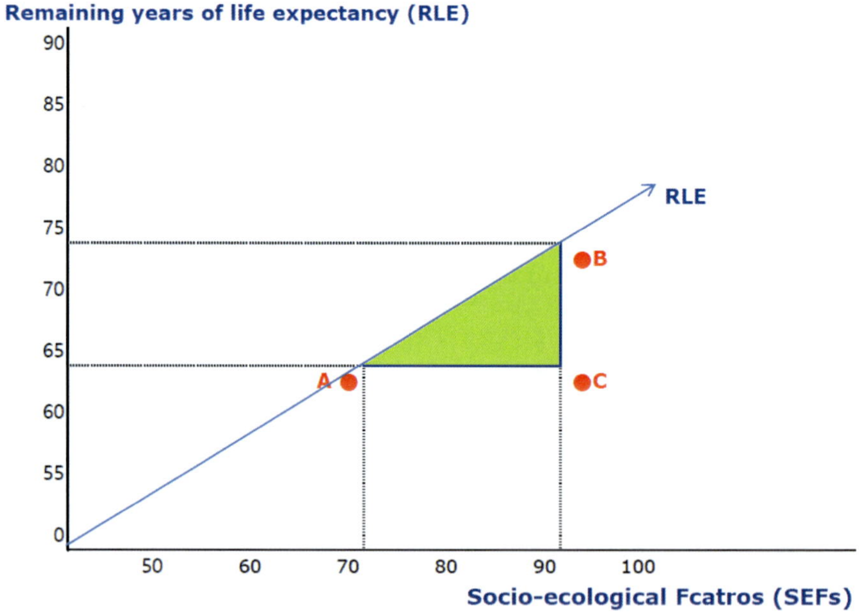

Fig. 3.3. Relationship between RLE and SEFs

(a) Gross national income (GNI)

Fig. 3.3.1 shows that as the GNI increases, RLE also increases. For example, as the national income index increases from $1,500 to $2,500 (Point B), the RLE increases from 65 to 75 years (Point C). Thus, income level is an essential requirement for RLE.

In addition, the RLE at age 65 is affected by income level. In this regard, most people retire at the age of 65, after which their health can significantly deteriorate due to sudden changes in their lifestyles. Hence, after age 65, it is crucial to have extra income to pay for certain expenses such as regular physical examinations, hobbies, exercise activities, and travel. In other words, if an individual's income level is high, they can afford to participate in social activities and contribute to their health promotion during old age.

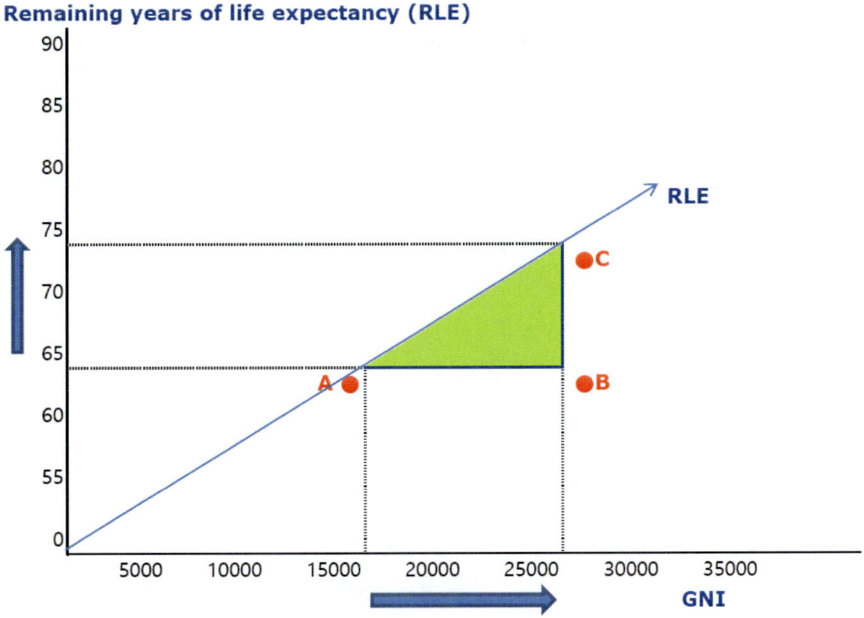

Fig. 3.3.1. Relationship between RLE and GNI

(b) Basic sanitation services (BSS)

Fig. 3.3.2 shows that RLE increases as the number of users of BSS or higher increases. For example, if the BSS rises from 80 to 100% (Point B), the RLE increases from 65 to 75 years (Point C). Thus, the higher the BSS level, the higher the RLE.

In addition, the higher the income, the higher the sanitation services level because many opportunities abound to receive sanitation services when financial support is available. However, not everyone with a high-income status has a high level of sanitation because the motivation to be healthy is a prerequisite. Therefore, since sanitation services keep the clean active, it is possible to prevent the onset of epidemics, thus supporting health promotion.

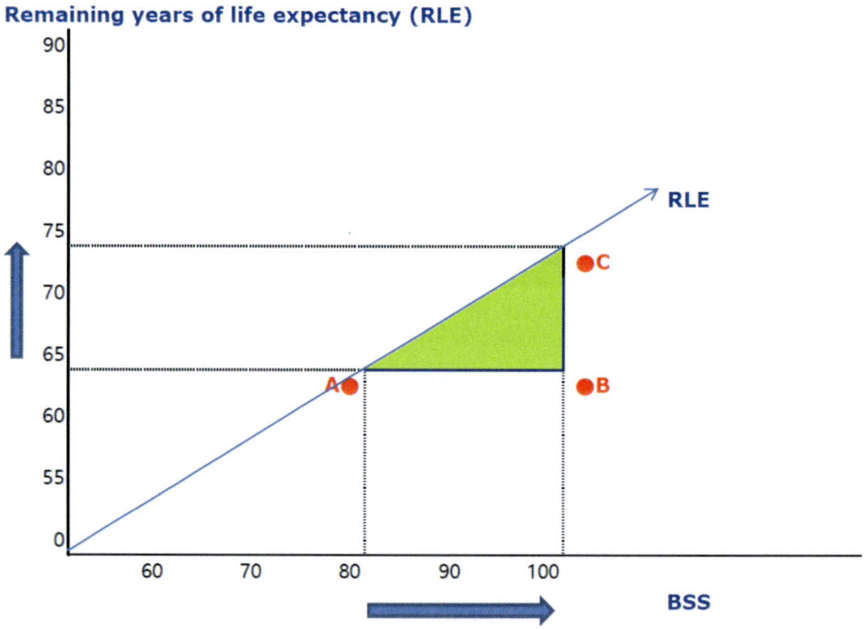

Fig.3.3.2. Relationship between RLE and the BSS

(c) Safely managed drinking water (SMDW)

Fig. 3.3.3 indicates that the higher the level of safe drinking water management, the higher the RLE. For example, when secure drinking water management increases from 80% to 100% (Point B), the RLE increases from 75 to 85 years (Point C).

In addition, SMDW is essential for human life. If drinking water is contaminated, then it can cause illnesses and other waterborne infections. In some underdeveloped countries, such as those in Africa, international support is necessary because drinking water is scarce, and there are no economic means to develop underground water. Therefore, we hope that developed countries will notice such issues and provide financial support for groundwater development.

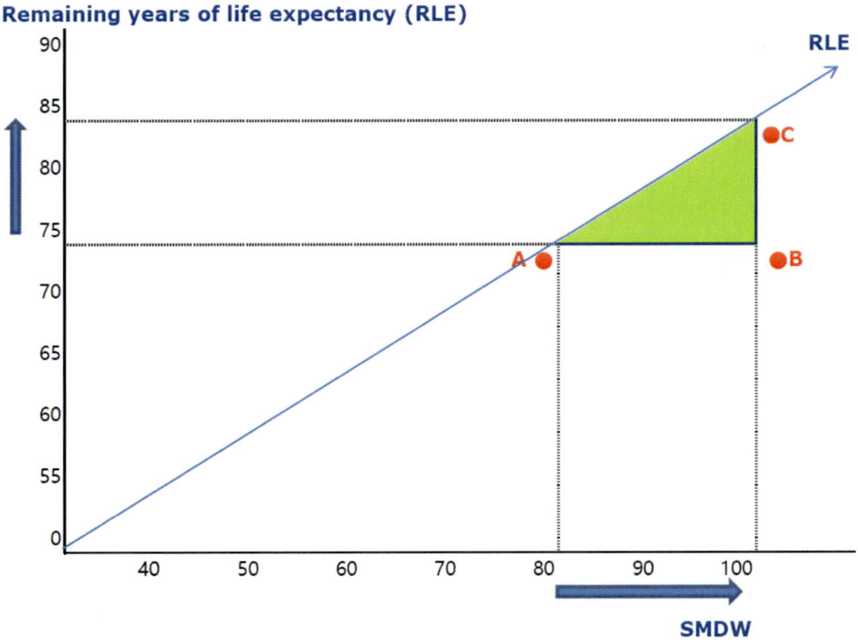

Fig.3.3.3. Relationship between RLE and SMDW

(b) Gender inequality index (GII)

Fig. 3.3.4 shows that RLE increases as the number of those with GII or lower increases. For example, if GII decreases from 0.8 to 0.6 (Point B), the RLE increases from 75 to 85 years (Point C). Thus, the lower the GII level, the higher the RLE.

In addition, the higher the gender equality, the higher women's education, and economic level. Because when gender equality support is available, opportunities abound for women to receive education and be economically active. However, not every woman with a high education level has a high level of gender equality because the motivation for gender equality is a prerequisite. Therefore, because gender equality maintains women's increased education and economic activities by improving income levels, it can prevent mental stress and promote health.

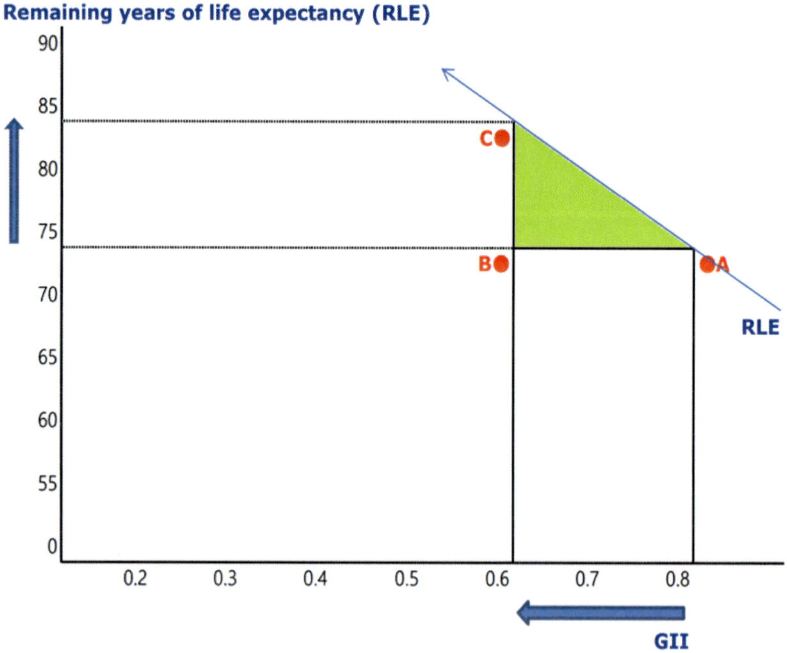

Fig.3.3.4. Relationship between RLE and the GII

3.3.2 An assessment of RLE (65)

RLE (65) refers to the number of remaining LE years for individuals 65 years and older (CDC, 2013). It can calculate with the following formula: RLE (65) = LE (–) aged 65 years (Kim & Kim, 2016b).

We need to focus on RLE (65) and its effects on SEFs as factors contributing to RLE (65). It might help distinguish them from PLI and CLSS. In addition, RLE (65) could use to compare health levels between countries.

Table 3.3 presents an assessment of RLE (65). The RLE (65) has a relationship of more than 50% in SEFs. It confirms that GNI, SMDW, BSS, and GII are significant factors in SEFs. Thus, at least for human survival, if one wants to achieve the remaining LE, major factors must increase, such as income level, safe drinking water, sanitation level, and gender equality in society.

Table 3.3. Correlations coefficient for the RLE (N = 39)

Variables		Correlations Coefficient	P-Value
RLE(65)	GNI	0.543	0.000
	SMDW	0.501	0.000
	BSS	0.524	0.001
	GII	-0.633	0.000

RLE(65): Remaining years of life expectancy in 65 years of age and old.

Fig. 3.3.5 presents the analysis methods of GNI, SMDW, BSS, and GII related to RLE (65). Significant relations between RLE (65) and SEFs can show by GNI, SMDW, BSS, and GII.

In addition, Fig. 3.2.5 presents direct relationships between RLE (65) and GNI, SMDW, BSS, and GII. These can be predictors because high GNI, SMDW, BSS, and GII affect RLE (65). Finally, predictors of high RLE (65) can be used to build a model of higher GNI, SMDW, BSS, and GII—all as SEFs.

The comprehensive assessment of RLE (65) shows that healthy aging increases with increased SEFs in a majority of the countries. The SEFs indicate that GNI, SMDW, BSS, and GII contribute to RLE (65). This increase in GNI, SMDW, BSS, and GII also increases RLE (65), suggesting that these indicators make essential contributions to RLE (65) (Fig. 3.3.5).

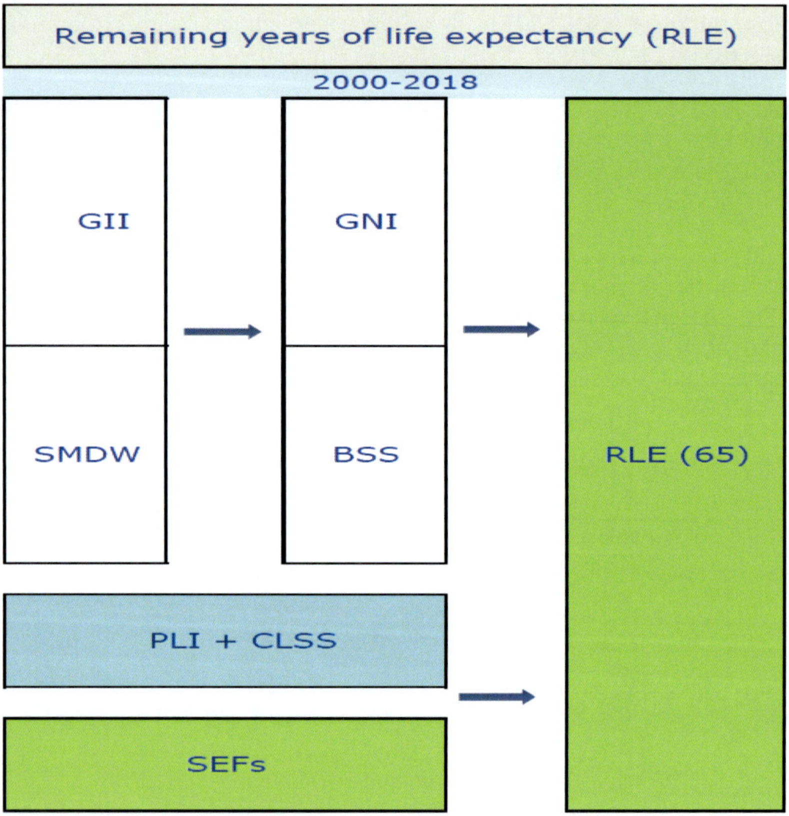

Fig.3.3.5. Relationship between RLE (65) and SEFs

3.4 Inequality in LE (ILE)

3.4.1 Impact on ILE of SEFs

ILE refers to the disparity of LE in the population. A gap in LE occurs if there is a significant difference in the influencing factors in LE, except for genetic factors. However, if genetic factors are constant and individuals living in the same area have similar lifestyles, there is no difference in LE.

ILE can arise from the differences in housing and social environment due to the income gap between individuals. In addition, the difference in higher education, which can improve the quality of life and OPR as an institutional device for national and social livelihood security, may cause ILE.

Fig.3.4 confirms the following. If labor productivity, educational attainment above SE, and the number of pensioners increases, then ILE 2 decreases from 8 to 2 points. However, if the GI increases, ILE 1 increases from 2 to 8 points. For example, at Point A for ILE, the proportion of GI for income inequality is 8 points. However, if the GI increases from 20% to 60% on the ILE 1 curve, the ILE1 increases to 14 points. In other words, if income inequality continues to increase, then ILE 1 will continue to increase. However, on the ILE 2 curve, if value-added per worker, the level of education, and the number of pensioners continue to increase from 40% to 60%, ILE 2 decreases, closing the gap to 2 points. Each of these variables is described as follows.

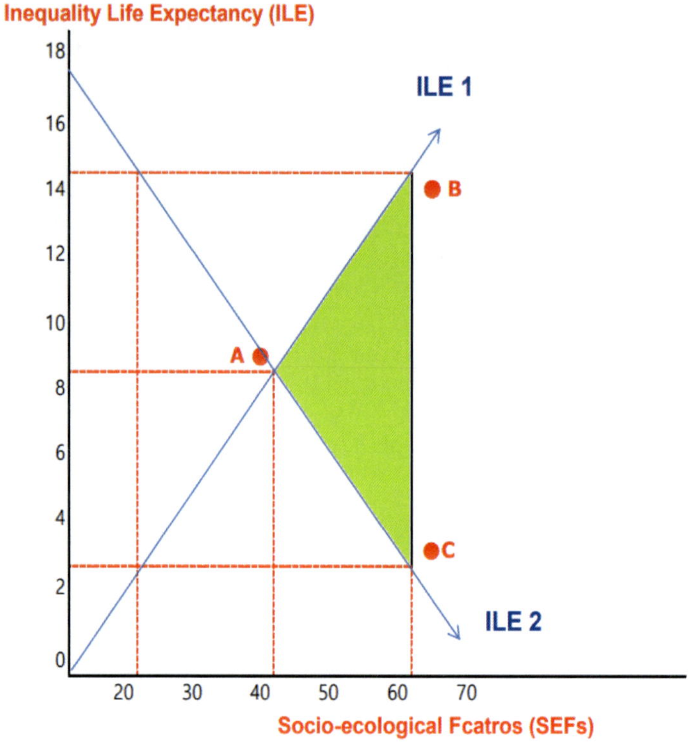

Fig. 3.4. Relationship between ILE and SEFs

(a) The Gini index (GI)

The GI ranges from 0 to 1 that the increases income inequality. If the GI increases, the ILE rises, showing an upward curve to the right. Since the GI is an income inequality curve, it moves in the same direction as the ILE (ILE 1 and ILE 2). For example, in the ILE 1 curve, if the GI is 0.3, then the ILE is 5 points. However, in the ILE 2 curve, when the GI is 0.6, the ILE increases to 8 points (Fig 3.4.1). As such, an increase in the GI means an increase in ILE. In other words, the higher the GI, the greater the disparity in income and the ILE. Thus, to improve ILE, economic support policies for the low-income class and short- and long term income conservation strategies must be implemented at the national and social levels.

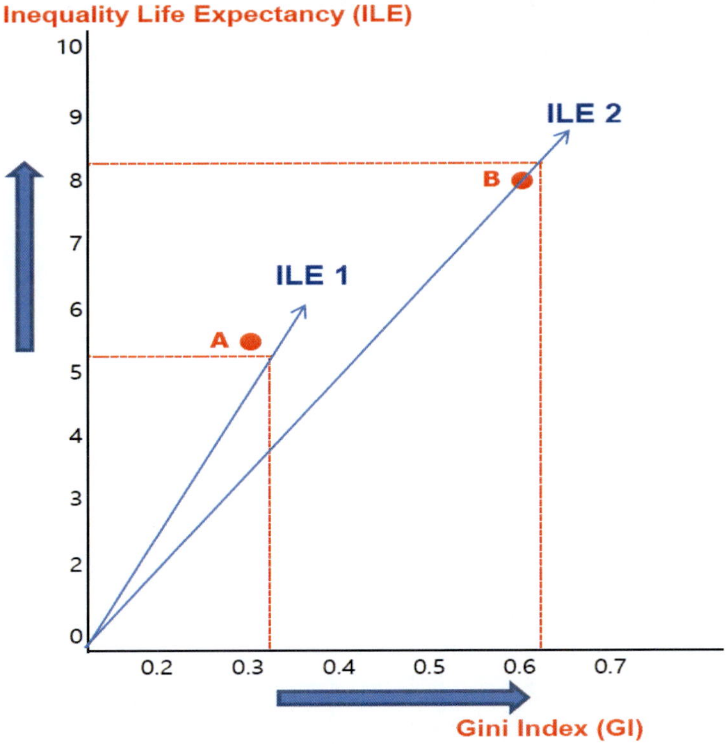

Fig. 3.4.1. Relationship between ILE and the GI

(b) Old age pension recipient (OPR)

Fig. 3.4.2 shows the association between OPR and ILE. For example, once the pension increases from 50% to 60%, the ILE decreases from 8 to 6 points. In other words, pension entitlement affects ILE. In addition, it indicates that economic income has a significant impact on the ILE.

As another factor of economic income, OPR significantly impacts the old population. In particular, it becomes a significant source for maintaining economic activity and health. Receiving a pension can result in a high level of economic satisfaction because it is an economic resource that improves health in old age. Therefore, pensions can be regarded as SEFs that positively affect the health of the elderly, especially if they do not receive financial support from their offspring.

In addition, from a long term perspective, if the countries can increase LE by implementing pensions and related policies, it can be an opportunity to increase 100 years of age population.

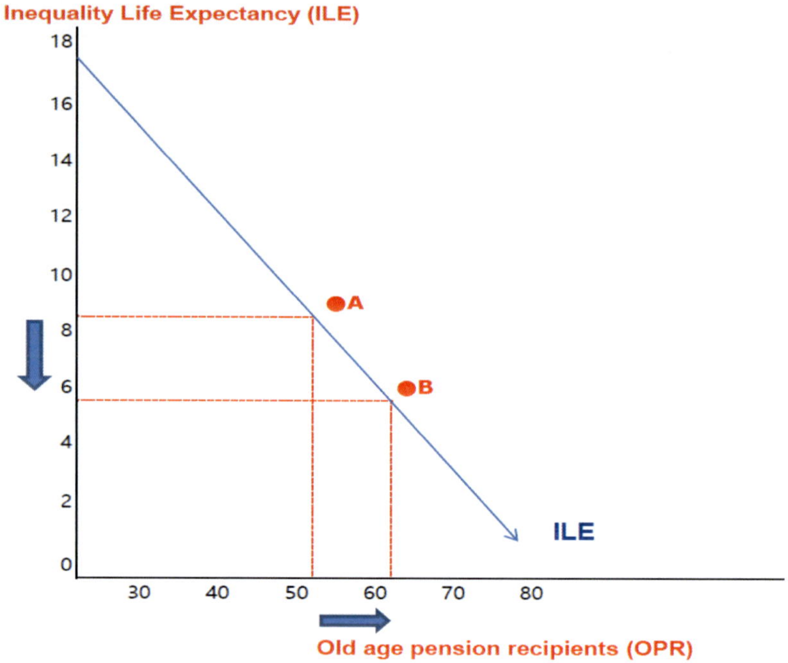

Fig. 3.4.2. Relationship between ILE and OPR

(c) Secondary education (SE)

Fig. 3.4.3 shows that an increase in the number of people receiving SE can reduce ILE. If the SE period lengthens from 14 to 16 years, the ILE decreases from 5 to 2 points. Therefore, if many people complete SE at the national level, then ILE will also reduce.

The proportion of the total population with SE can use to measure a country's healthy living standards. In other words, countries with lower SE levels generally have lower income levels. In addition, individuals with lower education and income levels tend to have poor eating and lifestyle habits.

Thus, policies that can increase a country's level of income/education and improve healthy living standards should devise. In this case, education programs, income businesses, and healthy living are all SEFs. Of course, promoting simultaneous cost-effective national projects is possible, but education should be a national priority.

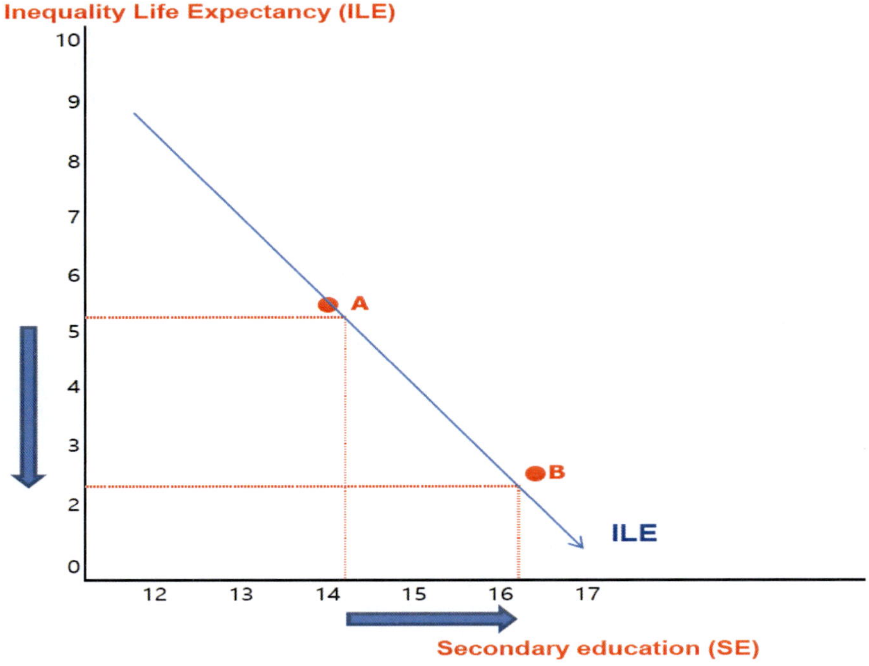

Fig. 3.4.3. Relationship between ILE and SE

(d) Services value-added per worker (SVPW)

Fig. 3.4.4 shows that an increase in SVPW can reduce ILE. For example, as the SVPW increases from $1,500 to $2,000, the ILE decreases from 8 to 6 points. In other words, when the value of labor productivity increases, the individual income of workers increases, while the ILE decreases.

The SVPW is a measure of labor productivity in which "value-added" refers to the net output of a sector after totaling all of the outputs and subtracting the intermediate inputs. Meanwhile, labor productivity can only increase when workers' mental and physical health is maintained, for example, through appropriate working hours. In this regard, employers should increase productivity and health by observing the appropriate number of working hours. Therefore, a national health management policy should devise to maintain the quality of health for workers.

Conversely, if we comprehensively analyze SEFs in a broader sense, then the higher the labor productivity of workers, the more they receive pension benefits. In addition, the more that individual obtains SVPW, the more that ILE can resolve. Finally, the national government's interest and various strategies, such as job creation expansion, must be prioritized to improve labor productivity.

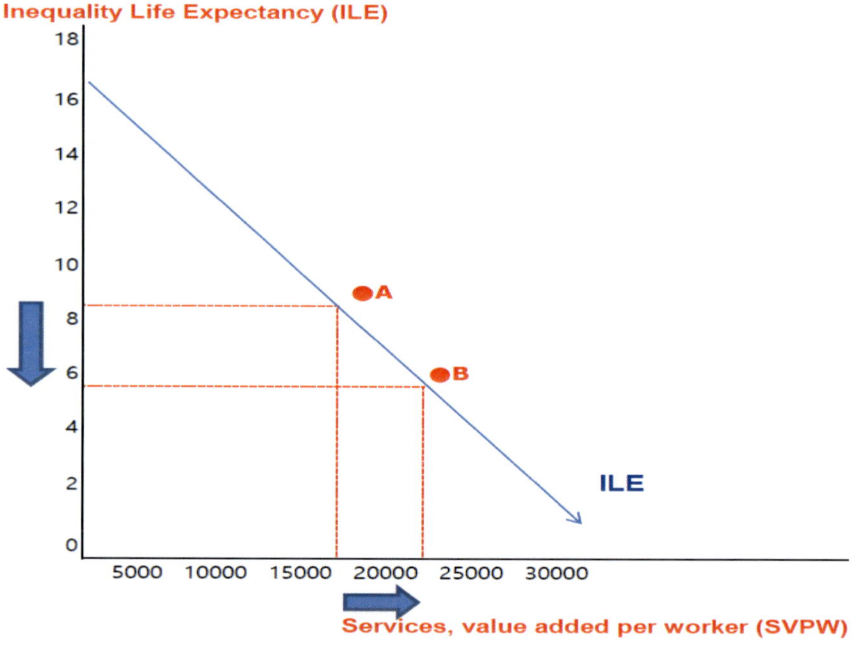

Fig. 3.4.4. Relationship between ILE and SVPW

3.4.2 A case study of ILE

This section identifies the country-level SEFs that affect ILE, based on the estimates from the Atkinson inequality index (Atkinson, 1970; UN, 2015). These estimates also rely on the data in the life table (UN, 2016b). The ILE can also influence country-level SEFs, including the Gini coefficient,

SE, output per worker, and OPR. Thus, ILE is an indicator that can help reduce health inequalities (Kim & Kim, 2016a).

Meanwhile, previous studies of various countries (2001–2012) (Hosseinpoor et al., 2012; Kim & Kim, 2016b) examined the relationship between black and white populations, social class, indigenous and non-indigenous people, and women and men in terms of ILE. In addition, the relationship between income disparity and LE was reported (Regidor et al., 2013; Rasella et al., 2013) and that between educational inequalities and LE (Van, 2012; Kim & Kim, 2014a). However, to date, the areas that have received less focus include the relationship between ILE and income inequality, education, labor productivity, and the number of OPR (Kim & Kim, 2018).

Thus, this chapter examines the associations between ILE and socio-ecological inequality by using the following indicators: (1) National income inequality on an individual level (Rasella et al., 2013; Kim & Kim, 2016a b, 2017b), (2) Education, at least SE (Kim & Kim, 2014a), (3) Labor productivity (Cervellati & Sunde, 2005), and (4) The number of OPR (Kim & Kim, 2018).

Framework from a socio-ecological perspective

The framework proposed in this chapter depicts the SEFs and ILE. This book examined the relationships between ILE and GI, SE, SVPW, and OPR in SEFs (Fig. 3.4.5).

This chapter proposes a socio-ecological framework for ILE on interpersonal economic factors, social environment, and public policies as targets for LE (Kim & Kim, 2018).

In addition, it assumes that appropriate changes in country-level SEFs will produce changes ILE. That is factors that; (1) the GI (a measure of economic deprivation from PLI perspective) and (2) SE attainment (a measure of the education of the female people from PLI perspective), (3) SVPW (a measure of labor productivity from CLSS perspective), and (4) the number of OPR (a measure of the welfare of the older population from CLSS perspective).

Moreover, based on standard statistical methods, we hypothesize that the association between output (ILE, including differences in ILE between countries) and progress (country-level GI, SE, SVPW, and OPR) predict the differences in ILE (Fig. 3.4.5).

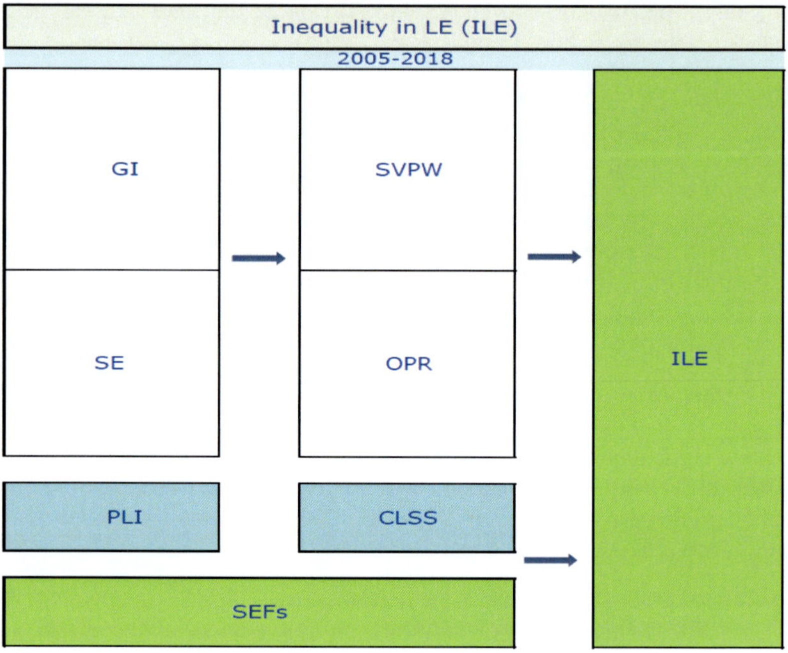

Fig. 3.4.5. Relationship between ILE and SEFs

Evaluating ILE

ILE has been defined as the inequality in the expected lifespan based on the life tables in the Atkinson inequality index (Atkinson, 1970; UN, 2015) and those in the 2010–2015 life tables from the United Nations Department of Economic and Social Affairs (UNDESA, 2015). Specifically, this distribution is presented in age intervals (0–1, 1–5, … , 85+ years), with the mortality rates and average estimated age at death specified for each interval. Meanwhile, ILE is estimated from the abridged life tables (5-year age cohorts) that reflect the current inequality in mortality patterns (UN, 2016b; Kim & Kim, 2018).

Predictive variables for the ILE

The data from the analysis of the SEFs for the 108 countries surveyed are presented in Tables 3.4. In this regard, the ILE was correlated with GI, SE, SE, SVPW, and OPR, while significant positive correlations were found between ILE and GI ($r = 0.335$, $p = 0.001$), SE ($r = -0.757$, $p = 0.001$),

SVPW (r = −0.631, p = 0.001), and OPR (r = −0.614, p = 0.001), (Kim & Kim, 2018).

Table 3.4. Correlation coefficients for the inequality in LE (ILE) (N = 108)

Variables		Correlations coefficient	p-value
ILE	GI	0.335	0.000
	SE	-0.757	0.000
	OPR	-0.641	0.000
	SVPW	-0.631	0.000

GI: The Gini coefficient, 2005–2013

SE: Female secondary education, 2005–2014

OPR: Old age pension recipients, 2005-2012

SVPW: Services value added per worker, 2018

Kim, J.I., Kim, G. Effects on inequality in life expectancy from a social ecology perspective. BMC Public Health 18, 243. 2018.

Suggestions for ILE

Shortcomings from a SEFs perspective are the primary sources of inequality. In this regard, inequalities in national income, education, labor productivity, and social security negatively impact health promotion development (Kim & Kim, 2014a, 2016a, 2017a, b; 2018). Although such aspects have significantly improved, it has not led to socio-ecological equality. Since socio-ecological inequality remains a barrier to human longevity (Kim & Kim, 2015, 2016a, 2017a, b; 2018), this chapter focused on the associations between ILE and SEFs indicators (Kim & Kim, 2018).

Based on the findings, GI, SE, SVPW, and OPR contribute to ILE (Khan et al., 2016; Kim & Kim, 2018). In addition, decreases in GI and increases in SE, SVPW, and OPR lead to reductions in ILE, suggesting that improving these factors can improve ILE.

SE, SVPW, and OPR values were the lowest in less developed regions and higher in more-developed countries. Thus, country-level SEFs that influence the living standard can predict ILE and corresponding country-level socio-ecological inequality. Consequently, SEFs are major contributing factors to ILE, and they indirectly reflect country-level socio-ecological conditions required for healthy living (Kim & Kim, 2018).

In addition, higher levels of income inequality and relative poverty occur in more-developed countries (Kim & Kim, 2017b, 2008). However, such countries also display higher education but lower ILE. In less developed countries, country-level income and educational inequality have likely contributed to slow progress in attaining health equality (Kim & Kim, 2014b, 2017b, 2018). Thus, ILE has a consistent influence, independent of income inequality and secondary education attainment (Kim & Kim, 2018).

Access to labor productivity and social security via SVPW and OPR can improve the quality of life and help individuals take charge of their health (Kim & Kim, 2017a, 2018). In this regard, better health increases labor supply and productivity and positively affects LE. Thus, SVPW and OPR can be seen as innovative tools for health promotion when viewed from a public policy perspective, and their values can help improve the standard of living (Kim & Kim, 2018).

In the proposed models, it is evident that if countries improve their GI, SE, SVPW, and OPR, they can obtain lower ILE. Hence, policies that will enhance these country-level SEFs can have latent effects on ILE.

Governments should reduce income inequality and increase access to education, labor productivity, and old age pensions. Meeting these goals could decrease the risk factors for ILE and raise the standard of living. Therefore, this chapter's findings can implement strategies related to ILE and address country-level socio-ecological indicators (Kim & Kim, 2018).

3.5 Healthy life expectancy (HLE)

3.5.1 Impact on HLE of SEFs

If HLE is affected by acquired factors at the national level, there will inevitably be a gap in such expectancy between individuals and countries. For example, although living in the same area is physically healthy, LE is inevitably affected by diet, lifestyle, and the social environment in which individuals live due to the disparity in national income. Additionally, the difference in education level can affect HLE, depending on the understanding of medical information and the urbanization of local communities.

Fig. 3.5 shows that if the national income, education level, Internet use, and urbanization rate increase to 40%, the HLE increases to 70 years

(Point A). Similarly, if these factors increase from 40% to 70% (Point B), the HLE will reach 85 years. Interestingly, if it rises to 100% (Point C), it is possible to maintain an HLE until 95 years of age.

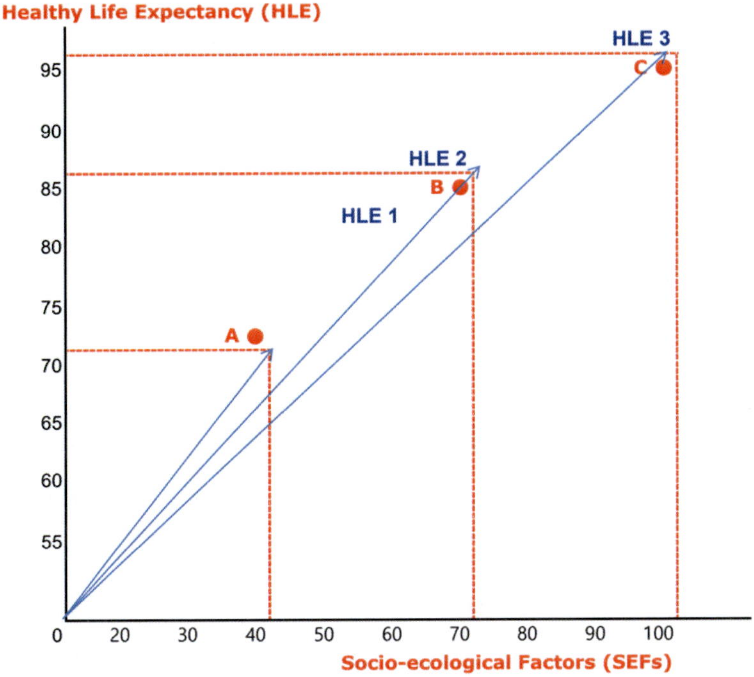

Fig. 3.5. Relationship between HLE and SEFs

(a) Gross national income (GNI)

Fig. 3.5.1 shows that HLE increases as the national income increases. For example, if the national income increases from \$25,000 to \$35,000, the HLE will increase from 80 to 95 years (Point B). In this regard, the national income allows individuals to pay medical expenses, either themselves or through an institutional healthcare system. However, HLE cannot be guaranteed if the national income is insufficient. Hence, to protect the health of its citizens and ensure HLE, the government should maintain its economic competitiveness and invest in primary healthcare sectors.

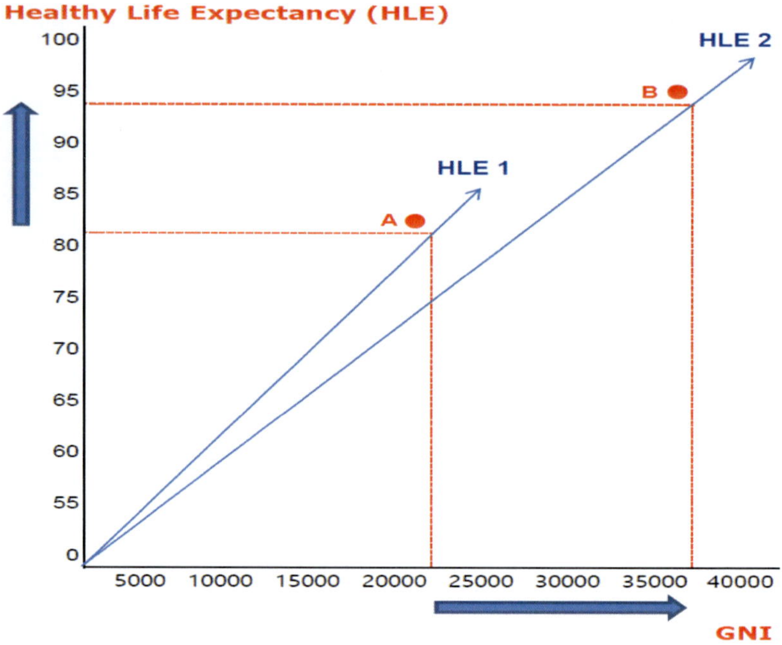

Fig. 3.5.1 Relationship between HLE and the GNI

(b) Individuals using the Internet (IUI)

Currently, we live in an era in which can immediately access medical information anywhere and anytime. For example, without physically visiting a doctor, it is possible to schedule an appointment online, receive a straightforward diagnosis, and go to the pharmacy with a prescription. Therefore, the Internet has brought tremendous development in health sections.

Fig. 3.5.2 shows that as IUI increases, HLE also increases. For example, if the number of Internet users increases from 75% to 90%, the HLE increases from 75 to 90 years (Point B). Thus, IUI is a significant variable in HLE.

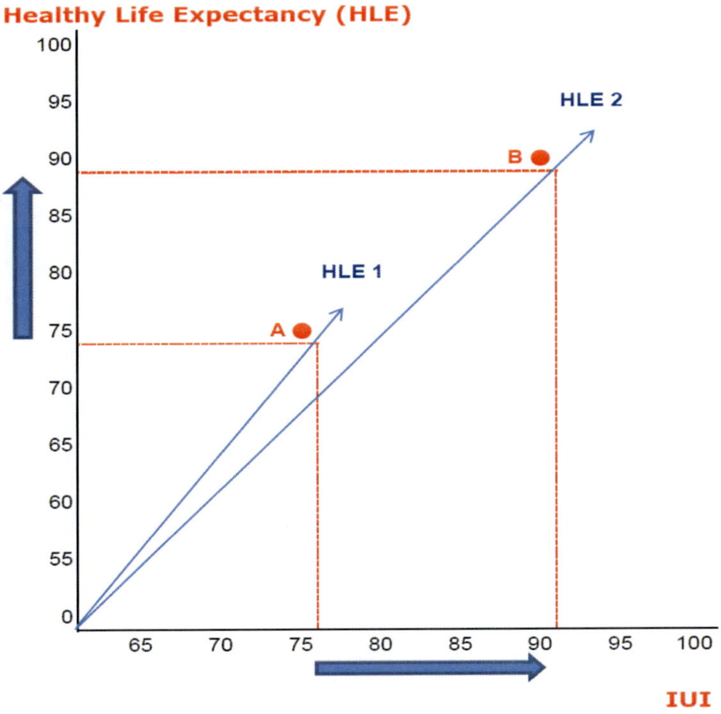

Fig. 3.5.2. Relationship between HLE and IUI

(c) Basic sanitation services (BSS)

Fig. 3.5.3 shows that as the BSS increases, HLE also increases. For example, if the BSS increases from 75% to 90%, HLE increases from 75 to 90 years (Point B). Thus, BSS is a significant variable in HLE. Sanitation services are an important factor for increasing HLE. For example, if there are no sanitation services at one's school, it cannot protect one from food poisoning and infectious diseases. Therefore, sanitation services can help save precious lives from contagious diseases.

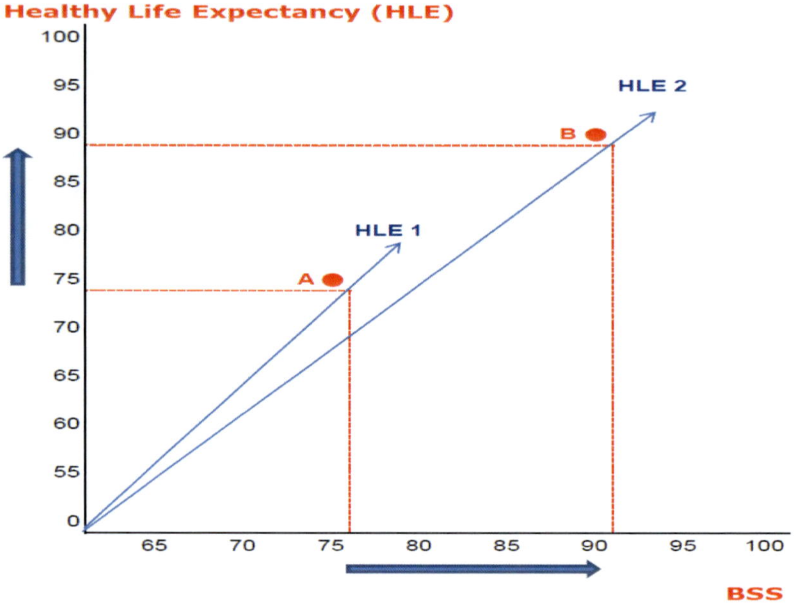

Fig. 3.5.3. Relationship between HLE and BSS

(d) Safely managed drinking water (SMDW)

Fig. 3.5.4 shows that HLE increases as the SMDW use increases. For example, when the SMDW increases from 75 to 90 %, HLE increases from 75 to 90 years (Point B). Thus, the greater the safely managed drinking water levels, the higher the HLE.

SMDW plays a pivotal role in increasing HLE. If the SMDW system raises the quality of drinking water by converting it into a compulsory healthy water supply, it can increase the HLE of citizens, including older persons.

In addition, because drinking water is closely related to HLE, non-safe drinking water can cause mental and physical stress. For instance, some individuals might have difficulty drinking water, while others might suffer from stress disorders. Therefore, the countries should implement a strategy toward improving the HLE of their citizens by preparing policies on the safe management of drinking water.

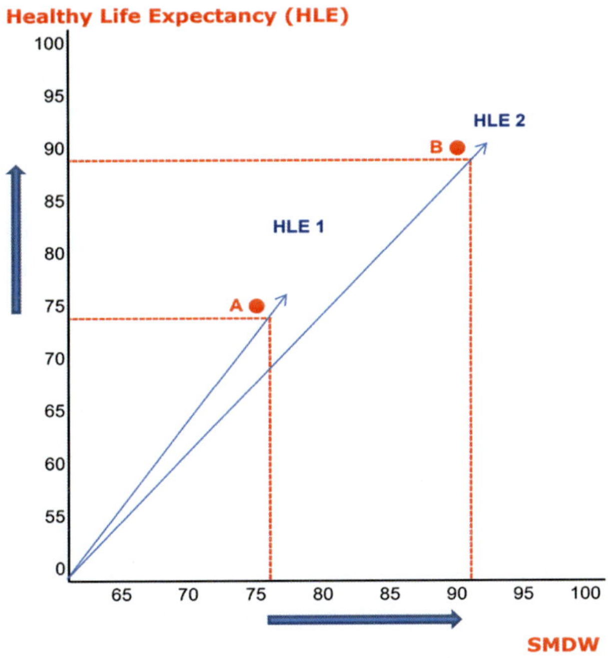

Fig.3.5.4. Relationship between HLE and SMDW

(e) Fixed telephone and mobile phone subscriber (FTMPS)

Fig. 3.5.5 indicates that HLE increases as the number of fixed telephone and mobile phone subscribers increases. For example, if the FTMPS increases from 75% to 90%, HLE would increase from 75 to 90 years (Point B). FTMPS allows individuals to subscribe, either by them or through an institutional communication system. However, HLE cannot guarantee if FTMPS is insufficient. Therefore, to protect the communication of its citizens and ensure HLE, the countries should maintain their communication competitiveness and invest in fundamental communication sectors.

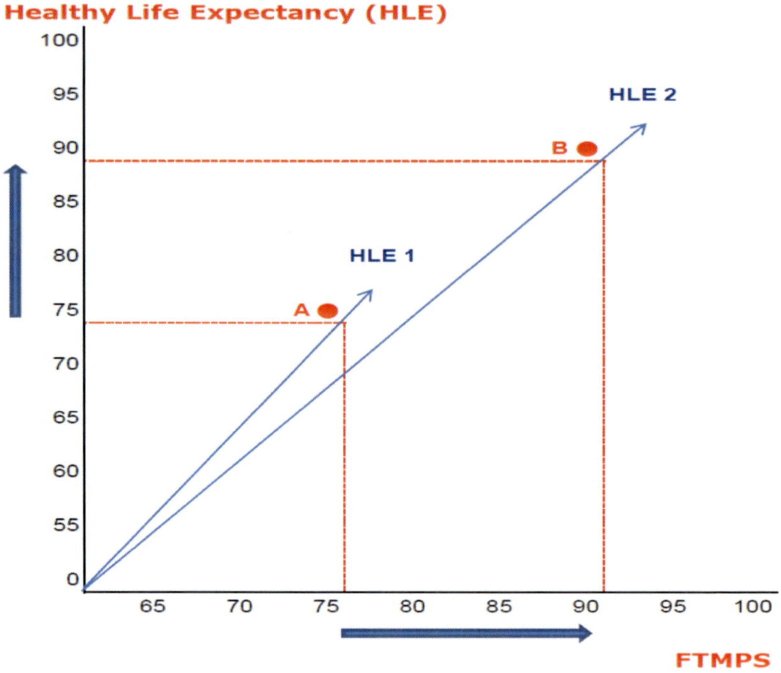

Fig. 3.5.5. Relationship between HLE and FTMPS

(f) GII

Fig. 3.5.6 shows that HLE increases as the GII decreases. For example, when the GII value increases from 0.6 to 0.9, HLE decreases from 80 to 75 years (Point B). Thus, the greater the gender equality levels, the higher the HLE.

Gender equality can play a pivotal role in mental health, which, in turn, can increase HLE. Therefore, if the gender equality system focuses on raising the quality of gender equality by alleviating stress, it could increase the HLE of citizens, including older persons.

In addition, since GII is closely related to HLE, it can cause mental and physical stress. For instance, if some women have difficulty finding employment opportunities due to gender inequality, they might suffer from stress disorders. Therefore, the countries should implement a strategy for improving the HLE of their citizens by preparing policies on gender equality.

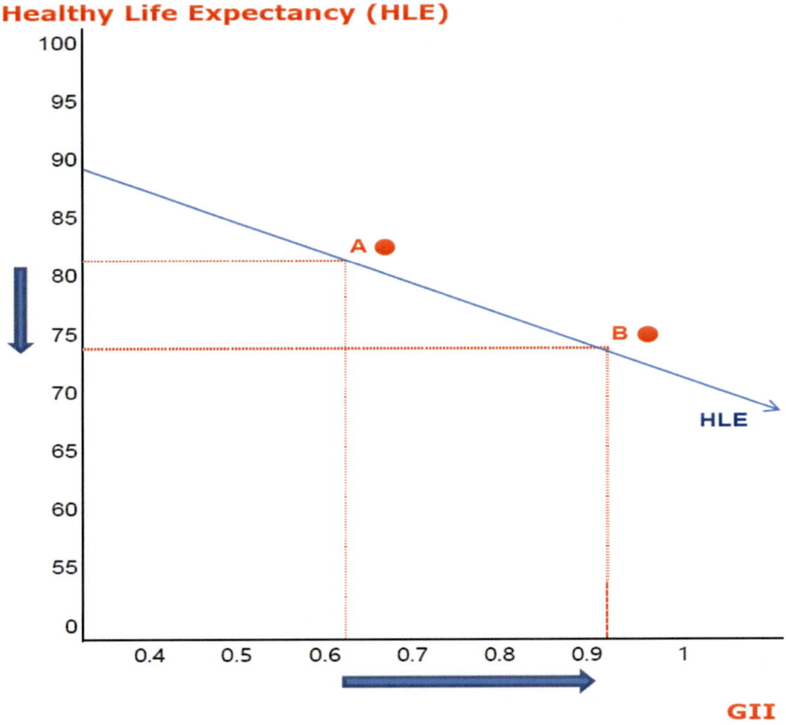

Fig. 3.5.6. Relationship between HLE and GII

(g) Services, value-added per worker (SVPW)

Fig. 3.5.7 indicates that HLE increases as SVPW increases. For example, if SVPW increases from \$15,000 to \$30,000, HLE would increase from 75 to 80 years (Point B). SVPW allows individuals to pay medical expenses, either by themselves or through an institutional healthcare system. However, HLE cannot guarantee if SVPW is insufficient. Therefore, to protect the health of its citizens and ensure HLE, the countries should increase SVPW by maintaining their economic competitiveness.

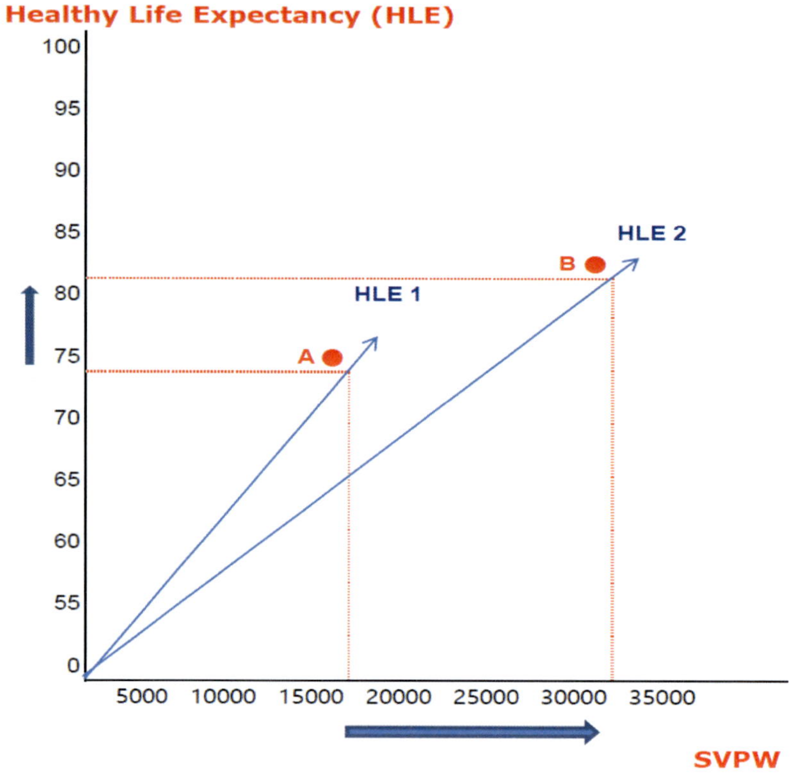

Fig. 3.5.7. Relationship between HLE and SVPW

3.5.2 An assessment of HLE

Table 3.5 presents an assessment of HLE. The GII and BSS have a relationship of more than 50% in the SEFs. This confirms that GNI, SMDW, BSS, FTMPS, IUI, SVPW, and GII are significant factors in HLE. Therefore, at least for human survival, if one wants to achieve HLE, it is important to increase major factors such as income level, safe drinking water, sanitation level, communication, Internet use, value-added productivity, and gender equality in society. We must also observe the seven elements that have a decisive influence on the basic survival probability of humanity.

Table 3.5. Correlations coefficient for the HLE (N = 39)

Variables		Correlations Coefficient	P-Value
	GNI	0.481	0.002
	SMDW	0.478	0.002
	IUI	0.383	0.016
HLE	GII	-0.625	0.001
	FTMPS	0.371	0.021
	SBB	0.528	0.001
	SVPW	0.483	0.002

Fig. 3.5.8 shows the GNI, SMDW, FTMPS, BSS, IUI, GII, and SVPW indicators of SEFs for HLE. Its significant relations are between HLE and seven factors. In addition, it can impact the direct relationship between HLE and these factors. Fig.3.5.8 of SEFs indicators reveal the predictors of HEL models: higher HLE can predict by higher factor values. It shows that the higher the SEFs indicator value, the greater the effect of the HLE. Thus, it indicates that countries with high SEFs levels have high expectations of HLE.

GNI, SMDW, FTMPS, BSS, IUI, GII, and SVPW values can be the lowest in less developed regions and highest in more-developed districts. Consequently, the contributing factors to high HLE reflect the SEFs required for healthy living. In addition, these factors are crucial determinants of HLE. In addition, if GNI, UP, SE, and IUI in SEFs were increased, HLE improved (Kim & Kim, 2016). Thus, as GNI, SMDW, FTMPS, BSS, IUI, GII, and SVPW levels increase, HLE also enhances. Consequently, HLE has a consistent influence, independent of these SEFs.

In addition, among the SEFs, GNI, SMDW, FTMPS, and BSS are fundamental factors that increase the survival probability of humanity. If these factors achieve, IUI and GII related to the local community can increase HLE. Ultimately, SVPW influences national economic development.

Finally, these factors might decrease the risk factors for unhealthy people. Higher GNI, SMDW, FTMPS, BSS, IUI, and SVPW and lower GII can help increase HLE. Therefore, HLE strategies and related policies should include the SEFs of GNI, SMDW, FTMPS, BSS, IUI, GII, and SVPW (Fig. 3.5.8).

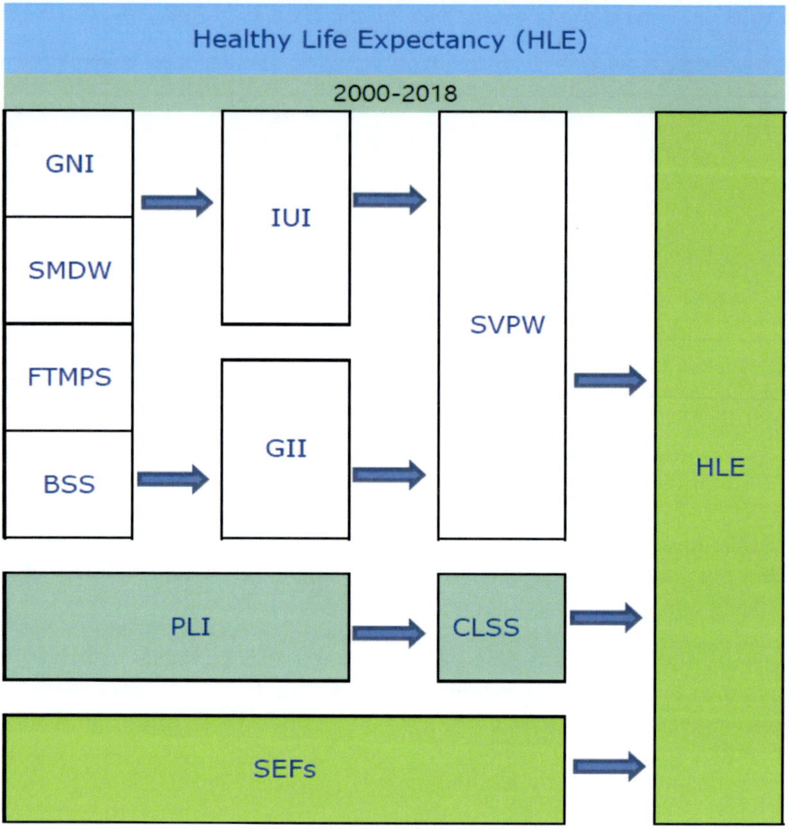

Fig.3.5.8. Relationship between HLE and SEFs

References

Asgeirsdóttir TL, Ragnarsdóttir DO. Health-income inequality: the effects of the Icelandic economic collapse. Int J Equity Health. 2014; 25: 13–50.

Atkinson AB. On the measurement of inequality. Journal of Economic Theory.1970; 2(3): 244–263.

Bain R, Cronk R, Wright J, Yang H, Slaymaker T, Bartram J. Fecal contamination of drinking-water in low-and middle-income countries: a systematic review and meta-analysis. *PLoS Med. 2014;* 11(5): e1001644.

Baruch GK, Biener L, Barnett RC. Women and gender in research on work and family stress. Am Psychol. 1987; 42(2): 130–136.

Bayati M, Akbarian R, Kavosi Z. Determinants of life expectancy in eastern Mediterranean region: A health production function. *International Journal of Health Policy and Management. 2013;* 1(1): 57–61.

Bennett JE, Li G, Foreman K, Best N, Kontis V, Pearson C, Hambly P, Ezzati M. The future of life expectancy and life expectancy inequalities in England and Wales: Bayesian spatiotemporal forecasting. Lancet. 2015; 386(9989): 163–70.

Bhavnani D, Goldstick JE, Cevallos W, Trueba G, Eisenberg JN. Impact of rainfall on diarrheal disease risk associated with unimproved water and sanitation. *The American Journal of Tropical Medicine and Hygiene. 2014;* 90(4): 705–711.

Biggs B, King L, Basu S, Stuckler D. Is wealthier always healthier? The impact of national income level, inequality, and poverty on public health in Latin America. *Social Science & Medicine*. 2010; 71(2), 266–273.

Bousquet J, Malva J, Nogues M, Mañas LR, Vellas B, Farrell J, MACVIA Research Group. Operational definition of active and healthy aging (AHA): The European innovation partnership (EIP) on AHA reference site questionnaire: Montpellier October 20–21, 2014, Lisbon July 2, 2015. Journal of the American Medical Directors Association. 2015; 16(12): 1020–1026.

Braveman PA, Cubbin C, Egerter S, Williams DR, Pamuk E. Socioeconomic disparities in health in the United States: what the patterns tell us. American Journal of Public Health. 2011; 100 Suppl 1: S186–96.

Cantu PA, et al. Increasing Education-Based disparities in healthy life expectancy among US non-Hispanic whites, 2000–2010. *The Journals of Gerontology: Series B*, 2021; 76(2): 319–329.

Candore G, Balistreri CR, Listì F, et al. Immunogenetics, gender, and longevity. *Annals of the New York Academy of Sciences*, 2006; 1089(1): 516–537.

Caserta M. Challenges, transitions, and healthy aging: introduction to the special issue. *The International Journal of Aging & Human Development*, 2011; 74(3): 189–191.

Castelló-Climent A, Doménech R. Human capital inequality, life expectancy and economic growth. The Economic Journal. 2008; 118(528): 653–677.

Centers for Disease Control and Prevention (CDC). State-specific healthy life expectancy at age 65 years-United States, 2007–2009. *MMWR. Morbidity and Mortality Weekly Report.* 2013; 62(28): 561.
Cervellati M, Sunde U. Human capital formation, life expectancy, and the process of development. The American Economic Review. 2005; 95(5): 1653–1672.
Colonna-Romano G, Franceschi C, Lio D, Caselli G, Caruso C. Immunogenetics, gender, and longevity. *Ann NY Acad Sci. 2006;* 1089: 516–37.
Crompton DW, Savioli L. Intestinal parasitic infections and urbanization. *Bull World Health Organ. 1993;* 71(1): 1–7.
De Vogli R. The financial crisis, health and health inequities in Europe: the need for regulations, redistribution and social protection. Int J Equity Health. 2014; 13:58.
Eckert S, Kohler S. Urbanization and health in developing countries: A systematic review. *World Health & Population. 2014:* 15(1): 7–20.
Elgar FJ, Pförtner TK, Moor I, De Clercq B, Stevens GW, Currie C. Socioeconomic inequalities in adolescent health 2002–2010: a time-series analysis of 34 countries participating in the Health Behaviour in School-aged Children study. The Lancet. 2015; 385(9982): 2088–2095.
Emery JH, Fleisch VC, McIntyre L. Legislated changes to federal pension income in Canada will adversely affect low income seniors' health. Preventive Medicine. 2013; 57(6): 963–966.
Engelaer FM, Koopman JJ, van Bodegom D, Eriksson UK, Westendorp RG. Determinants of epidemiologic transition in rural Africa: the role of socioeconomic status and drinking water source. *Transactions of The Royal Society of Tropical Medicine and Hygiene. 2014;* 108(6): 372–379.
Evans JG. Hypothesis: Healthy Active Life Expectancy (HALE) as an index of effectiveness of health and social services for elderly people. *Age and Ageing.* 1993; 22(4): 297–301.
Geronimus AT, Bound J, Waidmann TA, Colen CG, Steffick D. Inequality in life expectancy, functional status, and active life expectancy across selected black and white populations in the United States. Demography. 2001; 38(2), 227–251.
Granados JA. Health at advanced age: Social inequality and other factors potentially impacting longevity in nine high-income countries. Maturitas. 2013; 74(2): 137–147.
Gunnarsdottir MJ, Gardarsson SM, Bartram J. Developing a national framework for safe drinking water—Case study from Iceland. *International Journal of Hygiene and Environmental Health. 2015;*

218(2): 196–202.

Haw C, Hawton K, Gunnell D, Platt S. Economic recession and suicidal behaviour: Possible mechanisms and ameliorating factors. Int J Soc Psychiatry. 2015; 61(1): 73–81.

Hertog S. The association between two measures of inequality in human development: income and life expectancy. technical paper (No. 2013/7), Population Division, United Nations. New York. 2013.

Hosseinpoor AR, Harper S, Lee JH, Lynch J, Mathers C, Abou-Zahr C. International shortfall inequality in life expectancy in women and in men, 1950–2010. Bulletin of the World Health Organization. 2012; 90(8): 588–594.

Hsu HC. Impact of morbidity and life events on successful aging. Asia-Pacific Journal of Public Health. 2011; 23(4): 458–469.

Jagger C, Gillies C, Moscone F, Cambois E, Van Oyen H, Nusselder W, Robine JM. Inequalities in healthy life years in the 25 countries of the European Union in 2005: a cross-national meta-regression analysis. The Lancet. 2009; 372(9656): 2124–2131.

Jakovljevic M, Laaser U. Population aging from 1950 to 2010 in seventeen transitional countries in the wider region of South Eastern Europe (Original research). SEEJPH. 2015; posted: February 21, 2015. DOI 10.12908/SEEJPH-2014-42

Jakovljevic M, Vukovic M, Fontanesi J. Life expectancy and health expenditure evolution in Eastern Europe—DiD and DEA analysis. Expert Review of Pharmacoeconomics & Outcomes Research. 2016; 16(4): 537–546.

Kalckreuth S, Trefflich F, Rummel-Kluge C. Mental health related Internet use among psychiatric patients: A cross-sectional analysis. *BMC Psychiatry.* 2014; 14(1): 368–371.

Karanikolos M, Mladovsky P, Cylus J, Thomson S, Basu S, Stuckler D, Mackenbach JP, McKee M. Financial crisis, austerity, and health in Europe. Lancet. 2013; 381(9874): 1323–1331.

Kennedy BP, Kawachi I, Prothrow-Stith D. Income distribution and mortality: cross sectional ecological study of the Robin Hood index in the United States. BMJ. 1996; 312(7037): 1004–1007.

Khan HR, Asaduzzaman M. Literate life expectancy in Bangladesh: a new approach of social indicator. Journal of Data Science. 2007; 5: 131–142.

Khan HR, Islam AA, Ababneh F. Substantial gender gap reduction in Bangladesh explained by the proximity measure of literacy and life expectancy. Journal of Applied Statistics. 2016; 43(13): 2377–2395.

Kim JI, Kim G. Country-level socioeconomic indicators associated with healthy life expectancy: income, urbanization, schooling, and internet users: 2000–2012. Social Indicators Research. 2016a; 129(1): 391–402.

Kim JI, Kim G. Country-level socioeconomic indicators associated with survival probability of becoming a centenarian among older European adults: gender inequality, male labor force participation, and proportions of women in parliaments. Journal of Biosocial Science. 2017a; 49(2): 239–250.

Kim JI, Kim G. Effects on inequality in life expectancy from a social ecology perspective. BMC Public Health. 2018; 18:243.

Kim JI, Kim G. Factors affecting the survival probability of becoming a centenarian for those aged 70, based on the human mortality database: Income, health expenditure, telephone, and sanitation. BMC Geriatrics. 2014b; 14: 113.

Kim JI, Kim G. Labor force participation and secondary education of gender inequality index (GII) associated with healthy life expectancy (HLE) at birth. International Journal for Equity in Health. 2014a; 13(1): 106.

Kim JI, Kim G. Relationship between the remaining years of healthy life expectancy in older age and national income level, educational attainment, and improved water quality. The International Journal of Aging and Human Development. 2016b; 83(4): 402–417.

Kim JI, Kim G. Social structural influences on healthy aging: community-level socioeconomic conditions and survival probability of becoming a centenarian for those aged 65 to 69 in South Korea. The International Journal of Aging & Human Development. 2015; 81(4): 241–259.

Kim JI, Kim G. Socio-ecological perspective of older age life expectancy: income, gender inequality, and financial crisis in Europe. Globalization and Health. 2017b; 13: 58.

Kim JI. Social factors associated with centenarian rate (CR) in 32 OECD countries. BMC International Health and Human Rights. 2013; 13: 16.

Kim JI, Kim G, Choi Y. Effects of air pollution on children from a socioecological perspective. BMC Pediatrics.2019; 19: 442.

King NB, Harper S, Young ME. Who cares about health inequalities? Cross-country evidence from the World Health Survey. *Health Policy and Planning.* 2013; 28(5): 558–571.

Kondilis E, Giannakopoulos S, Gavana M, Ierodiakonou I, Waitzkin H, Benos A. Economic crisis, restrictive policies, and the population's health and health care: the Greek case. Am J Public Health. 2013; 103(6): 973–979.

Kontis V, Bennett JE, Mathers CD, Li G, Foreman K, Ezzati M. Future life expectancy in 35 industrialised countries: projections with a Bayesian model ensemble. The Lancet. 2017; 389(10076): 1323–1335.

LaVeist TA, Gaskin D, Richard P. Estimating the economic burden of racial health inequalities in the United States. Int J Health Serv. 2011; 41(2): 231–238.

Lee BX, Marotta PL, Blay-Tofey M, Wang W, de Bourmont S. Economic correlates of violent death rates in forty countries, 1962–2008: A cross-typological analysis. Aggress Violent Behav. 2014 Nov-Dec; 19(6): 729–737.

Mäki N, Martikainen P, Eikemo T, et al. Educational differences in disability-free life expectancy: A comparative study of long-standing activity limitation in eight European countries. *Social Science & Medicine. 2013;* 94(1): 1–8.

Martín U, Esnaola S. Changes in social inequalities in disability-free life expectancy in Southern Europe: the case of the Basque Country. Int J Equity Health. 2014; 20; 13(1): 74.

Mathers CD, Stevens GA, Boerma T, White RA, Tobias MI. Causes of international increases in older age life expectancy. Lancet. 2015; 385(9967): 540–548.

Mathers CD, Sadana R, Salomon JA, et al. Healthy life expectancy in 191 countries, 1999. *The Lancet,* 2001; 357(9269), 1685–1691.

Martinez R., Morsch P, Soliz P, Hommes C, Ordunez P, Vega E. Life expectancy, healthy life expectancy, and burden of disease in older people in the Americas, 1990–2019: a population-based study. *Revista Panamericana de Salud Pública*, *45*. 2021

McLeroy KR, Bibeau D, Steckle A, Glanz K. An ecological perspective on health promotion programs. Health Education & Behavior. 1988; 15(4): 351–377

Messias E. Income inequality, illiteracy rate, and life expectancy in Brazil. American Journal of Public Health. 2003; 93(8): 1294–1296.

Mitsutake S, Shibata A, Ishii K, et al. Association of eHealth literacy with colorectal cancer knowledge and screening practice among internet users in Japan. *Journal of Medical Internet Research.2012;* 14(6): e153.

Murray CJ, Salomon JA, Mathers C. A critical examination of summary measures of population health. Bulletin of the World Health Organization, 2000; 78(8), 98–994.

National Association of Student Personnel Administrators (NASPA). Leadership for a healthy campus: an ecological approach for student success, 2004. http://www.naspa.org/help/index.cfm. Accessed June 8, 2017.

Neiderud CJ. How urbanization affects the epidemiology of emerging infectious diseases. *Infection Ecology & Epidemiology*, 2015; 5: 27060.

Nölke L, Mensing M, Krämer A, et al. Sociodemographic and health-(care-) related characteristics of online health information seekers: a cross-sectional German study. *BMC Public Health*, 2015; 15(1): 31–43.

Nygren BL, Blackstock AJ, Mintz ED. Cholera at the crossroads: The association between endemic cholera and national access to improved water sources and sanitation. *The American journal of tropical medicine and hygiene*, 2014; 91(5): 1023–1028.

O'Sullivan J, Ashton T. A minimum income for healthy living (MIHL)–older New Zealanders. Ageing & Society. 2012; 32(5): 747–768.

Osborne K, Patel K. Evaluation of a website that promotes social connectedness: lessons for equitable e-health promotion. *Australian Journal of Primary Health*, 2013; 19(4): 325–330.

Ostrom E. A general framework for analyzing sustainability of social-ecological systems. Science. 2009; 325(5939): 419–422.

Paranthaman K, Harrison H. Drinking water incidents due to chemical contamination in England and Wales, 2006–2008. Journal of Water and Health, 2010; 8(4): 735–740.

Pullan RL, Freeman MC, Gething PW, Brooker SJ. Geographical inequalities in use of improved drinking water supply and sanitation across sub-Saharan Africa: mapping and spatial analysis of cross-sectional survey data. *PLoS Med*, 2014; 11(4): e1001626.

Rasella D, Aquino R, Barreto ML. Impact of income inequality on life expectancy in a highly unequal developing country: the case of Brazil. Journal of Epidemiology and Community Health. 2013; jech–2012.

Regidor E, Calle ME, Navarro P, Domínguez V. Trends in the association between average income, poverty and income inequality and life expectancy in Spain. Social Science & Medicine. 2003; 56(5): 961–971.

Robinson T. Applying the socio-ecological model to improving fruit and vegetable intake among low-income African Americans. Journal of Community Health. 2008; 33(6): 395–406.

Rowe JW, Kahn RL. Human aging: usual and successful. Science. 1987; 237(4811): 143–149

Salomon JA, Wang H, Freeman MK, Vos T, Flaxman AD, Lopez AD, Murray CJ. Healthy life expectancy for 187 countries, 1990–2010: a systematic analysis for the Global Burden Disease Study 2010. The Lancet. 2013; 380(9859): 2144–2162.

Simmons BE. Average rate of change. http://www.mathwords.com. Accessed June 2, 2015.

Stuckler D, Basu S, Suhrcke M, Coutts A, McKee M. The public health effect of economic crises and alternative policy responses in Europe: an empirical analysis. Lancet. 2009; 374(9686): 315–323.

Szwarcwald CL, da Mota JC, Damacena GN, Pereira TG. Health inequalities in Rio de Janeiro, Brazil: lower healthy life expectancy in socioeconomically disadvantaged areas. Am J Public Health. 2011; 101(3): 517–523.

Tapia Granados JA, Rodriguez JM. Health, economic crisis, and austerity: A comparison of Greece, Finland and Iceland. Health Policy. 2015; 119(7): 941–953.

Tarkiainen L, Martikainen P, Laaksonen M. The changing relationship between income and mortality in Finland, 1988–2007. *Journal of Epidemiology and Community Health.* 2013; 67(1): 21–27.

UNDESA (United Nations Department of Economic and Social Affairs). 2015 Revision. World Population Prospects. Population Division Database. Detailed Indicators. https://esa.un.org/unpd/wpp/ Accessed June 14, 2016a.

UNDESA (United Nations Department of Economic and Social Affairs). World Population Prospects: The 2012 Revision. New York. http://esa.un.org/unpd/wpp/ Accessed April 15, 2016b.

United Nations (UN). Gender inequality index (value). In: Human development report. http://hdr.undp.org/en/content/gender-inequality-index -Accessed Feb 16, 2015d.

United Nations (UN). Human development report 2015: Work for human development, Table A1.1 Work with Exploitation, Risks and Insecurities, Security from Employment, Old Age Pension Recipients 2004–2012, 47–50, Published for the United Nations Development Programme (UNDP), New York, USA. http://hdr.undp.org/sites/default/files/2015_human_development_report_1.pdf -Accessed August 16, 2016c.

United Nations (UN). Human development report 2015d: Statistical annex, Statistical Table 3: Inequality-adjusted Human development index, inequality in life expectancy and Gini coefficient, 216–219; Table 5: Gender Inequality Index, Secondary education, 224–227; Table 13: Work and employment, Labour productivity, 254–257.

United Nations (UN). Human Development Report, Gender inequality index. http://hdr.undp.org/en/statistics/gii/. Accessed on August 15, 2016: Comments and limitations. http://mdgs.un.org/unsd/mdg/Metadata.aspx?IndicatorId=0&SeriesId=557. Accessed on July 28, 2016.

United Nations (UN). Human development report: Income index. http://hdr.undp.org/en/content/income-index. Accessed February 16, 2015a.

United Nations (UN). Human development report: Inequality-adjusted Human Development Index. http://hdr.undp.org/en/faq-page/inequality-adjusted-human-development-index-ihdi#t293n97_Accessed August 16, 2016b.

United Nations (UN). Human development report: Mean years of schooling (of adults) (years), http://hdr.undp.org/en/content/mean-years-schooling-adults-years. Accessed February 16, 2015b.

United Nations (UN). Human development report: Population, urban (% of population). http://hdr.undp.org/en/content/population-urban-population. Accessed February 16, 2015c.

United Nations (UN). Human development report 2015: Statistical annex, Statistical Table 3: Inequality-adjusted Human Development Index, Inequality in life expectancy and Gini coefficient, 216–219; Table 5: Gender Inequality Index, Secondary education, 224–227; Table 13: Work and employment, Labour productivity, 254–257.

Welsh CE, Matthewa FE, Jagger C. Trends in life expectancy and healthy life years at birth and age 65 in the UK, 2008–2016, and other countries of the EU28: An observational cross-sectional study. *The Lancet Regional Health-Europe*, 2021; 2: 100023.

Wilkinson RG, Pickett KE. Income inequality and socioeconomic gradients in mortality. American Journal of Public Health. 2008; 98(4): 699–704.

World Bank (WB). Depth of credit information index, (0 = low to 8 = high). http://data.worldbank.org/indicator/IC.CRD.INFO.XQ/countries/1W?display=default. Accessed Jun 16, 2015a.

World Bank (WB). World Bank, International Comparison Program database. GNI per capita, PPP (current international $), http://data.worldbank.org/indicator/NY.GNP.PCAP.PP.CD?view=chart. Accessed Jan 16, 2016.

World Bank (WB). World Development Indicators, Improved water source, urban, http://data.worldbank.org/indicator/SH.H2O.SAFE.UR.ZS?page=1, Accessed on January 12, 2015b.

World Bank (WB). World development indicators: Internet users (per 100 people), http://data.worldbank.org/indicator/IT.NET.USER.P2. Accessed February 16, 2015.

World Health Organization (WHO), Regional Office for Europe. Healthy ageing. http://www.euro.who.int/en/health-topics/Life-stages/healthy-ageing/healthy-ageing. Accessed June 16, 2017.

World Health Organization (WHO). Healthy life expectancy at birth. http://apps.who.int/gho/indicatorregistry/App_Main/view_indicator.aspx?iid=66. Accessed February 12, 2015a.

World Health Organization (WHO). Life expectancy at birth. In: Global Health Observatory Data Repository. http://apps.who.int/gho/data/view.main.680?lang=en. Accessed Feb 16, 2015c.

World Health Organization (WHO). WHO Methods for Life Expectancy and Healthy Life Expectancy. 2014; Geneva: WHO.

World Health Origination (WHO). Global Health Observatory Data Repository. Life expectancy. http://apps.who.int/gho/data/node.main.3?lang=en.ccessed on January 6, 2015b.

Yang H, Bain R, Bartram J, Gundry S, Pedley S, Wright J. Water safety and inequality in access to drinking-water between rich and poor households. *Environmental Science & Technology.* 2013; 47(3): 1222–1230.

Zhao Y, Dempsey K. Causes of inequality in life expectancy between and non-indigenous people in the Northern Territory, 1981–2000: a decomposition analysis. Medical Journal of Australia. 2006; 184(10): 490–494.

PART 4

APPLICATION OF SEFS AS DETERMINANTS FOR BECOMING A CENTENARIAN

Part 4 discusses the application of SEFs as determinants for becoming a centenarian:

(1) It estimates regression and correlation between SEFs and SPBC and between SEFs and LE.

(2) It proposes estimation formulas for becoming centenarians.

(3) These 14 factors' values and the estimation formulas are applied to analyze global trends in SEFs and present graphs of variables.

Subsequently, Part 4 applies factors identified in SEFs to provide both short- and long-term plans for humanity. Finally, causes of increases and decreases in SEFs suggest short- and long-term individual and national policy alternatives.

CHAPTER 4

INFLUENCE OF SEFs ON LE AND SPBC

4.1 Correlation between LE and SEFs and SPBC and SEFs

4.1.1 Planning to nurture healthy centenarians

First, this chapter describes the LE plan in which humans live to be 100 years of age (see Fig. 4.1).

The next step is to select the variables of SEFs that affect this goal. These variables can predict the probability of reaching a healthy 100 years of age at a certain age.

The third and fourth step is creating an estimation formula for reaching the age of 100 at 82 (ISS). Each country's SEFs are centered on the estimation equations to measure and confirm people's health levels.

The fourth to ninth step is to establish short- and long-term plans to improve the health levels reaching centenarians of each country. In this step, we consider the factors and variables from the standpoint of individuals, the national government, and overall medical expenditures, after which the probability of becoming a centenarian is, confirmed according to the survival probability and improvement measures.

Finally, the plan is revised and supplemented based on quality feedback. Therefore, the details of each step are shown in Fig. 4.1.

Goal:
(1) Achieve healthy centenarians

▼▲

Planning:
(2) Correlation between LE and SEFs, SPBC and SEFs
(3) Developing estimation formula of ISS
(4) Prediction of estimates for SEFs of LE and SPBC

▼▲

Managing:
(5) Establishment of short and long-term plans (1, 5 to 10 years)
(6) PLI: GNI, BSS, SMDW, and use of the ECLE
(7) Social environment as CLSS: GII, IUI, and UP, and use of the ECLE
(8) Hospital visit: GHE and HEPGDP as CLSS
(9) Achievement of the health level and SPBC feasibility review

▼▲

Feedback and reinforcement:
(10) Healthcare system based on CLSS
(11) Health resource mobilization

▼▲

Assessment:
(12) Assessment of the health level based on CLSS

Fig. 4.1. Plan for achieving healthy centenarians

4.1.2 Correlation between LE and SEFs and SPBC and SEFs

At this point, the following question is raised. How do we select the SEFs that influence 82-year-olds to live a healthy life until the age of 100? Chapter 2 described nine significant variables by summarizing all of the previous studies published by the author, while Chapter 3 explained the 14 SEFs that affect LE. Therefore, 14 important variables are estimated, including nine variables that have a common influence on SPBC and LE and five variables that only affect LE.

Among the 14 variables that were valid for LE, five variables excluded from SPBC (82) were pension receipt, education level, Gini coefficient, government medical expenditure, and national creditworthiness. The majority of the 39 countries in SPBC (82) were developed countries as a sample. There were almost no gaps in education and income and public healthcare expenditure. In addition, there was no gap in pension receipt as it is a welfare system implemented by nearly all developed countries. Therefore, the relationship between the LE and SPBC (82) is described in Table 4.1.

Table 4.1. Correlation coefficients for LE and SPBC (82) and SEFs

Variables		Correlations coefficient	p-value
LE	GNI	0.647	0.000
	OPR	0.621	0.000
	SE	0.706	0.000
	SMDW	0.821	0.000
	FTMPS	0.727	0.000
	BSS	0.853	0.000
	GI	-0.352	0.000
	UP	0.636	0.000
	GII	-0.861	0.000
	IUI	0.859	0.000
	GHE	0.708	0.000
	HEGDP	0.317	0.000
	SVPW	0.668	0.000
	DCI	0.279	0.005
SPBC (82 to 100)	GNI	0.487	0.002
	SMDW	0.484	0.002
	BSS	0.554	0.000
	UP	0.481	0.002
	GII	-0.471	0.003
	IUI	0.535	0.000
	HEGDP	0.544	0.000
	SVPW	0.491	0.002
	FTMPS	0.493	0.001

In this case, the 14 variables in which CLSS and PLI affect LE and SPBC have a negative (−) sign in two of the variables and a positive (+) sign in the remaining 12.

In Fig. 4.2, the curves of LE and SPBC 1 are upwards, and to the right, i.e., curve 1 moves from Point A to Point B. In this regard, as the SEFs increase from 70% to 90%, the LE and survival probability increase from 60 to 90 years of age.

However, the curves of LE and SPBC 2 are downward and to the right, i.e., curve 2 moves from Point A to Point C. Thus, as the SEFs increase from 70% to 90%, the LE and survival probability decrease from 60 to 30 years. This indicates that triangle ABC is the area in which the increase/decrease in gain changes the survival probability according to the increase/decrease of the SEFs.

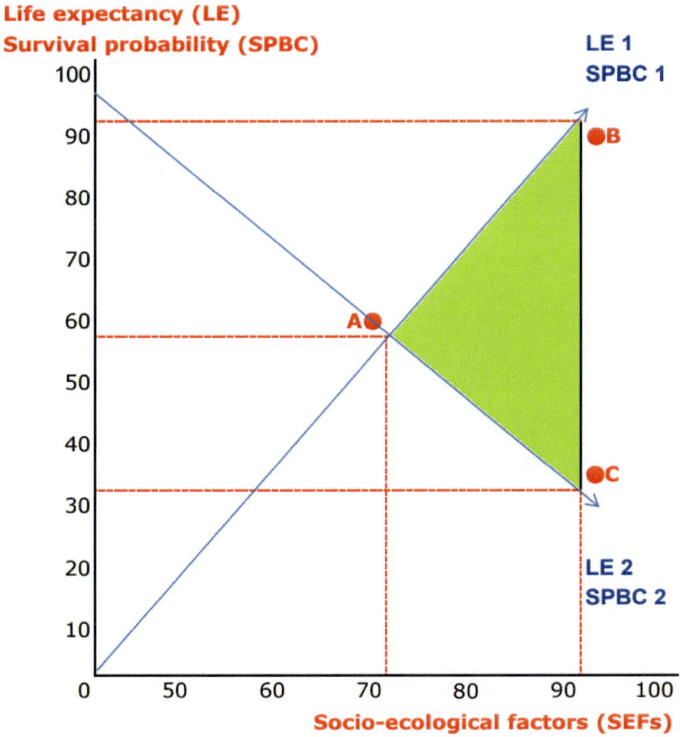

Fig. 4.2 Relationship between SPBC and LE and SEFs

Among the SEFs, the Gini index (GI) and Gender inequality index (GII) have a negative correlation in the direction of their Gini coefficients. In other words, the lower the GII, the higher the SPBC. Specifically, Fig. 4.2.1 shows the correlation between SPBC and LE and the GI and GII. For example, when the SEFs are 0.5, the survival rate is 80 years, but when the SEFs are 0.7, it decreases to 50 years (Point B).

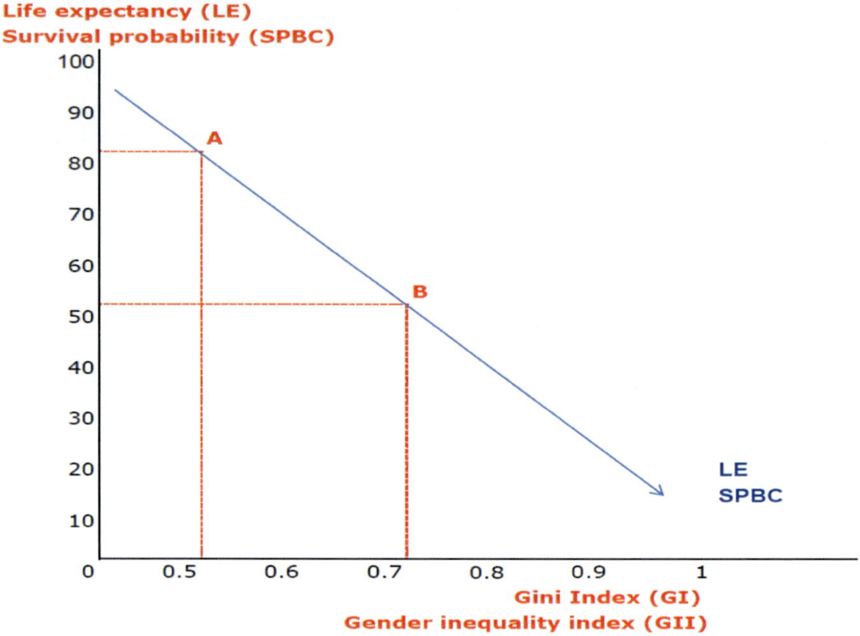

Fig. 4.2.1 Relationship between SPBC, LE, and the GI and GII

The factors for PLI include Gross national income (GNI) and Services value-added per worker (SVPW). Fig. 4.2.2 explains the relationship between SPBC and LE and GNI and SVPW. For instance, when the SEFs are $10,000, the survival rate is 60 years, but when the SEFs are $25,000, it increases to 90 years (Point B). This indicates that if the income level of the people in a country is high and the added productivity per worker can increase, then the survival probability can further improve.

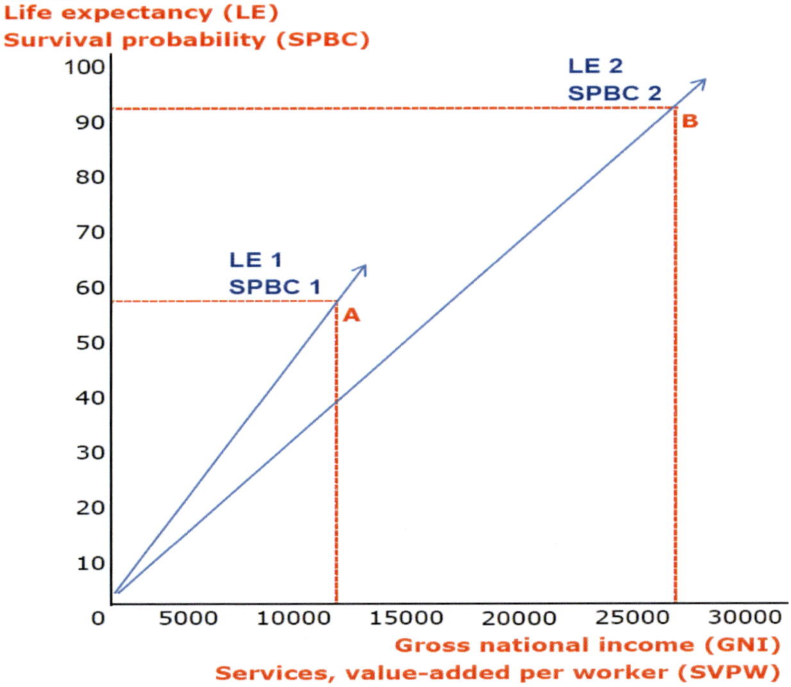

Fig. 4.2.2 Relationship between SPBC, LE, and GNI and SVPW

The SEFs of LE and CLSS include UP, IUI, OPR, BSS, SMDW, and FTMPS. In Table 4.1, we can see the correlation between LE and SPBC and UP, BSS, OPR, IUI, SMDW, and FTMPS. Additionally, as shown in Fig. 4.2.3, when the SEFs are 60%, the survival rate is 60 years, but when the SEFs are 70%, it increases to 80 years (Point B). This indicates that the higher the SEFs (i.e., UP, BSS, OPR, IUI, SMDW, and FTMPS), the higher the survival probability. In other words, if the national welfare and health facilities are well-maintained, then the probability of surviving until the age of 100 is high.

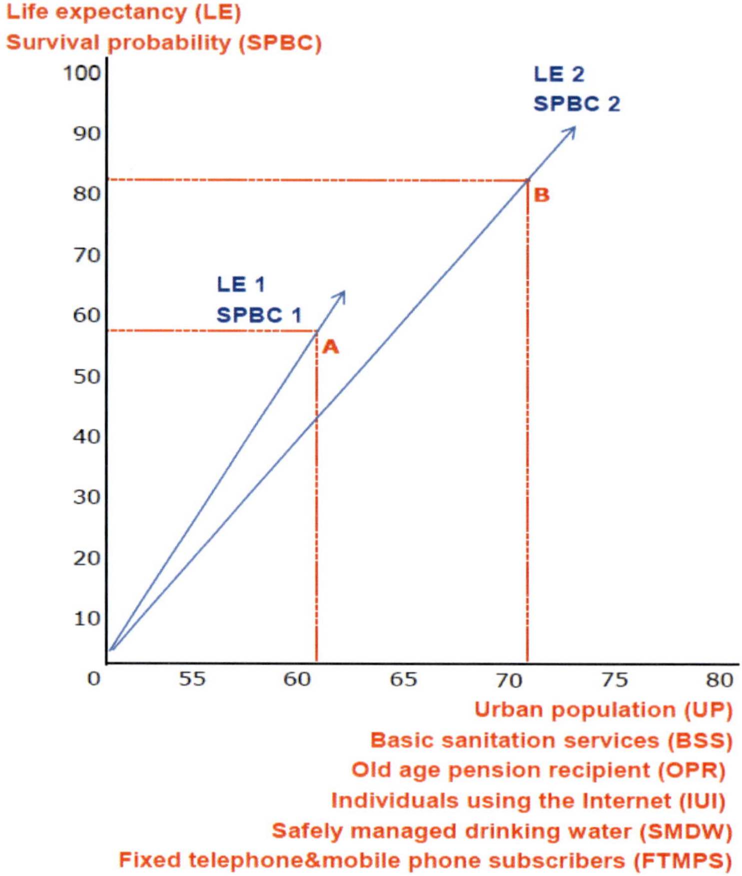

Fig. 4.2.3 Relationship between SPBC, LE, and UP, BSS, OPR, IUI, SMDW, and FTMPS

Among the factors of PLI, there is secondary education (SE). In Table 4.1, we can see the correlation between LE and SPBC, and SE. Moreover, as shown in Fig. 4.2.4, the survival rates can be increased to 60 years when the SE period is 12 years; to 80 years when the SE period is 14 years; and 90 years (Point C) when the SE period is 17 years. This indicates that as the SE increases in the positive (+) direction, LE and SPBC increase. In other words, countries with a high national education level have a higher survival probability.

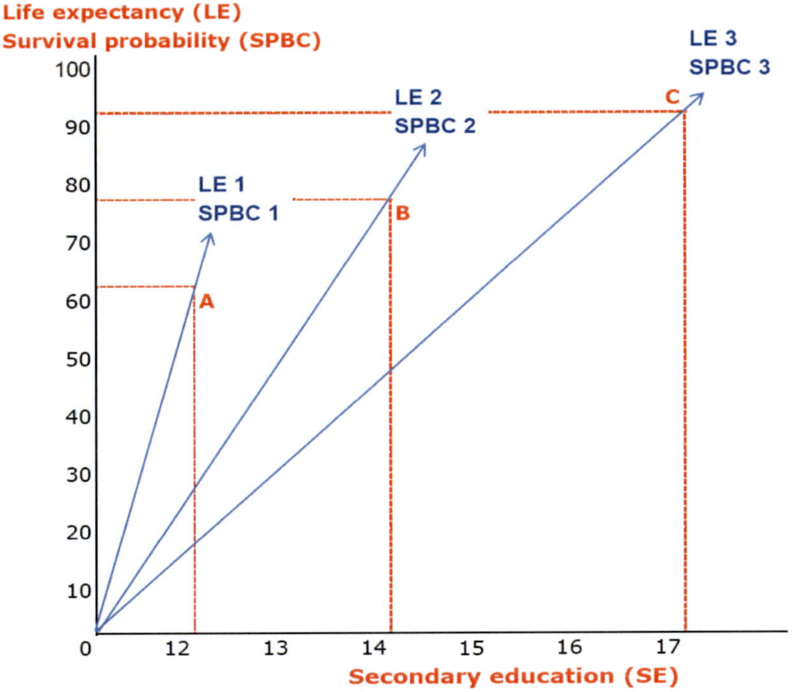

Fig. 4.2.4 Relationship between SPBC, LE, and SE

The factors of CLSS include GHE, DCI, and HEPGDP. Table 4.1 shows the correlation between LE and SPBC, and GHE, DCI, and HEPGDP. Additionally, in Fig. 4.2.5, when the SEFs are 5%, the survival rate is 60 years, but when the SEFs are 7%, it increases to 80 years (Point B). This indicates that if a country has a high GHE, DCI, and HEPGDP, the LE and SPBC are high.

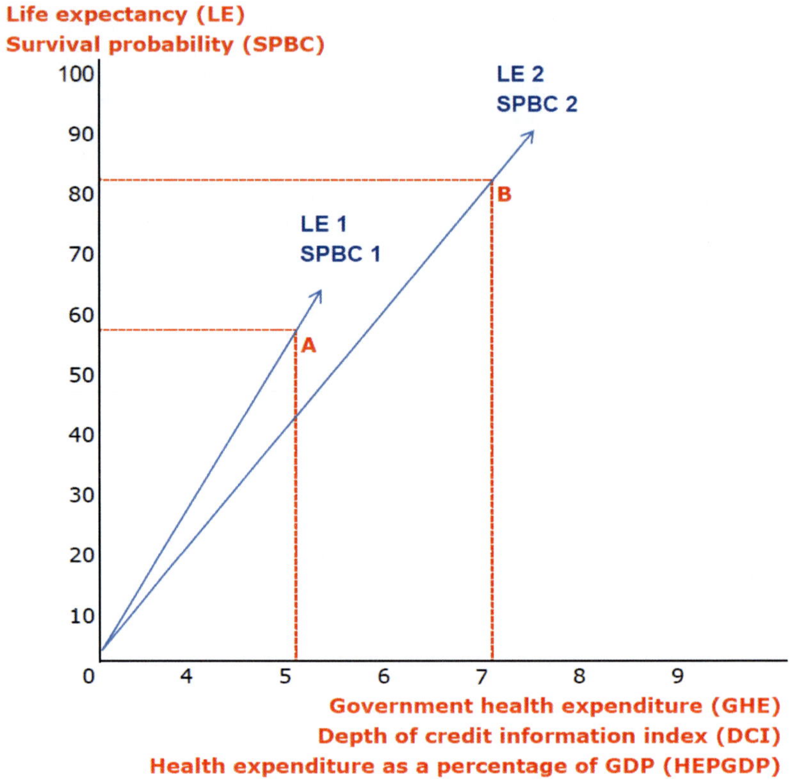

Fig. 4.2.5 Relationship between SPBC, LE, and the GI and GII

4.2 Measures for SPBC

As previously mentioned, nine variables were related to SBPC were discovered.
Thus, Chapter 4 will perform the following actions:
(1) Create estimation ISS based on nine variables' influence on SPBC,
(2) Derive estimates of SPBC (82) based on each country's SEFs, and
(3) Discuss a response strategy.

4.2.1 Developing the estimation formula of ISS

In this chapter, an estimation formula is essential for quantifying and measuring the lifespan of each country based on their respective health levels. Additionally, an effective plan for health and longevity must include specific SEFs such as those described earlier. Thus, the following is a customized and practical approach for achieving a healthy 100 years of age.

First, it is crucial to set the LE standard before creating the estimation formula for reaching the age of 100. As shown in Fig. 4.3, if the LE is 82 years, this estimation formula's index systematically improves the national health level by predicting the attainable healthy lifespan from 82 to 100 years. The variables applied to this estimation formula are the re-evaluated nine factors. In other words, it is an estimation of the SEFs for the nine re-tested variables essential for LE, starting from 82 to 100 years of age. Put precisely, the probability of surviving to 100 years is calculated by the mean score of the highest standard of 100% to each of the nine correlated SEFs (i.e., the actual measured value of each indicator is converted into 100% and evaluated for comparison necessary for becoming a centenarian).

In this regard, the nine variables include (1) GNI, (2) SMDW, (3) IUI, (4) SVPW, (5) UP, (6) BSS, (7) HEPGDP, (8) FTMPS, and (9) the GII. Thus, it is possible to predict the impact on centenarians by finding and substituting their indicators in the database of international organizations.

Based on SEFs, the formula for estimating ISS is as follows. The survival probability is estimated by calculating the highest, middle, and lowest values of the nine variables of SEFs that affect SPBC.

Impact of SEFs on SPBC: ISS

$$ISS = \sum_{x=1}^{n} A + PLICLSS\,x1 + \dots + PLICLSS\,xn \text{ ------------------(1)}$$

$$ISS = \sum [(PLICLSS)_{x1} + (PLICLSS)_{x2} + \cdots + (PLICLSS)_{x9}] \text{ -------(2)}$$

(Category)
PLICLSS x1: GNI (Low 1 to high 100)
PLICLSS x2, x3: IUI (Low 1 to high 100) + UP (Low 1 to high 100)
PLICLSS x4, x5: FTMPS (Low 1 to high 100) + GII (Low 1 to high 100)
PLICLSS x6, x7: BSS (Low 1 to high 100) + HEPGDP (Low 1 to high 100)
PLICLSS x8, x9: SMDW (Low 1 to high 100) + SVPW (Low 1 to high 100)

(Impact Ranking)
Highest: $\sum$ [PLI CLSS x_1 + ··· + 9 PLI CLSS x_9] ≤ 800 to 900 (A++)
High: $\sum$ [PLI CLSS x_1 + ··· + 9 PLI CLSS x_9] ≤ 700 to 799 (A+)
Middle: $\sum$ [PLI CLSS x_1 + ··· + 9 PLI CLSS x_9] ≤ 600 to 699 (A)
Low: $\sum$ [PLI CLSS x_1 + ··· + 9 PLI CLSS x_9] ≤ 500 to 599 (B+)
Lowest: $\sum$ [PLI CLSS x_1 + ··· + 9 PLI CLSS x_9] ≤ 400 to 499 (B)

Fig.4.3 Estimate the impact of SEFs on SPBC: (ISS)

▶ The maximum 100-year SPBC prediction is calculated by substituting 100% for the highest scores of the PLI and CLSS factors in the nine valid variables. The calculation is as follows (see Fig. 4.3).

Highest: $\sum$ [PLICLSS x_1 + ···+ PLICLSS x_9] ≤ 800–900 (A++)

This formula estimates the impact of the highest survival probability—$\sum$ (90% [the highest scores in the PLI and CLSS factors] X 9 factors [the valid variables for SPBC]) = Total 810 points. The impact of the highest survival probability can extend from 800 to 900 points. The calculation is as follows:

Highest: (90 X 9 ≤ 810 [A++]).

▶ The high 100-year SPBC prediction is calculated by substituting 100% for each of the PLI and CLSS factors in the nine valid variables. The calculation is as follows:

High: $\sum$ [PLICLSS x_1 + ···+ PLICLSS x_9] $\leq$ 700–799 (A+)

This formula estimates the high SEFs in the process of reaching centenarians—$\sum$ (88% [the medium scores in the PLI and CLSS factors] X 9 factors [the valid variables for SPBC]) = total 792 points. The impact of the medium survival probability can extend from 700 to 799 points. The calculation is as follows:

High: (88 X 9 $\leq$ 792 [A+]).

▶ The middle 100-year SPBC prediction is calculated by substituting 100% for each of the PLI and CLSS factors in the nine valid variables. The calculation is as follows:

Middle: [PLICLSS x_1 + ···+ PLICLSS x_9] $\leq$ 600–699 (A)

This formula estimates the medium SEFs in the process of reaching centenarians—$\sum$ (77% [the medium scores in the PLI and CLSS factors] X 9 factors [the valid variables for SPBC]) = total 693 points. The impact of the medium survival probability can extend from 600 to 699 points. The calculation is as follows:

Middle: (77 X 9 $\leq$ 693 [A]).

▶ The low 100-year SPBC prediction is calculated by substituting 100% for each of the PLI and CLSS factors. The calculation is as follows:

Low: [PLICLSS x_1 + ···+ PLICLSS x_9] $\leq$ 500–599 (B+)

This formula estimates the lower SEFs in reaching centenarians—$\sum$ (66% [the low scores in the PLI and CLSS factors] X 9 factors [the valid variables for SPBC]) = total 594 points. The impact of the low survival probability can extend from 500 to 599 points. The calculation is as follows:

Low: (66 X 9 $\leq$ 594 [B+]).

▶ The lowest 100-year SPBC prediction is calculated by substituting 100% for each of the PLI and CLSS factors. The calculation is as follows:

Lowest: [PLICLSS x_1 + ···+ PLICLSS x_9] ≤ 400–499 (B)

This formula estimates the lowest SEFs in reaching centenarians—∑ (55% [the lowest scores in the PLI and CLSS factors] X 9 factors [the valid variables for SPBC]) = total 495 points. The impact of the lowest survival probability can extend from 400 to 499 points. The calculation is as follows:

Lowest: (55 X 9 ≤ 495 [B]).

4.2.2 Output for ISS

Based on each country's SEFs, the SPBC (82) can be estimated by using the ISS formulas (Table 4.2).

If we use these formulas, and input actual data, then it is possible to determine the possible impact in a country. As SEFs are the default, the value of ISS is substituted as 100%. For example, the actual GNI in the UK is 41770$. In this case, we can obtain the substituted values 100% and substitute them into ISS formula (1) as follows:

ISS = ∑ ([PLICLSS] x_1 + [PLICLSS] x_2 + ···· + [PLICLSS] x_9) ---------- (1)

The latest UK GNP data (2018) is estimated to be 50% if the substituting is based on ISS formula (1) values. For example, if GNI $41770 is estimated to be the UK's GNP value of ISS, then the UK outputs an ISS of 50% as substituted, when—with the highest value in all 39 countries—Switzerland is set as the standard of 100%.

In the UK, notably, those who have achieved SPBC (82) can impact 50% on SPBC through just GNI. Meanwhile, if indicators of CLSS and PLI increase, the chances of reaching 100 years will be even higher. Thus, countries should try to replace CLSS and PLI as 100%.

In this case, by substituting the ISS formula, the present situation of each country can be analyzed, and a vision for the survival probability of reaching centenarians can be established.

4.2.3 Differences between countries for ISS

Based on each country's SEFs, we have estimated the ISS (Table 4.2).

With regard to GNI, among the 39 countries, Switzerland is the highest with 1.00, and Ukraine is the lowest with 0.03. However, Ukraine is the weakest in SPBC (82) with 21 (Additional File 1).

In SMDW, among the 39 countries, Belgium, the Netherlands, Germany, Sweden, the United Kingdom, New Zealand, Finland, Greece, and the Slovak Republic are the highest with 1.00, and the Russian Federation is the lowest with 0.76. In contrast, the Russian Federation is weak in SPBC (82) with 31 as survival probability (Additional File 1).

In BSS, Switzerland, the United States, Japan, Denmark, Australia, New Zealand, Austria, Israel, Spain, the Republic of Korea, Portugal, and Chile are the highest with 1.00, and Bulgaria is the lowest with 0.86. Japan is the highest in SPBC (82) with 185, and Bulgaria is weak in SPBC (82) with 30 as survival probability (Additional File 1).

In UP, Belgium is the highest with 1.00 and the Slovak Republic is the lowest with 0.55. Belgium, however, is high in SPBC (82) with 93, and the Slovak Republic is weak in SPBC (82) with 52 as its survival probability (Additional File 1).

In gender equality, Switzerland, Sweden, Denmark, and New Zealand are the highest with 1.00, Ukraine is low with 0.74. In IUI, Iceland is the highest with 1.00 and Bulgaria the lowest with 0.65. In HEPGDP, the United States is the highest with 1.00, and the Russian Federation and Luxembourg are the lowest with 0.31. In SVPW, Luxembourg is the highest with 1.00, and Ukraine is the lowest with 0.04. Lastly, in FTMTS, France is the highest with 1.00 and Finland is the lowest with 0.11.

In addition, we found that the overall evaluation in ISS, Switzerland, Luxembourg, the United States, Iceland, France, Japan, Belgium, the Netherlands, Germany, Sweden, Denmark, and Norway are grade A+. However, Bulgaria, the Russian Federation, and Ukraine are rated B.

Overall, we know that these high-scoring country groups have the highest SPBC (82), but the low-scoring countries have the lowest SPBC (82).

Table 4.2 Example ISS in the 39 countries

Countries	GNI	SMDW	BSS	UP	GII	IUI	HEPGDP	SVPW	FTMTS	TOTAL	Ranking
Switzerland	1.00	0.95	1.00	0.75	1.00	0.91	0.70	0.64	0.70	765	A+
Luxembourg	0.85	0.92	0.98	0.93	0.91	0.79	0.31	1.00	0.78	747	A+
United States	0.75	0.99	1.00	0.84	0.85	0.89	1.00	0.53	0.60	745	A+
Iceland	0.81	1.00	0.99	0.96	0.98	1.00	0.50	0.35	0.73	732	A+
France	0.49	0.98	0.99	0.82	0.98	0.82	0.67	0.50	1.00	725	A+
Japan	0.49	0.98	1.00	0.94	0.94	0.93	0.65	0.44	0.84	721	A+
Belgium	0.55	1.00	0.99	1.00	0.99	0.89	0.61	0.49	0.63	715	A+
Netherlands	0.61	1.00	0.98	0.94	0.96	0.99	0.59	0.44	0.64	715	A+
Germany	0.56	1.00	0.99	0.79	0.95	0.86	0.68	0.40	0.90	713	A+
Sweden	0.66	1.00	0.99	0.89	1.00	0.95	0.65	0.47	0.44	705	A+
Denmark	0.73	0.97	1.00	0.90	1.00	0.99	0.60	0.54	0.32	705	A+
Norway	0.96	1.00	0.98	0.84	0.90	0.92	0.60	0.63	0.22	705	A+
United Kingdom	0.50	1.00	0.99	0.86	0.91	0.92	0.59	0.39	0.80	696	A
Canada	0.54	0.99	0.99	0.83	0.95	0.94	0.64	0.41	0.66	695	A
Australia	0.64	0.98	1.00	0.88	0.93	0.88	0.55	0.50	0.58	694	A
New Zealand	0.50	1.00	1.00	0.88	1.00	0.95	0.55	0.31	0.64	683	A
Austria	0.59	0.99	1.00	0.60	0.96	0.89	0.61	0.43	0.70	677	A
Ireland	0.71	0.97	0.91	0.65	0.94	0.86	0.41	0.60	0.66	671	A
Israel	0.49	0.99	1.00	0.94	0.93	0.83	0.45	0.33	0.66	662	A
Spain	0.35	0.98	1.00	0.82	0.96	0.86	0.53	0.35	0.70	655	A
Republic of Korea	0.39	0.95	1.00	0.83	0.95	0.75	0.45	0.21	0.88	641	A
Finland	0.58	1.00	0.99	0.87	0.99	0.89	0.54	0.42	0.11	639	A
Greece	0.23	1.00	0.99	0.81	0.91	0.71	0.46	0.31	0.82	624	A
Portugal	0.26	0.99	1.00	0.67	0.91	0.77	0.56	0.24	0.79	619	A
Italy	0.40	0.95	0.99	0.72	0.97	0.64	0.51	0.44	0.57	619	A
Slovenia	0.29	0.98	0.99	0.56	0.97	0.80	0.49	0.28	0.60	596	B+
Estonia	0.25	0.93	0.99	0.70	0.94	0.90	0.40	0.18	0.46	575	B+
Belarus	0.07	0.95	0.98	0.81	0.91	0.76	0.33	0.05	0.80	566	B+
Czech Republic	0.25	0.98	0.99	0.75	0.90	0.80	0.45	0.23	0.26	561	B+
Chile	0.17	0.99	1.00	0.89	0.74	0.84	0.54	0.13	0.29	559	B+
Poland	0.17	0.98	0.98	0.61	0.99	0.98	0.37	0.18	0.33	559	B+
Latvia	0.20	0.98	0.92	0.70	0.98	0.97	0.37	0.16	0.29	557	B+
Hungary	0.18	0.90	0.98	0.73	0.77	0.78	0.40	0.17	0.54	545	B+
Croatia	0.17	0.90	0.97	0.58	0.91	0.68	0.40	0.18	0.56	535	B+
Lithuania	0.21	0.95	0.93	0.69	0.86	0.82	0.39	0.16	0.29	530	B+
Slovak Republic	0.22	1.00	0.98	0.55	0.84	0.83	0.40	0.20	0.23	525	B+
Bulgaria	0.10	0.97	0.86	0.77	0.81	0.65	0.44	0.09	0.30	499	B
Russian Federation	0.12	0.76	0.90	0.76	0.77	0.77	0.31	0.10	0.37	486	B
Ukraine	0.03	0.92	0.96	0.70	0.74	0.60	0.46	0.04	0.28	473	B

Life expectancy at birth, total (years): LE

Life expectancy at birth indicates the number of years a newborn infant would live if prevailing patterns of mortality at the time of its birth were to stay the same throughout its life.

Source: United Nations Population Division. World Population Prospects: 2019 Revision.

4.3 Prediction of the estimates for SEFs

4.3.1 Gross national income (GNI)

GNI (World Bank Atlas method, in $US) is a SEFs that affects the LE and SPBC (82) of each country. Income level has also been shown to have a decisive effect on the two dependent variables of LE and survival probability (see Fig. 4.4).

As of 2019, the highest GNI in the world was Switzerland, at $US 85,500, while the lowest was Burundi at $US 280. In this regard, income level not only has a decisive effect on surviving from birth to LE in each country, but it is also the most influential economic variable for surviving from 82 to 100 years of age. This is because the economic environment can influence health and longevity.

Estimating ISS based on income level is as follows. The maximum value of GNI in the 39 countries is substituted at the rate of 100%. For this ISS, if the variables verified in the relevant country are excellent, we substitute 100 points (%) in each variable. Consequently, if all nine variables are excellent in a country with SPBC (82), the highest probability of reaching 100 years of age can be predicted by ISS.

Applying the ISS formula for GNI

Switzerland has one of the highest GNI in the world. Based on Switzerland's income level, the probability of an 82-year-old surviving to 100 receives the highest score of 100% in nine example countries (Table 4.3). This indicates the importance of income level on SEFs and SPBC (82). Examples of the GNI scores by country are shown in Table 4.3.

Table 4.3. Example of a score for GNI per capita, 2019 (current US$)

Countries	Switzerland	Norway	United States	United Kingdom	Italy	Korea, Rep.	Spain	Russian Federation	Brazil
GNI	85,500	82,500	65,850	42,220	34,530	33,790	30,390	11,260	9130
ISS (%)	100	96	77	49	40	40	36	13	11

GNI per capita, Atlas method (current US$):

GNI per capita (formerly GNP per capita) is the gross national income (GNI), converted to US dollars using the World Bank Atlas method, divided by the midyear population. GNI is the sum of value-added by all resident producers plus any product taxes not included in the valuation of output plus net receipts of primary income (compensation of employees and property income) from abroad. To smooth fluctuations in prices and exchange rates, the World Bank uses a special Atlas method of conversion.

Source: World Bank national accounts data, and OECD National Accounts data files.

Impact of GNI on LE and SPBC (82)

Tables 4.3.1 and 4.3.2 show that GNI, as the sole independent variable, influences 23% of SPBC (82) and 42% of LE. Additionally, Fig. 4.4 shows that the higher the national income, the higher the likelihood of achieving LE and reaching 100 years of age. Additionally, if the income is high, then the interest in health is naturally high. The possibility of reaching the age of 100 is very high because the healthcare system is well-maintained.

Table 4.3.1. Multiple regression models of predicting the GNI and SPBC(82)

(N = 39)

Term	Coefficients	SE Coef	T-Value	P-Value	VIF	R^2
GNI	0.000785	0.000232	3.39	0.002	1	0.237
R-sq	R-sq(adj)					
23.72%	21.66%					

Table 4.3.2. Multiple regression models of predicting the GNI and LE

(N = 170)

Term	Coefficients	SE Coef	T-Value	P-Value	VIF	R^2
GNI	0.000246	0.000022	11	0.001	1	0.418
R-sq	R-sq(adj)					
41.86%	41.52%					

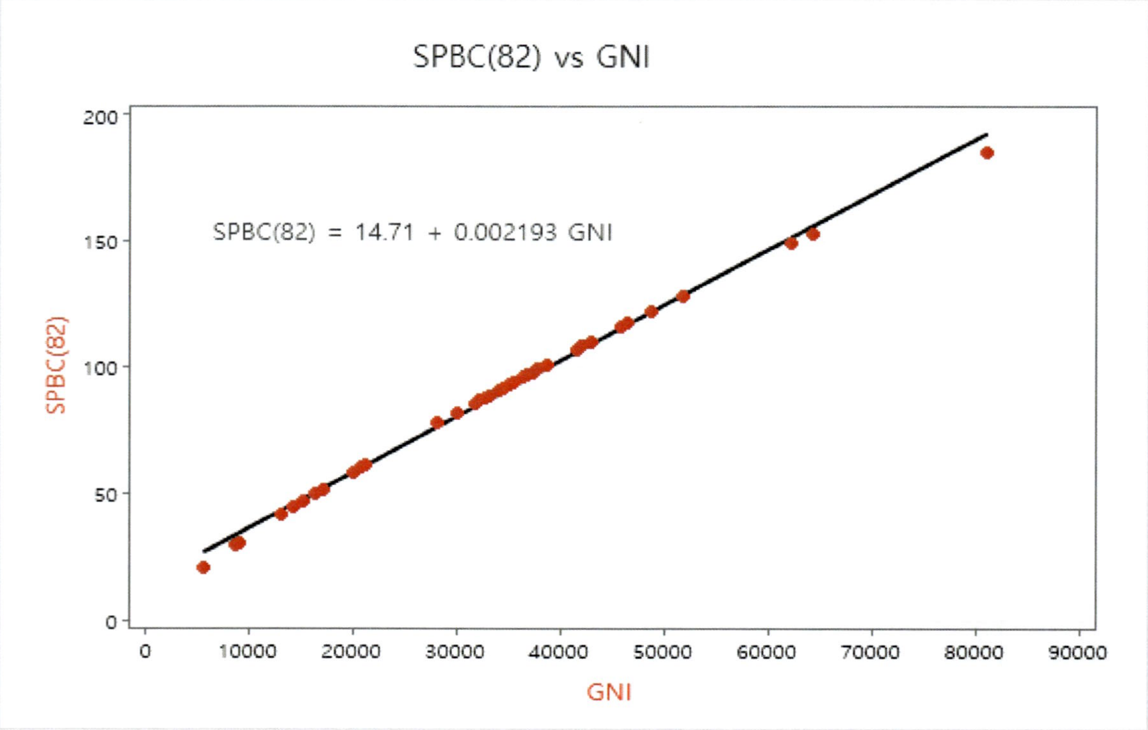
SPBC(82) vs GNI
SPBC(82) = 14.71 + 0.002193 GNI
SPBC(82)
200
150
100
50
0
0
10000
20000
30000
40000
50000
60000
70000
80000
90000
GNI

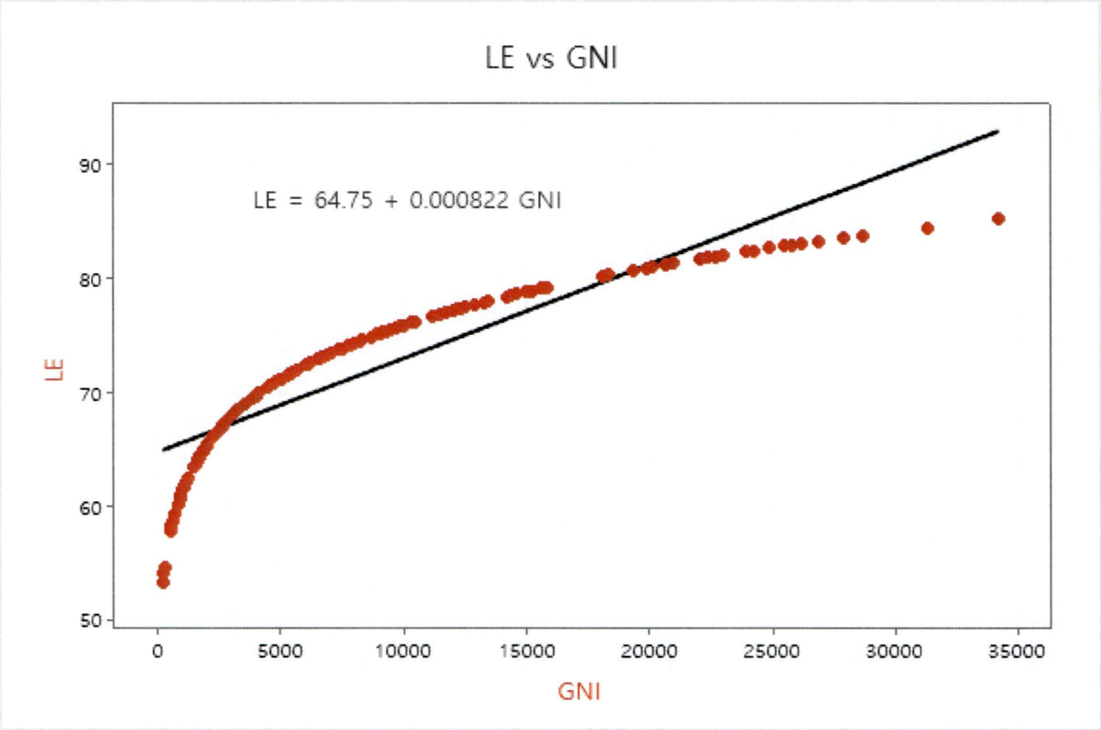

Fig. 4.4 GNI associated with SPBC (82) & LE

4.3.2 Old age pension recipient (OPR)

As of 2014–2019, among the 53 countries surveyed, the UK had the highest OPR, at 100%, while Malawi had the lowest at 2.3%. This indicates that OPR only affects LE, with no difference in the probability of surviving to 100 years of age (see Fig. 4.5). This is because many countries have recently implemented short-term pensions. However, pensions are considered an important source of income that can sustain healthy life in old age and increase LE. Examples of the OPR by country are shown in Table 4.4.

Table 4.4 Example for old age pension recipients (OPR), 2014–2019

Countries	United Kingdom	Russian Federation	Korea, Rep.	United States	Australia	Jamaica	India.	Malaysia	Malawi
OPR	100	100	100	100	71.3	30.3	25.2	19.8	2.3

Source: United Nations. Human development report: Old age pension recipients (% of statutory pension age population) http://hdr.undp.org/en/indicators/123806. Accessed on October 8, 2021.

Impact of OPR on LE

Table 4.4.1 shows that OPR alone has an influence of 38.4% on LE. Moreover, Fig. 4.5 shows that the higher the OPR, the more likely they will achieve LE. This is because those receiving pensions refer to guaranteed income in old age. In particular, since pensioners are not afraid of the economy, they have less mental stress and greater interest in healthcare.

Table 4.4.1 . Multiple regression models of predicting the OPR and LE

(N = 129)

Term	Coefficients	SE Coef	T-Value	P-Value	VIF	R^2
OPR	0.1129	0.0127	8.9	0.001	1	0.384
R-sq	R-sq(adj)					
38.39%	37.90%					

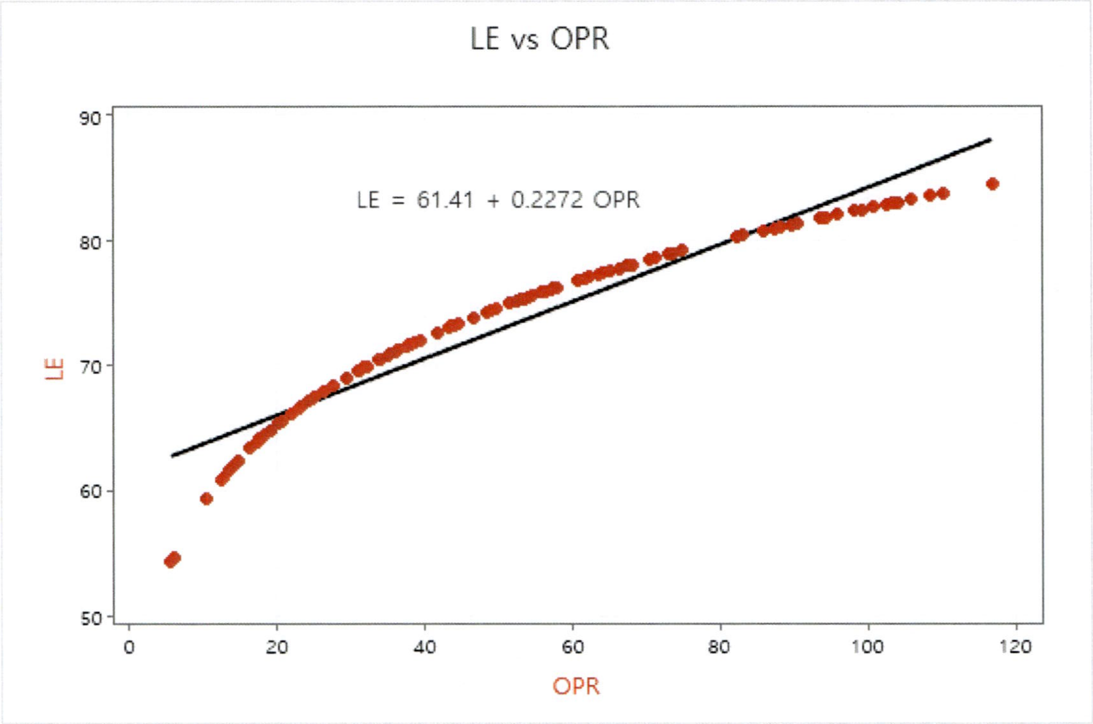

Fig. 4.5 OPR associated with LE

4.3.3 Secondary education (SE)

The proportion of the population with at least some SE (%, ages 25 and older, male and female) showed a significant correlation in LE (see Fig. 4.6). Meanwhile, the level of SE can be proportional to an individual's income level, while the secondary effect of such education is that it improves mental health.

Interestingly, since the majority of the current 100-year-olds do not have SE (or higher), it indicates that there is no significant effect on SPBC. However, studies have confirmed that LE cannot be reached without a minimum education. Thus, the government should establish short- and long-term education policies that improve this aspect so that the population can reach LE.

Finally, the education level is as follows. As of 2018, Austria and Finland accounted for 100%, following by the United States at 96%, Japan at 93.6%, the Rep. of Korea at 86%, and the UK at 78.2%. Meanwhile, Burkina Faso had the lowest level of education at 9%. Examples of the SE by country are shown in Table 4.5.

Table 4.5 Example for population with at least secondary education (SE), 2018

Countries	Austria	United Kingdom	Spain	Peru	India	Pakistan	Bhutan	Sudan	Burkina Faso
SE	100	78.2	77.7	64.1	39.2	37.2	27.6	17.5	8.8

Source: United Nations. Human development report: Population with at least some secondary education (% ages 25 and older).
http://hdr.undp.org/en/indicators/23806. Accessed on October 8, 2021.

Impact of SE on LE

Table 4.5.1 shows that SE alone has an influence of approximately 50% on LE. In other words, SE is the PLI that is important for reaching LE. Additionally, Fig. 4.6 shows that the more people complete SE, the more they will achieve LE. However, the majority of those who are 100 years old do not have SE, since there was insufficient economic power to support such education. Hence, if education contributes to mental health, then such participation can help achieve LE from birth to at least 82 years of age.

Table 4.5.1 . Multiple regression models of predicting the SE and LE

(N = 157)

Term	Coefficients	SE Coef	T-Value	P-Value	VIF	R^2
SE	0.1853	0.0149	12.42	0.001	1	0.499

R-sq	R-sq(adj)
49.90%	49.57%

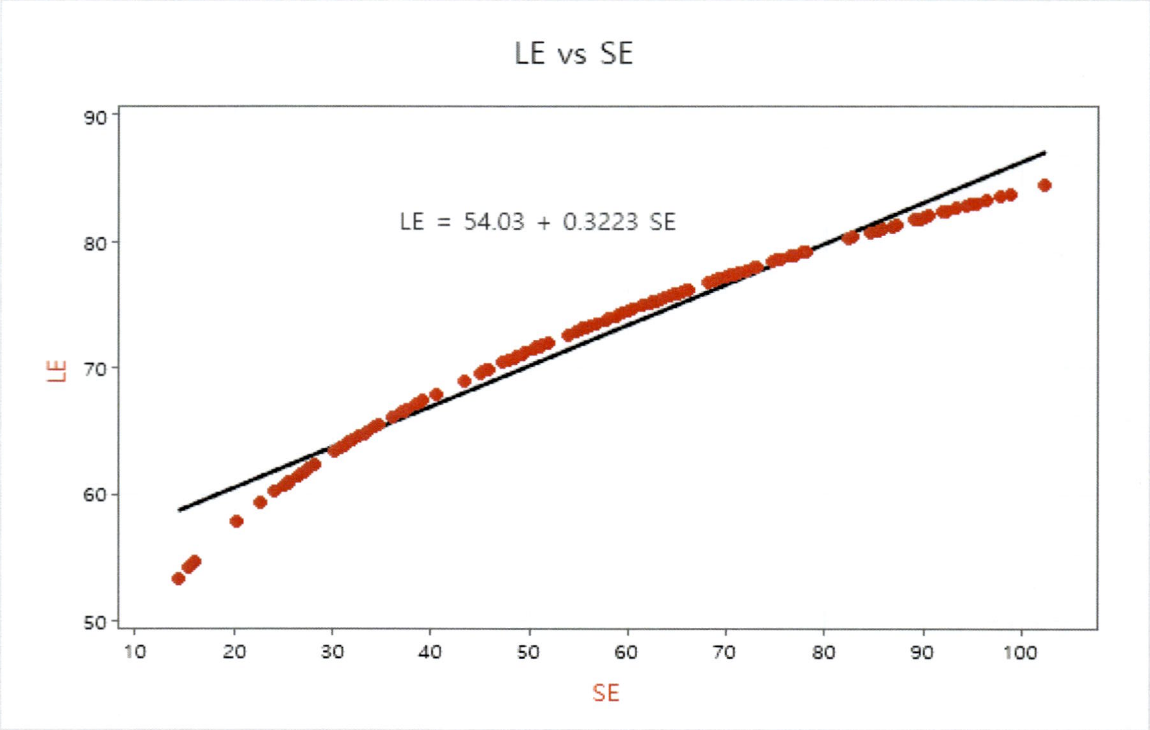

Fig. 4.6 SE associated with LE

4.3.4 Safely managed drinking water (SMDW)

SMDW (% of the population) is a factor that influences LE from birth to 82 years and SPBC (82) (see Fig. 4.7) ($r = 0.843$, $p = 0.000$). In this regard, drinking water refers to water free from contamination, including bottled and delivered drinking water.

Safe drinking water is an essential factor for reducing child mortality and morbidity. In addition, secure access to and the supply of drinking water can also improve the quality of life over the long-term. Specifically, it improves the quality of life by increasing household income (through increased labor productivity) and reducing medical expenses due to a healthy body. Thus, political leaders should recognize the importance of critical SEFs in prolonging peoples' lifespans and devise policies to ensure that they can receive safe drinking water.

Applying the ISS formula for SMDW

As of 2017, countries such as the United Kingdom, Iceland, and Greece accounted for 100% of the world's SMDW, followed by the United States and Canada at 99%. Meanwhile, Uganda had the lowest SMDW at 7%. SMDW is a variable that affects SPBC. In the case of 100%, such as the UK, ISS is calculated by the highest score of 100%. Then, this score is substituted as a reference point for conversion into each country's SMDW. Examples of the SMDW scores by country are shown in Table 4.6.

Table 4.6 Example of a score for using safely managed drinking water (SMDW), 2017

Countries	United Kingdom	Iceland	United States	Korea, Rep.	Italy	Hungary	Russian Federation	Philippines	Uganda
SMDW	100	100	99	98	95	90	76	47	7
ISS (%)	100	100	99	98	95	90	76	47	7

People using safely managed drinking water services (% of population):

People using safely managed drinking water services (% of the population): The percentage of people using drinking water from an improved source accessible on-premises, available when needed and free from fecal and priority chemical contamination. Improved water sources include piped water, boreholes or tube wells, protected dug wells, protected springs, and packaged or delivered water.

Source: WHO/UNICEF Joint Monitoring Programme (JMP) for Water Supply, Sanitation and Hygiene (washdata.org).

Impact of SMDW on LE and SPBC (82)

Tables 4.6.1 and 4.6.2 show that SMDW affects 23% of SPBC (82) and 67% of LE as a single independent variable. In addition, Fig. 4.7 indicates that the greater the SMDW, the higher the likelihood of achieving LE and SPBC.

Table 4.6.1 . Multiple regression models of predicting the SMDW and SPBC(82)

(N = 39)

Term	Coefficients	SE Coef	T-Value	P-Value	VIF	R^2
SMDW	3.76	1.12	3.36	0.002	1	0.234

R-sq	R-sq(adj)
23.42%	21.35%

Table 4.6.2 . Multiple regression models of predicting the SMDW and LE

(N = 88)

Term	Coefficients	SE Coef	T-Value	P-Value	VIF	R^2
SMDW	0.1926	0.0145	13.27	0.001	1	0.672

R-sq	R-sq(adj)
67.20%	66.81%

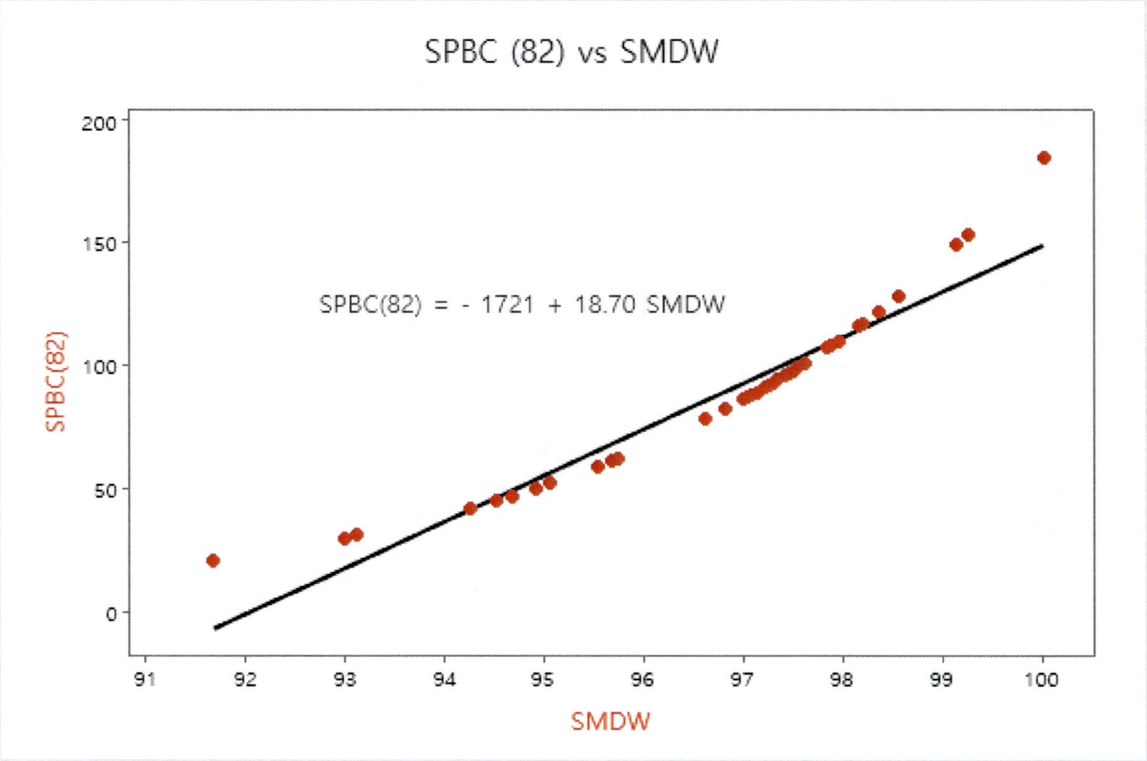
SPBC (82) vs SMDW
SPBC(82) = - 1721 + 18.70 SMDW
SPBC(82)
SMDW
0
50
100
150
200
91
92
93
94
95
96
97
98
99
100

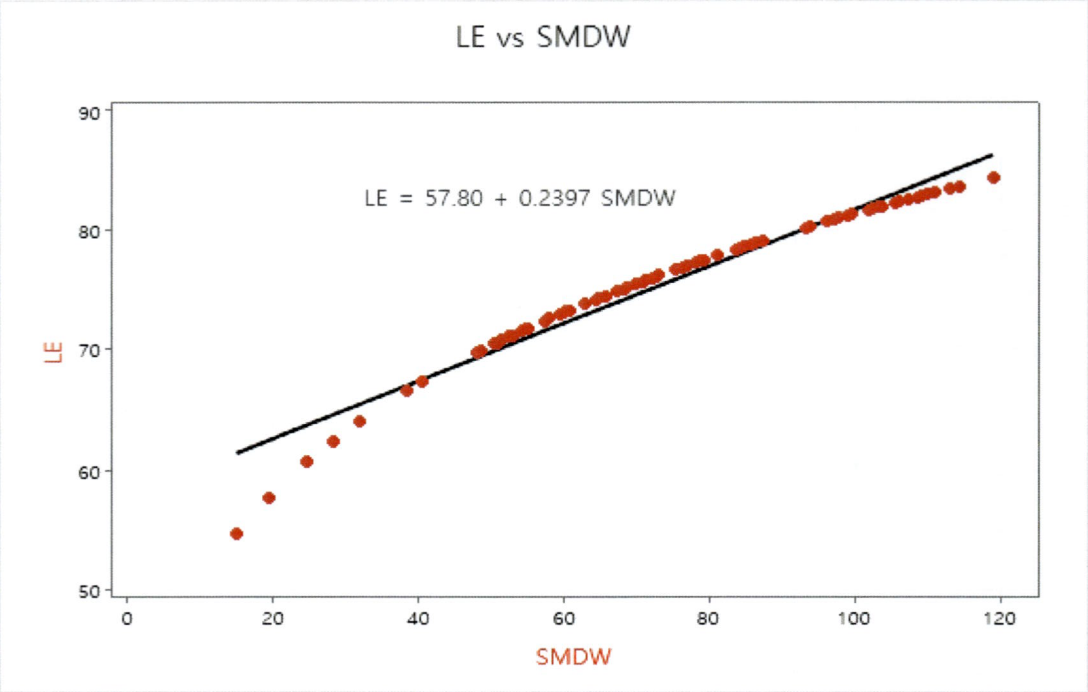

Fig. 4.7 SMDW associated with SPBC (82) & LE

4.3.5 Fixed telephone and mobile phone subscribers (FTMPS)

FTMPS is a significant variable that affects LE and SPBC (see Fig. 4.8). In this regard, communication through such devices can strengthen relationships and have a positive impact on mental health and the quality of life. Thus, FTMPS is a SEFs that positively affects mental health, LE, and SPBC.

Applying the ISS formula for FTMPS

As of 2017, France was the largest country with 60 members per 100 people, followed by Australia with 34. Meanwhile, Finland had the lowest FTMPS at seven. FTMPS is a variable that affects SPBC. As of 2017, France had the highest FTMPS in the world. Thus, ISS receives the highest score of 100%. Examples of the FTMPS scores by country are shown in Table 4.7.

Table 4.7 Example of a score for fixed telephone and mobile phone subscribers, 2017

Countries	France	Germany	Rep.of Korea	Japan.	Australia	Italy	Denmark	Chile	Finland
FTMPS	60	54	53	50	34	34	19	17	7
ISS (%)	100	90	88	83	57	57	32	28	12

Fixed telephone subscriptions (per 100 people):

Fixed telephone subscriptions refer to the sum of the active number of analog fixed telephone lines, voice-over-IP (VoIP) subscriptions, fixed wireless local loop subscriptions, ISDN voice-channel equivalents, and fixed public payphones.

Mobile cellular subscriptions (per 100 people):

Mobile cellular telephone subscriptions are subscriptions to a public mobile telephone service that provide access to the PSTN using cellular technology. The indicator includes (and is split into) the number of postpaid subscriptions and the number of active prepaid accounts (i.e., used during the last three months).

The indicator applies to all mobile cellular subscriptions that offer voice communications.

Source: International Telecommunication Union (ITU) World Telecommunication/ICT Indicators Database

Impact of FTMPS on LE and SPBC (82)

Tables 4.7.1 and 4.7.2 show that FTMPS affects 24% of SPBC (82) and 53% of LE as the sole independent variable. Moreover, Fig. 4.8 shows that as FTMPS increases, LE and SPBC also increase. In this regard, the frequent use of mobile and fixed phones contributes to the promotion of mental health by strengthening communication with family and friends. In addition, FTMPS is a SEFs that can prevent depression (by improving communication with the elderly) and safely respond to emergencies, thus increasing LE and the likelihood of reaching 100 years of age.

Table 4.7.1 . Multiple regression models of predicting the FMTS and SPBC(82)

(N = 39)

Term	Coefficients	SE Coef	T-Value	P-Value	VIF	R^2
FTMPS	1.261	0.366	3.45	0.001	1	0.243
R-sq	R-sq(adj)					
24.33%	22.29%					

Table 4.7.2 . Multiple regression models of predicting the FMTS and LE

(N = 140)

Term	Coefficients	SE Coef	T-Value	P-Value	VIF	R^2
FTMPS	0.3161	0.0254	12.44	0.001	1	0.529
R-sq	R-sq(adj)					
52.88%	52.54%					

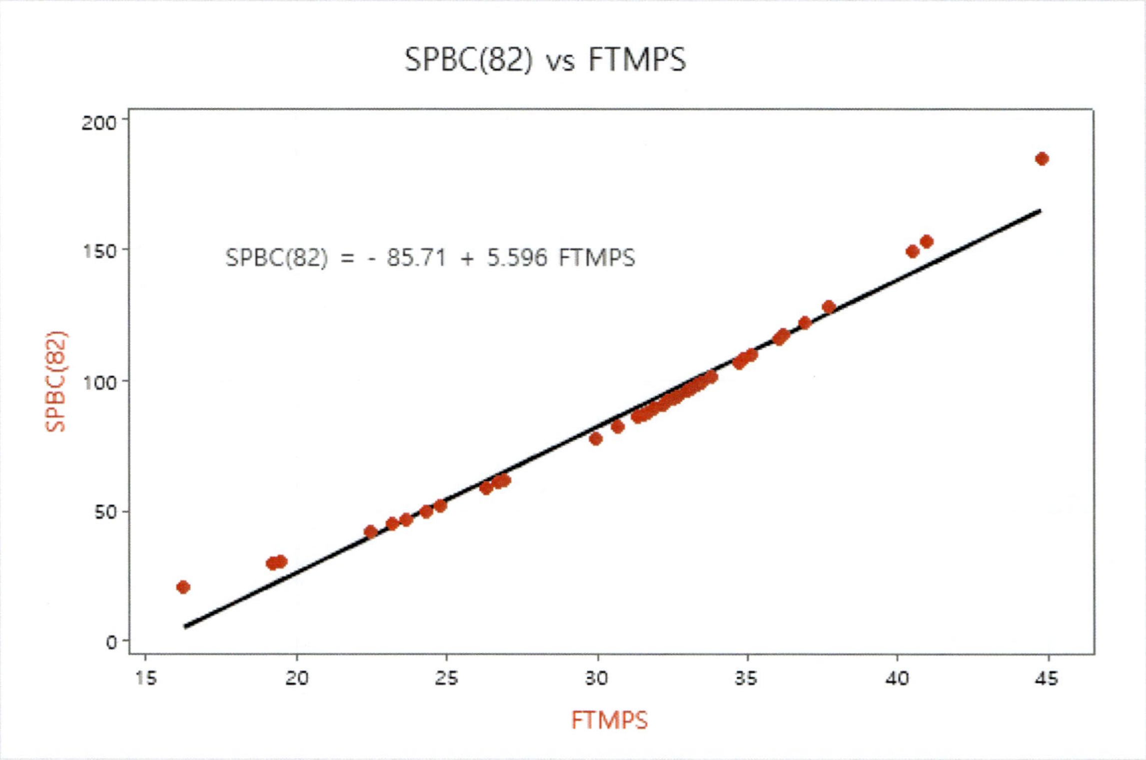
SPBC(82) vs FTMPS
SPBC(82) = - 85.71 + 5.596 FTMPS
SPBC(82)
FTMPS
0
50
100
150
200
15
20
25
30
35
40
45

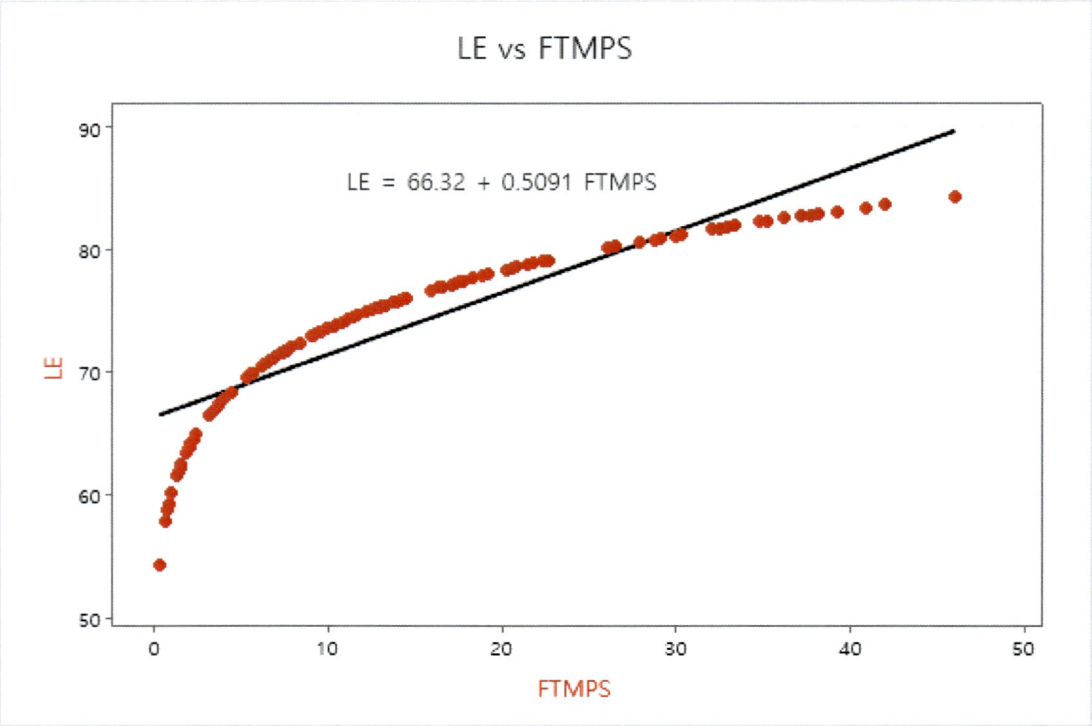

Fig. 4.8 FTMPS associated with SPBC (82) & LE

4.3.6 Basic sanitation services (BSS)

BSS (% of the population) is an essential SEFs for LE and SPBC (82) (see Fig. 4.9). This indicator covers both basic sanitation and safely managed sanitation services. In this case, such services include sewage systems and flush toilets. Meanwhile, inadequate hygiene is a significant cause of various infectious diseases.

Applying the ISS formula for BSS

As of 2017, Palau had the highest BSS at 100%, followed by South Africa at 75%. Meanwhile, Ethiopia had the lowest BSS at 7%. BSS is a variable that affects ECLE. Since Palau has the highest rate of BSS at 100%, the ECLE receives 100% points. Examples of the BSS scores by country are shown in Table 4.8.

Table 4.8. Example of a score for using at least basic sanitation services (BSS), 2017

Countries	Korea, Rep.	Palau	United Kingdom	Argentina	China	South Africa	India	Malawi	Ethiopia
BSS	100	100	99	94	83	75	57	26	7
ISS (%)	100	100	99	94	83	75	57	26	7

People using at least basic sanitation services (% of population):

The percentage of people using at least basic sanitation services, that is, improved sanitation facilities that are not shared with other households. This indicator encompasses both people using basic sanitation services as well as those using safely managed sanitation services. Improved sanitation facilities include flush/pour flush to piped sewer systems, septic tanks, or pit latrines; ventilated improved pit latrines, compositing toilets, or pit latrines with slabs.

Source: WHO/UNICEF Joint Monitoring Programme (JMP) for Water Supply, Sanitation and Hygiene (washdata.org).

Impact of BSS on LE and SPBC (82)

Tables 4.8.1 and 4.8.2 show that BSS affects 31% of SPBC (82) and 73% of LE. Additionally, Fig. 4.9 shows that the greater the BSS, the higher the LE and SPBC. Again, since inadequate hygiene is a significant cause of human disease, it is necessary to keep the primary source of infection clean by focusing on health and hygiene management. Thus, BSS is a significant variable that can enhance primary healthcare services, prevent infectious diseases over the long term, and improve both LE and SPBC.

Table 4.8.1 . Multiple regression models of predicting the BSS and SPBC (82)

(N = 39)

Term	Coefficients	SE Coef	T-Value	P-Value	VIF	R^2
BSS	6.05	1.49	4.05	0	1	0.308
R-sq	R-sq(adj)					
30.75%	28.87%					

Table 4.8.2 . Multiple regression models of predicting the BSS and LE

(N = 166)

Term	Coefficients	SE Coef	T-Value	P-Value	VIF	R^2
BSS	0.2197	0.0105	20.89	0	1	0.727
R-sq	R-sq(adj)					
72.69%	72.52%					

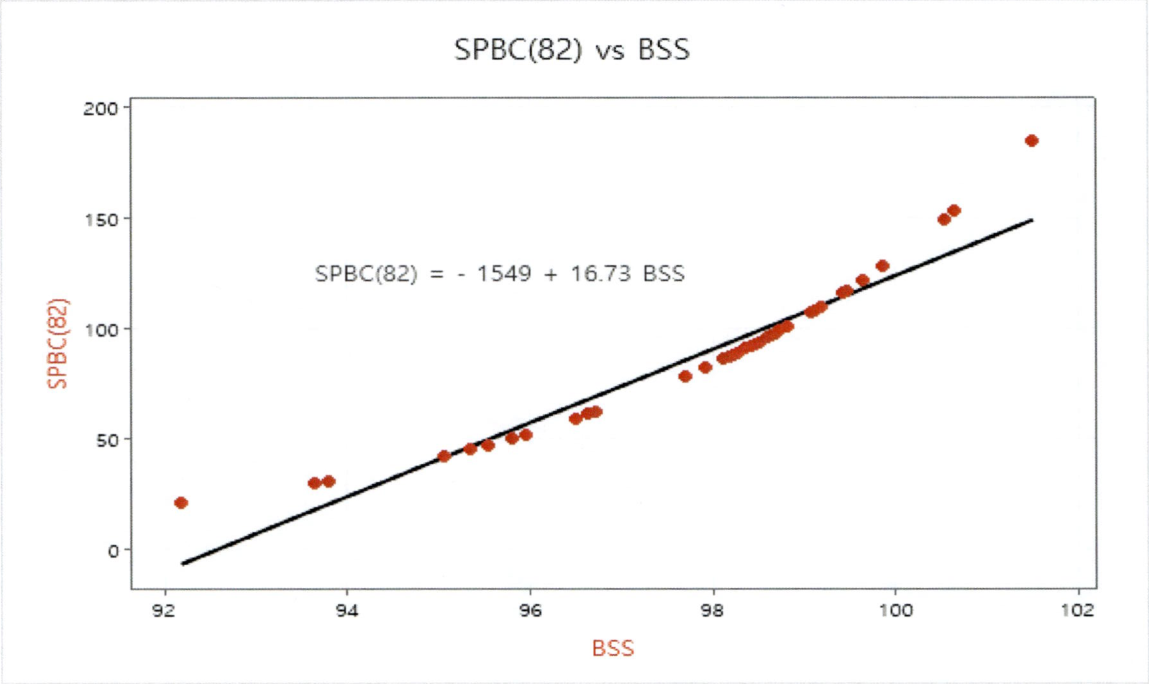
SPBC(82) vs BSS
SPBC(82) = - 1549 + 16.73 BSS
SPBC(82)
BSS
200
150
100
50
0
92
94
96
98
100
102

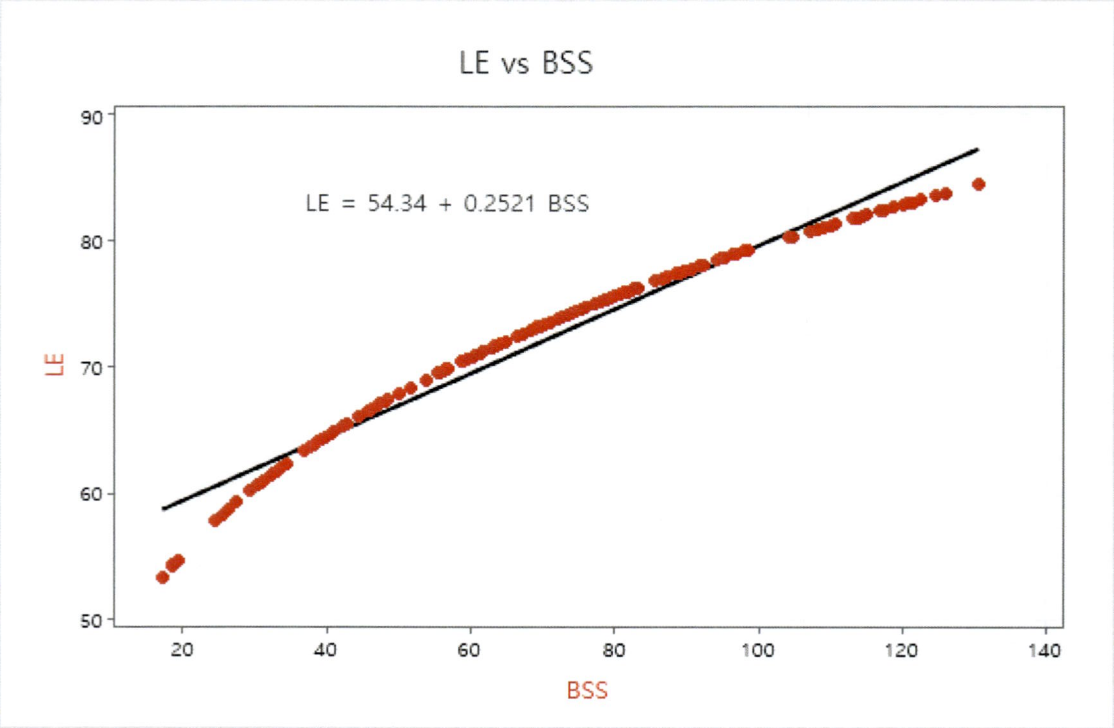

Fig. 4.9 BSS associated with SPBC (82) & LE

4.3.7 The Gini index (GI)

The GI, representing the income inequality index, is the only valid variable in LE (see Fig. 4.10). Specifically, a GI of zero means perfect equality, while an index of 100 means perfect inequality. The limiting point is that as the GI of developing countries increases, the absolute poverty population decreases. This is because the GI measures relative wealth.

Income inequality can also indicate inequality in the level of health. In this regard, households with high-income levels are more interested in healthcare than their low-income counterparts. Interestingly, income inequality has little effect on SPBC. Those who have reached the age of 100 have either overcome income inequality or have never experienced inequality due to their high-income level.

However, it is significant that income inequality can affect LE. Specifically, if the income level is low, then individuals have no choice but to invest more time and effort in their family's livelihood, rather than for their health. Therefore, since income disparities inevitably lead to differences in health level, health economic policies that can resolve income inequality are required.

As of 2021, Brazil has the highest GI at 53.4, followed by the United States at 41.4. Meanwhile, Slovenia has the lowest GI at 24.6. Examples of the GI scores by country are shown in Table 4.9.

Table 4.9. Example for Gini index (World Bank estimate), 2017–2019

Countries	Slovenia	Norway	Sweden	France	Spain	Lithuania	United States	Iran	Brazil
GI	24.6	27.6	30	32.4	34.7	35.7	41.4	42	53.4

Gini index (World Bank estimate):

Gini index measures the extent to which income distribution among individuals or households within an economy deviates from a perfectly equal distribution. A Lorenz curve plots the cumulative percentages of total income received against the cumulative number of recipients, starting with the poorest individual or household. Thus, a Gini index of 0 represents perfect equality, while an index of 100 implies perfect inequality.

Source: World Bank, Development Research Group. Gini index (World Bank estimate)
https://data.worldbank.org/indicator/SI.POV.GINI?end=2019&start=1967&view=chart

Impact of the GI on LE

Table 4.9.1 shows that the GI affects 12% of LE as a single independent variable. Moreover, Fig. 4.10 indicates that the lower the income inequality index, the more people can survive up to 82 years of age. As stated earlier, people with low-income inequality are more interested in healthcare than others because they can afford to live economically. However, people with high-income inequality experience a sense of economic deprivation and tend to neglect their healthcare. This income gap makes it challenging to guarantee fundamental health rights and solve mental stress. Thus, the GI is an essential variable with a high possibility of increasing LE if the minimum income gap is resolved through CLSS.

Table 4.9.1 . Multiple regression models of predicting the GI and LE

(N = 105)

Term	Coefficients	SE Coef	T-Value	P-Value	VIF	R^2
GI	-0.2734	0.0717	-3.81	0.001	1	0.124

R-sq	R-sq(adj)
12.38%	11.52%

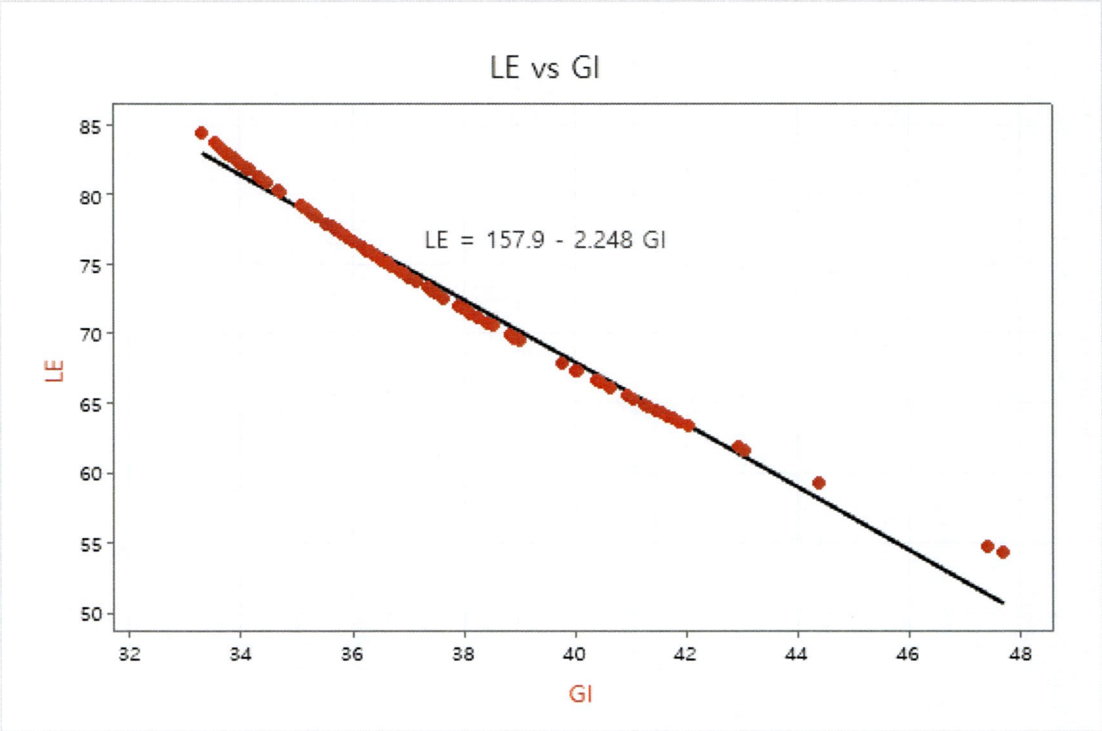

Fig. 4.10 The GI associated with LE

4.3.8 Urban population (UP)

UP (% of the total population) is a variable that affects the LE and SPBC of each country (see Fig. 4.11). As stated earlier, the increase in UP is due to the migration of the rural population. In addition, cities are more favorable environments for health promotion than rural societies because the healthcare system is well-structured and better maintained.

Applying the ISS formula for UP

As of 2018, six countries, including Singapore, had the highest UP at 100%, following by the UK at 84%. Meanwhile, Burundi had the lowest UP at 13%. Since Singapore has the highest UP, it receives 100% points. Examples of the UP scores by country are shown in Table 4.10.

Table 4.10. Example of a score for urban population (UP), 2018

Countries	Singapore	Iceland	United Kingdom	Korea, Rep.	Iran	Italy	South Africa	China	Burundi
UP	100	94	84	81	75	71	67	60	13
ISS (%)	100	94	84	81	75	71	67	60	13

Urban population (% of total population):

Urban population refers to people living in urban areas as defined by national statistical offices. The data are collected and smoothed by United Nations Population Division.

Source: United Nations Population Division. World Urbanization Prospects: 2018 Revision.

Impact of UP on LE and SPBC (82)

Tables 4.10.1 and 4.10.2 show that UP affects 23% of SPBC (82) and 40% of LE as a single independent variable. In addition, Fig. 4.11 shows that the more urbanized the population, the greater the LE and SPBC. This indicates that emergencies can be quickly addressed and that the quality of life is high due to the convenience of living environments.

Table 4.10.1 . Multiple regression models of predicting the UP and SPBC (82)

(N = 39)

Term	Coefficients	SE Coef	T-Value	P-Value	VIF	R^2
UP	0.2058	0.0198	10.42	0.001	1	0.232
R-sq	R-sq(adj)					
23.18%	21.11%					

Table 4.10.2 . Multiple regression models of predicting the UP and LE

(N = 162)

Term	Coefficients	SE Coef	T-Value	P-Value	VIF	R^2
UP	1.436	0.43	3.34	0.002	1	0.404
R-sq	R-sq(adj)					
40.42%	40.05%					

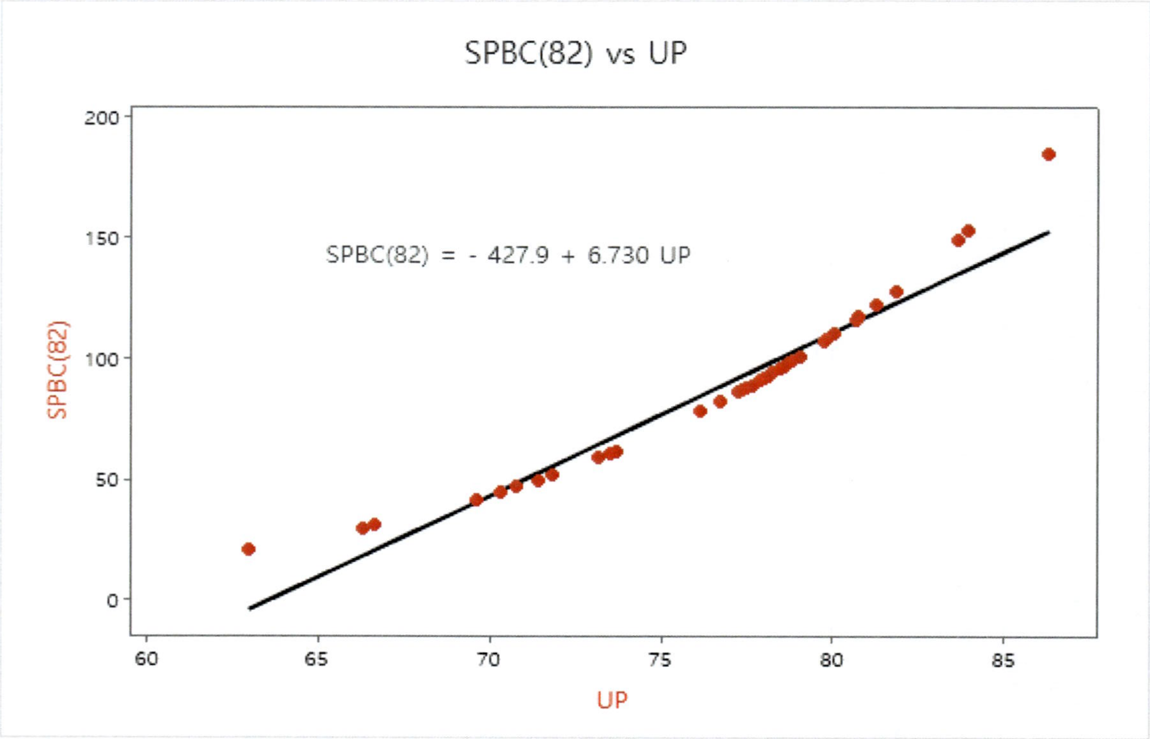
SPBC(82) vs UP
SPBC(82) = - 427.9 + 6.730 UP
SPBC(82)
UP
200
150
100
50
0
60
65
70
75
80
85

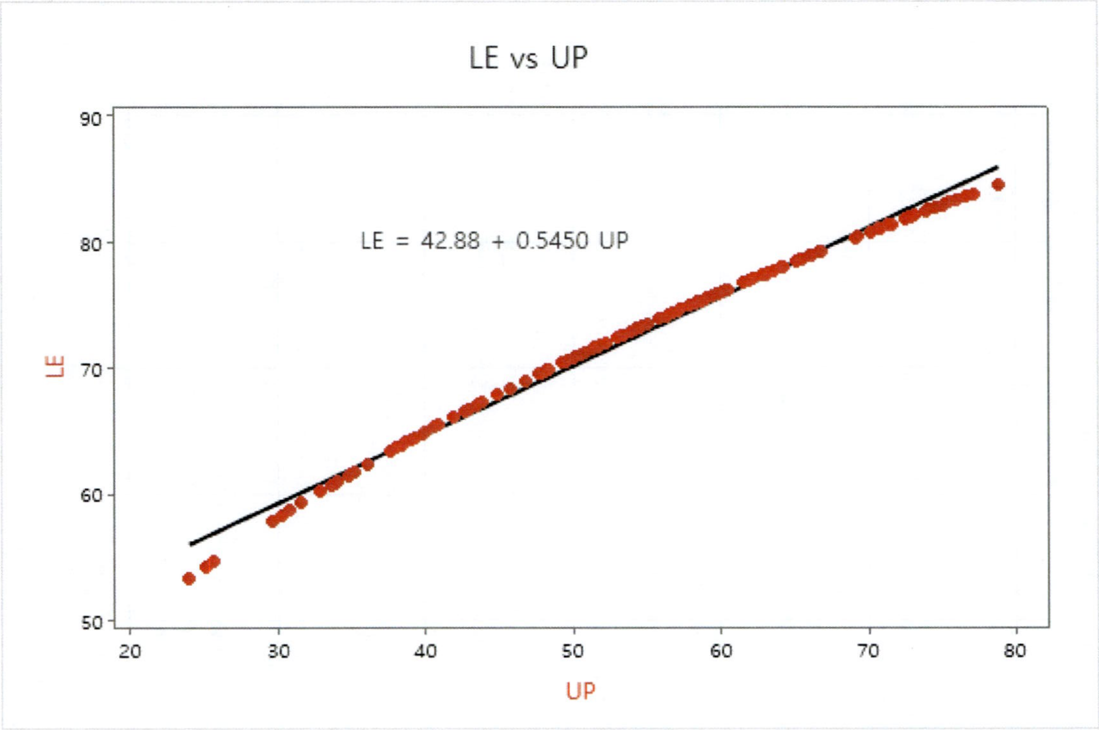

Fig. 4.11 UP associated with SPBC (82) & LE

4.3.9 Gender inequality index (GII)

The GII is a variable that significantly impacts LE and SPBC (82) (see Fig. 4.12). Additional details are as follows:

The GII measures gender disadvantages in the following three dimensions (Human Development Index, 2010):

(a) Women's reproductive health index, due to maternal mortality and adolescent childbirth;
(b) The minimum share of the population with SE and the proportion of male and female parliamentary seats; and
(c) The participation rate of males and females in the labor market.

As such, in these three dimensions, gender disadvantages occur that can decrease health levels.

Gender equality ranges from 0 (inequality) to 1 (low equality). Meanwhile, the maternal mortality rate that occurs during pregnancy and childbirth is representative of the health inequality due to gender discrimination. In addition, the roles and rights of males and females should be equal. However, if they are not, then mental stress can occur.

In particular, if employment restrictions and job losses occur due to gender discrimination, then the quality of life will be reduced due to uncertainties in household income and mental health. Hence, the higher the GII value, the more significant the gender gap and the greater the loss in the quality of life. In this regard, political leaders of each country should implement social changes that promote a gender-equal society.

Applying the ISS formula for the GII

As of 2018, Switzerland had the lowest GII at 0.037, followed by the UK at 0.119, and the United States at 0.182. Meanwhile, Yemen had the highest GII at 0.0834. Based on the same findings, 100% points are given to Switzerland. This value is calculated by multiplying the value by reversely converting the country's GI. Examples of the GII scores by country are shown in Table 4.11.

Table 4.11 Example of a score for gender inequality index (GII), 2018

Countries	Switzerland	Korea, Republic of	United Kingdom	United States	Fiji	Myanmar	Iraq	Malawi	Yemen
GII	0.037	0.058	0.119	0.182	0.357	0.458	0.549	0.615	0.834
ISS (%)	100	98	92	85	67	56	47	41	18

Gender inequality index:

Gender inequality remains a significant barrier to human development. The disadvantages facing women and girls are an essential source of inequality. The GII is an inequality index. The higher the GII value, the more disparities between females and males and the more loss to human development.

UN, Human Development Reports, Gender Inequality Index (GII), http://hdr.undp.org/en/content/gender-inequality-index-gii

Impact of the GII on LE and SPBC (82)

Tables 4.11.1 and 4.11.2 show that the GII affects 22% of SPBC (82) and 74% of LE. Additionally, Fig. 4.12 shows that both LE and SPBC increase in a gender-equal society. Specifically, equal economic activity and social participation by males and females can increase family income and improve the quality of life, increasing LE and SPBC.

Table 4.11.1 . Multiple regression models of predicting the GII and SPBC (82)

(N = 39)

Term	Coefficients	SE Coef	T-Value	P-Value	VIF	R^2
GII	-234.1	72.1	-3.25	0.002	1	0.222

R-sq	R-sq(adj)
22.19%	20.08%

Table 4.11.2 . Multiple regression models of predicting the GII and LE

(N = 154)

Term	Coefficients	SE Coef	T-Value	P-Value	VIF	R^2
GII	-32.7	1.56	-20.9	0.001	1	0.742

R-sq	R-sq(adj)
74.18%	74.01%

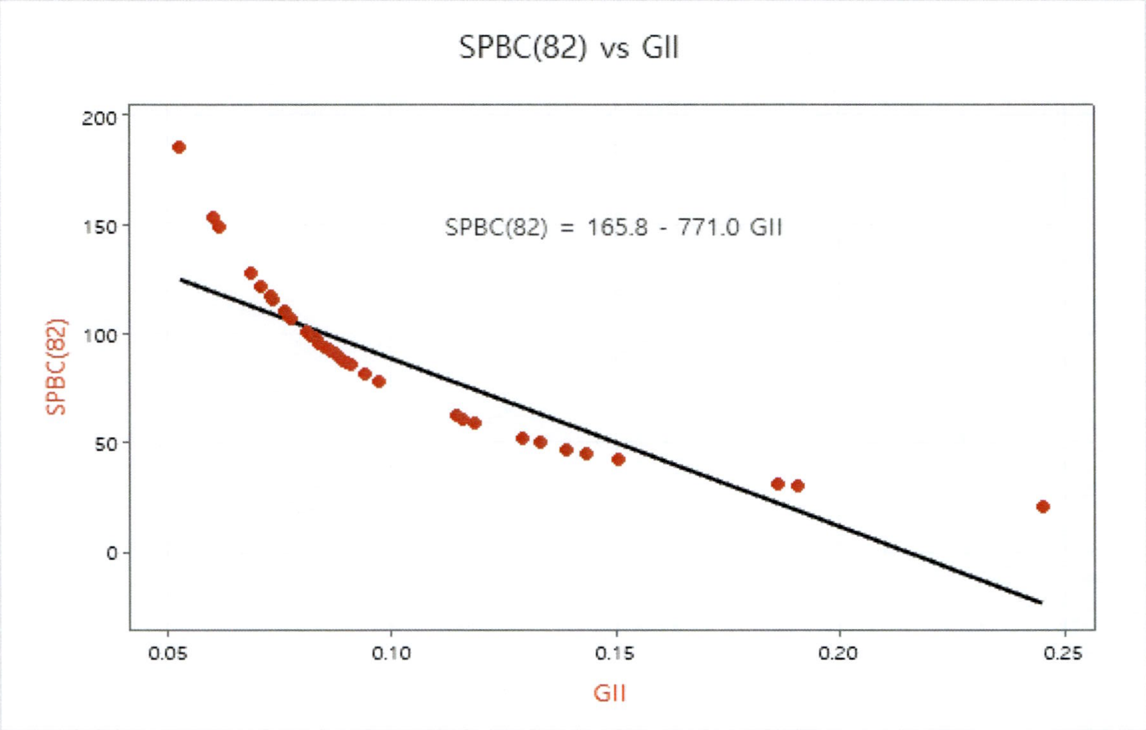
SPBC(82) vs GII
SPBC(82) = 165.8 - 771.0 GII
200
150
100
50
0
SPBC(82)
0.05
0.10
0.15
0.20
0.25
GII

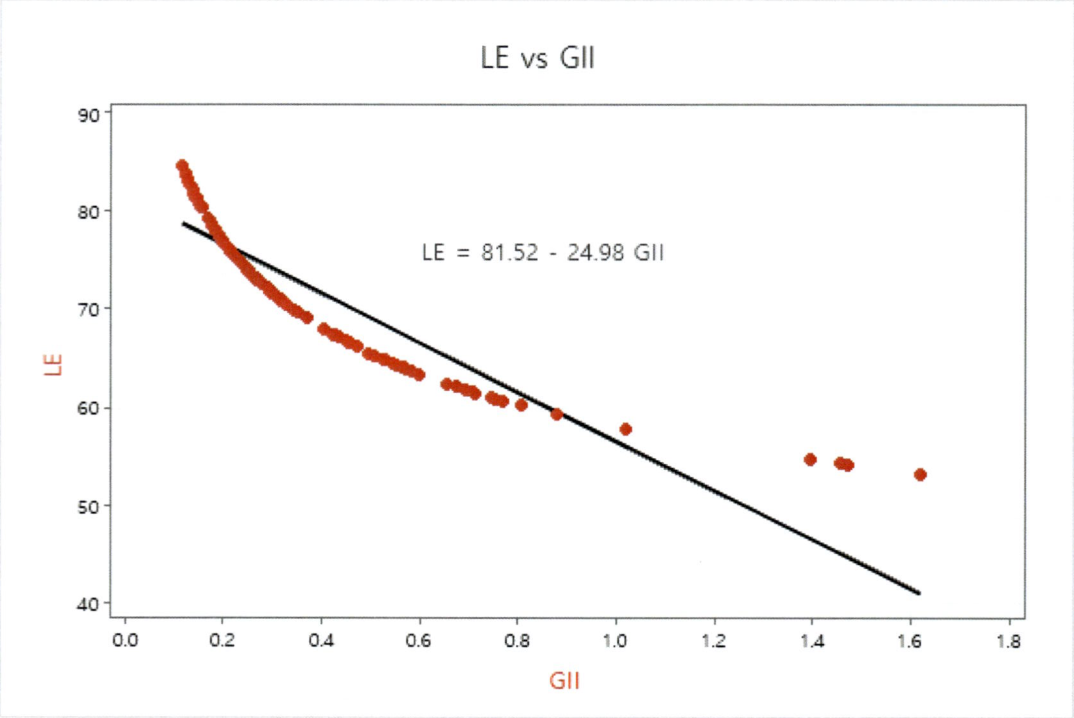

Fig. 4.12 GII associated with SPBC (82) & LE

4.3.10 Individuals using the Internet (IUI)

IUI is an essential SEFs for increasing LE and SPBC (see Fig. 4.13). In this case, the population of IUI refers to those who have used the Internet in all locations for at least the last three months (WB, 2012). Meanwhile, this information industry revolution has brought about advanced technological changes in finding the causes of diseases and treating them. However, the development of information and communication technology has created a gap between healthcare services and the level of health. Thus, the political leaders of countries should collaborate so that all countries can improve the health levels of humanity as a whole.

Applying the ISS formula for IUI

As of 2017, Iceland had the highest IUI globally at 100%, followed by the UK at 90%. Since Iceland's IUI was 100%, the ISS received the highest score of 100% points. Examples of the IUI scores by country are shown in Table 4.12.

Table 4.12. Example of a score for individuals using the Internet (IUI), 2017

Countries	Iceland	Norway	Korea, Rep.	United Kingdom	United States	France	Greece	India	Pakistan
IUI	98	96	95	90	87	81	70	32	17
ISS (%)	100	98	97	92	89	83	71	33	17

Individuals using the Internet (% of the population):

Internet users are individuals who have used the Internet (from any location) in the last three months. The Internet can use via a computer, mobile phone, personal digital assistant, games machine, digital TV, etc.

Source: International Telecommunication Union (ITU) World Telecommunication/ICT Indicators Database

Impact of IUI on LE and SPBC (82)

Tables 4.12.1 and 4.12.2 show that the IUI affects 28% of the SPBC (82) and 74% of the LE as a single independent variable. In addition, Fig. 4.13 indicates that the greater the number of Internet users, the more the LE and SPBC increase. Therefore, if the health and medical information obtained from the Internet influences individuals to seek advice and treatment, the LE and possibility of reaching 100 years of age can be increased.

Table 4.12.1 . Multiple regression models of predicting the UI and SPBC (82)

(N = 39)

Term	Coefficients	SE Coef	T-Value	P-Value	VIF	R^2
IUI	1.862	0.483	3.85	0.001	1	0.286
R-sq	R-sq(adj)					
28.62%	26.69%					

Table 4.12.2 . Multiple regression models of predicting the UI and LE

(N = 160)

Term	Coefficients	SE Coef	T-Value	P-Value	VIF	R^2
IUI	0.2277	0.0108	21.05	0.001	1	0.737
R-sq	R-sq(adj)					
73.72%	73.55%					

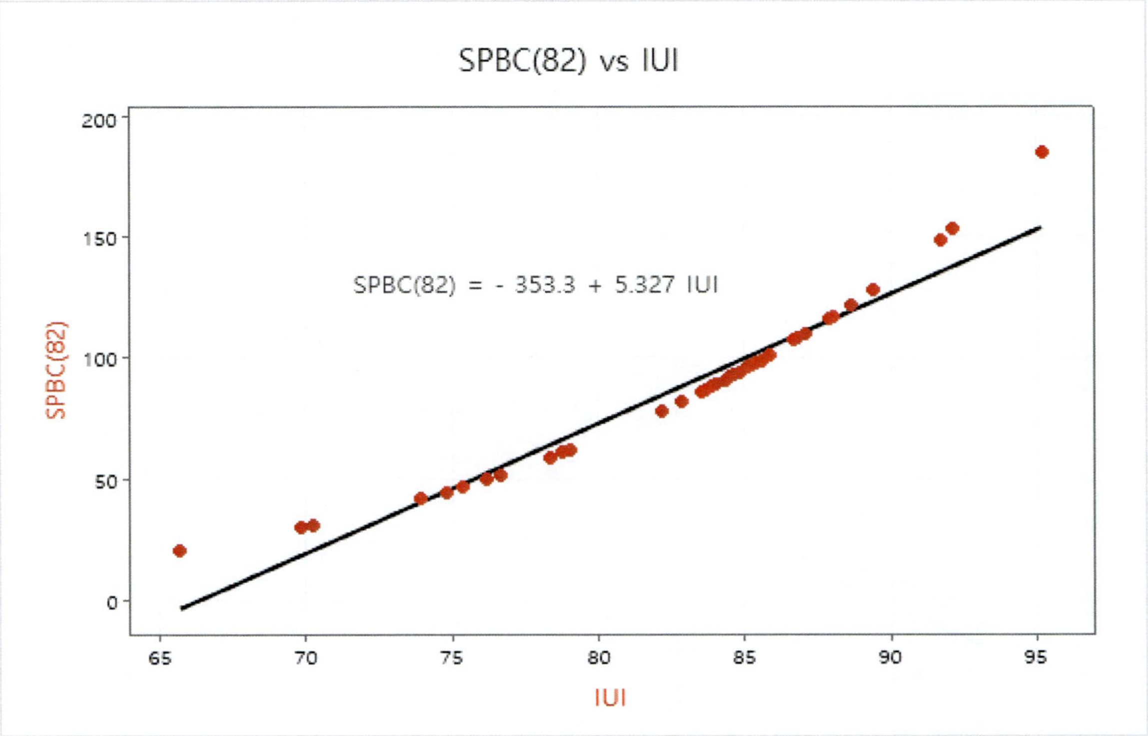
SPBC(82) vs IUI
SPBC(82) = - 353.3 + 5.327 IUI
SPBC(82)
IUI
200
150
100
50
0
65
70
75
80
85
90
95

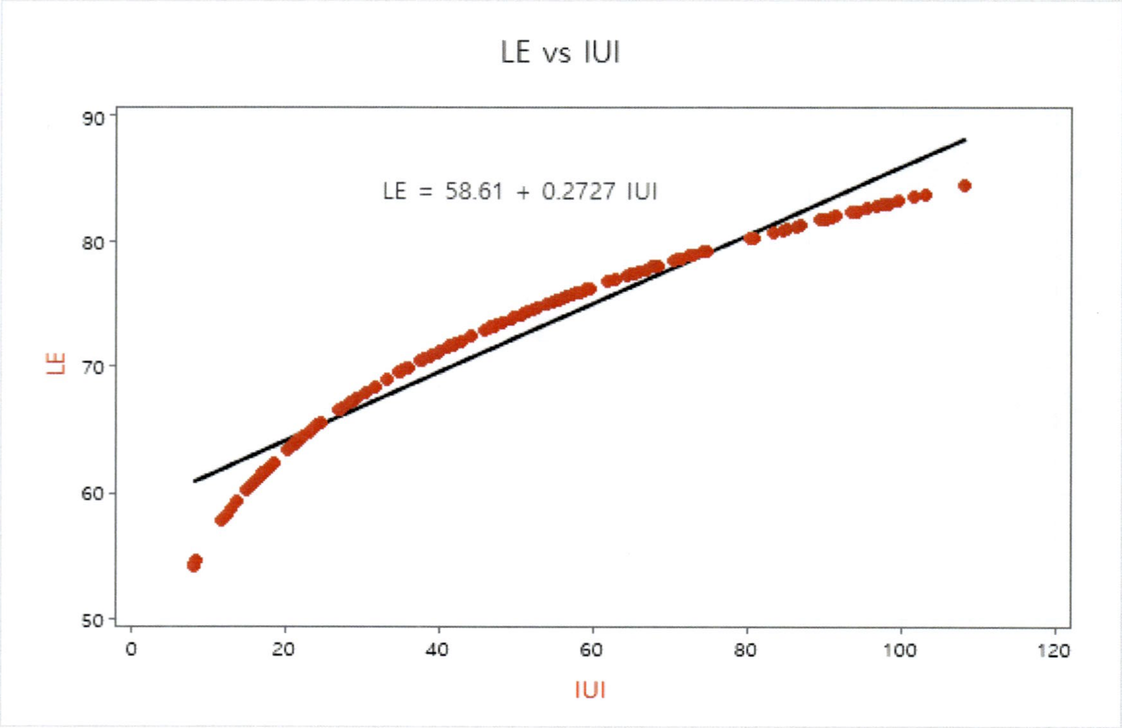

Fig. 4.13 IUI associated with SPBC (82) & LE

4.3.11 Government health expenditure (GHE)

As a variable of CLSS, only GHE affects LE (see Fig. 4.14). This indicates that when the current 100-year-olds were born, the GHE was insufficient. However, it shows that the proportion of government spending on healthcare directly affects national health, thus impacting LE.

In general, public resources include health insurance and related subsidies. Additionally, a portion of each country's health and medical expenses are spent on establishing or expanding health and medical institutions and training health and medical personnel. In this process, the role of the government is significant. In particular, financial support for healthcare in underdeveloped countries that lack government spending should be shared to promote the health of humanity as a whole. For example, when an infectious disease, such as COVID-19, spreads worldwide, all countries must focus on healthcare. However, in reality, since there are countries with insufficient government budgets, their interest in other countries is limited. Therefore, it is hoped that the political leaders of each country will collaborate so that all individuals, regardless of nationality, will have adequate health and medical resources.

As of 2018, Cuba had the highest GHE at 100%, followed by the UK at 79%. In addition, Afghanistan had the lowest GHE at 5%. Examples of the GHE scores by country are shown in Table 4.13.

Table 4.13 Example for domestic general government health expenditure (GHE), 2018

Countries	Cuba	Norway	Japan	United Kingdom	Canada	Spain	Australia	India	Afghanistan
GHE	88	85	84	79	73	70	69	27	5

WHO. Domestic general government health expenditure as a CHE (%):

Share of current health expenditures funded from general government sources, social health insurance, and compulsory prepayment.

https://www.who.int/data/gho/indicator-metadata-registry/imr-details/4953

Impact of GHE on LE

Table 4.13.1 shows that GHE affects 50% of LE as a single independent variable. In addition, Fig. 4.14 shows that LE increases as the proportion of GHE increases. The government spends a significant amount on healthcare because it invests directly in the public sector without relying on the private sector. Therefore, if the countries contribute to public health promotion by increasing medical expenses, LE and SPBC are expected to increase.

Table 4.13.1 . Multiple regression models of predicting the GHE and LE

(N = 167)

Term	Coefficients	SE Coef	T-Value	P-Value	VIF	R^2
GHE	0.2459	0.0191	12.88	0.001	1	0.501

R-sq	R-sq(adj)
50.14%	49.84%

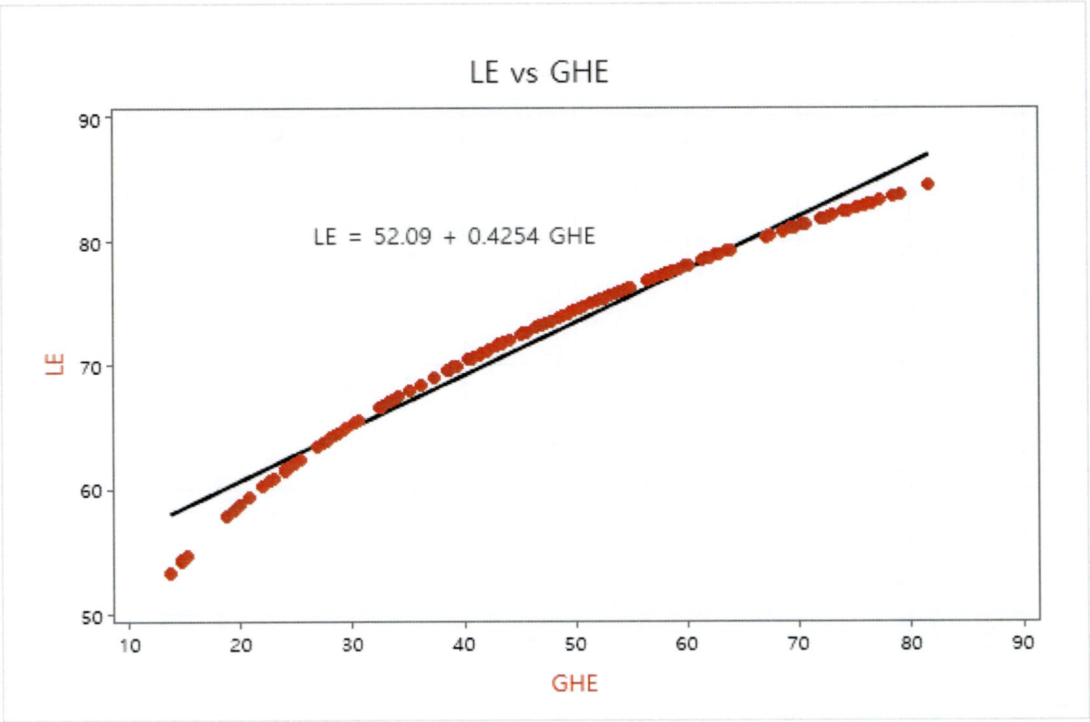

Fig. 4.14. GHE associated with LE

4.3.12 Health expenditure as a percentage of GDP (HEPGDP)

The HEPGDP is an index that indicates the degree of government expenditure on healthcare resources compared to other expenditures. In this regard, the proportion spent in the healthcare sector suggests the importance of health-related spending. In short, national health spending has a high priority in terms of cost/effectiveness.

The gross domestic product (GDP) is highly related to health since unhealthy people cannot work and add to the GDP. Thus, the government should increase the national budget for health- and medical-related projects.

Applying the ISS formula for HEPGDP

As of 2018, the United States had the highest HEPGDP at 16.89%, followed by the UK at 10%. Meanwhile, Monaco had the lowest HEPGDP at 1.6%. By converting and substituting the nine indicators, including HEPGDP, it is possible to predict the age at which individuals will survive from 82 years of age to centenarians.

HEPGDP is a variable that affects SPBC (see Fig. 4.15). For example, since the United States has the highest HEPGDP, the probability of surviving to 100 at age 82 receives the highest score of 100% points. Examples of the HEPGDP scores by country are shown in Table 4.14.

Table 4.14 Example of a score for health expenditure as a % of GDP, 2018

Countries	United States	Germany	United Kingdom	Italy	Republic of Korea	China	India	Indonesia	Monaco
GHE	16.89	11.43	10	8.67	7.56	5.35	3.54	2.87	1.6
ISS (%)	100	68	59	51	45	32	21	17	9

Health expenditure as a percentage of gross domestic product (GDP) (%):

The definition of HEPGDP is the level of current health expenditure expressed as a percentage of GDP. Current health expenditure as a share of GDP indicates the resources channeled to health relative to other uses. It shows the importance of the health sector in the whole economy and demonstrates the societal priority which health measures in monetary terms.

https://apps.who.int/gho/data/node.main.GHEDCHEGDPSHA2011?lang=en

Impact of HEPGDP on LE and SPBC (82)

Tables 4.14.1 and 4.14.2 show that HEPGDP affects 30% of SPBC (82) and 10% of LE as a single independent variable. Additionally, Fig. 4.15 shows that the higher the HEPGDP, the higher the LE and SPBC. Thus, improving workers' health can lead to increased productivity and a higher GDP, which, in turn, can provide better healthcare and extend their LE.

Table 4.14.1. Multiple regression models of predicting the HEPGDP and SPBC (82)

(N = 39)

Term	Coefficients	SE Coef	T-Value	P-Value	VIF	R^2
HEPGDP	8.33	2.11	3.94	0.001	1	0.296
R-sq	R-sq(adj)					
29.58%	27.68%					

Table 4.14.2. Multiple regression models of predicting the HEPGDP and LE

(N = 165)

Term	Coefficients	SE Coef	T-Value	P-Value	VIF	R^2
HEPGDP	0.897	0.21	4.27	0.001	1	0.101
R-sq	R-sq(adj)					
10.07%	9.52%					

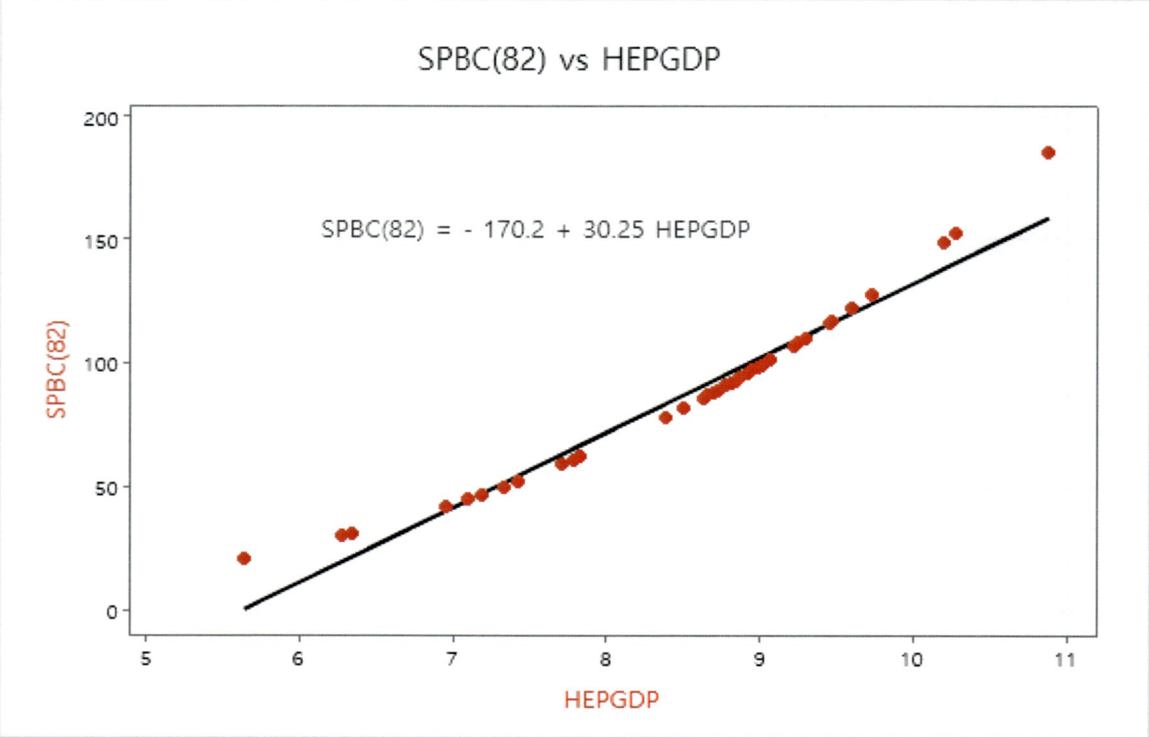
SPBC(82) vs HEPGDP
SPBC(82) = - 170.2 + 30.25 HEPGDP
200
150
100
50
0
SPBC(82)
5
6
7
8
9
10
11
HEPGDP

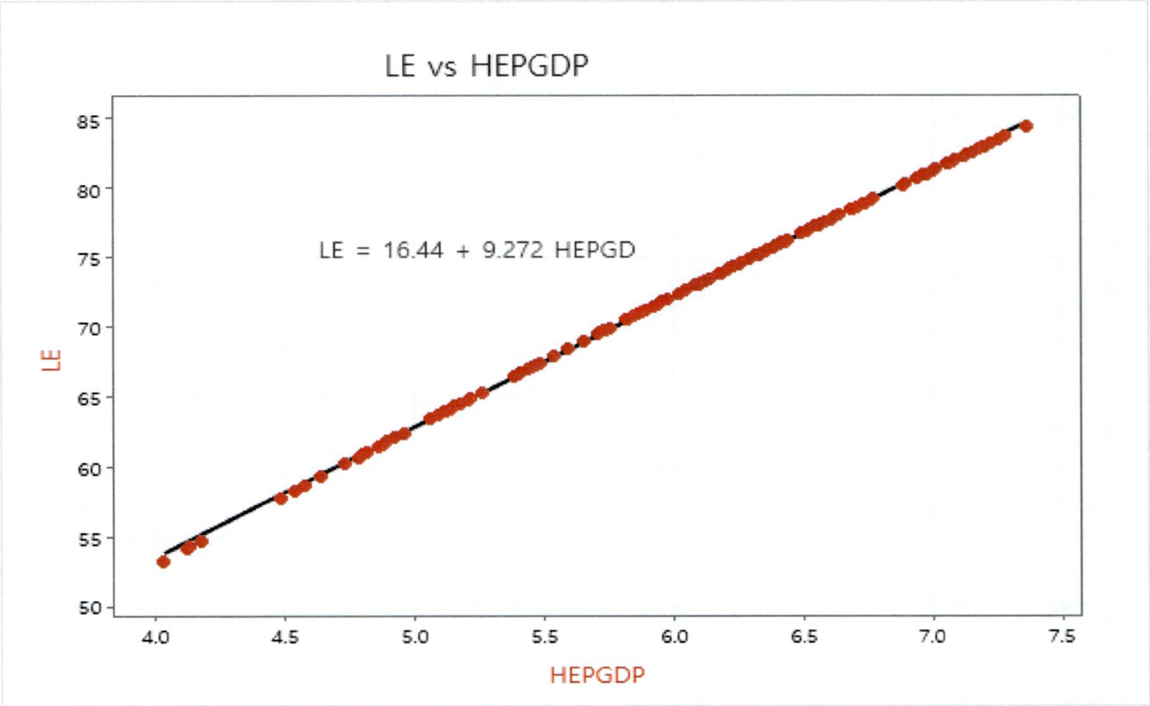

Fig. 4.15 HEPGDP associated with SPBC (82) & LE

4.3.13 Services value-added per worker (SVPW)

As a measure of labor productivity at the individual standard of living, SVPW is calculated by dividing the added value per worker by the number of employed workers. In this regard, an increase in SVPW means that the value of the net output increases. As mentioned earlier, the net productivity of workers is highly correlated with their health. Thus, political leaders should recognize that the health level of workers is directly related to the increase/decrease in the net output per worker. Moreover, since the added value per worker in a country is highly correlated with workers' LE, it is crucial to establish and implement innovative health and welfare policies.

Applying the ISS formula for SVPW

In 2018, Luxembourg had the highest SVPW at $207,763, whereas Sierra Leone had the lowest at $1,407. SVPW is a variable that affects SPBC. For example, Luxembourg, with the highest SVPW, receives the highest score of 100% points. Examples of the SVPW scores by country are shown in Table 4.15.

Table 4.15 Example of a score for services value-added per worker index, 2018

Countries	Luxembourg	United Kingdom	Iceland	Republic of Korea	Kuwait	Brazil	Bulgaria	Iraq	Sierra Leone
SVPW	207,763	78,078	70,459	42,709	36,456	20,927	18,129	14,227	1,407
ISS (%)	100	38	34	21	18	10	9	7	1

Services, value-added per worker (constant 2010 US$):

The value-added per worker is a measure of labor productivity—value-added per unit of input. Value-added denotes the net output of a sector after adding up all results and subtracting intermediate inputs. Data are in constant 2010 US dollars.

Source: Derived using World Bank national accounts data and OECD National Accounts data files, and employment data from International Labor Organization, ILOSTAT database.

Impact of SVPW on LE and SPBC (82)

Tables 4.15.1 and 4.15.2 show that SVPW affects 24% of SPBC (82) and 45% of LE as a single independent variable. In addition, Fig. 4.16 indicates that the higher the SVPW, the higher the LE and SPBC. Hence, the value of the net output of each worker increases when the national health level improves.

Table 4.15.1 . Multiple regression models of predicting the SVPW and SPBC (82)

(N = 39)

Term	Coefficients	SE Coef	T-Value	P-Value	VIF	R^2
SVPW	0.000426	0.000125	3.42	0.002	1	0.241
R-sq	R-sq(adj)					
24.11%	21.96%					

Table 4.15.2 . Multiple regression models of predicting the SVPW and LE

(N = 151)

Term	Coefficients	SE Coef	T-Value	P-Value	VIF	R^2
SVPW	0.000149	0.000014	10.94	0.001	1	0.446
R-sq	R-sq(adj)					
44.56%	44.19%					

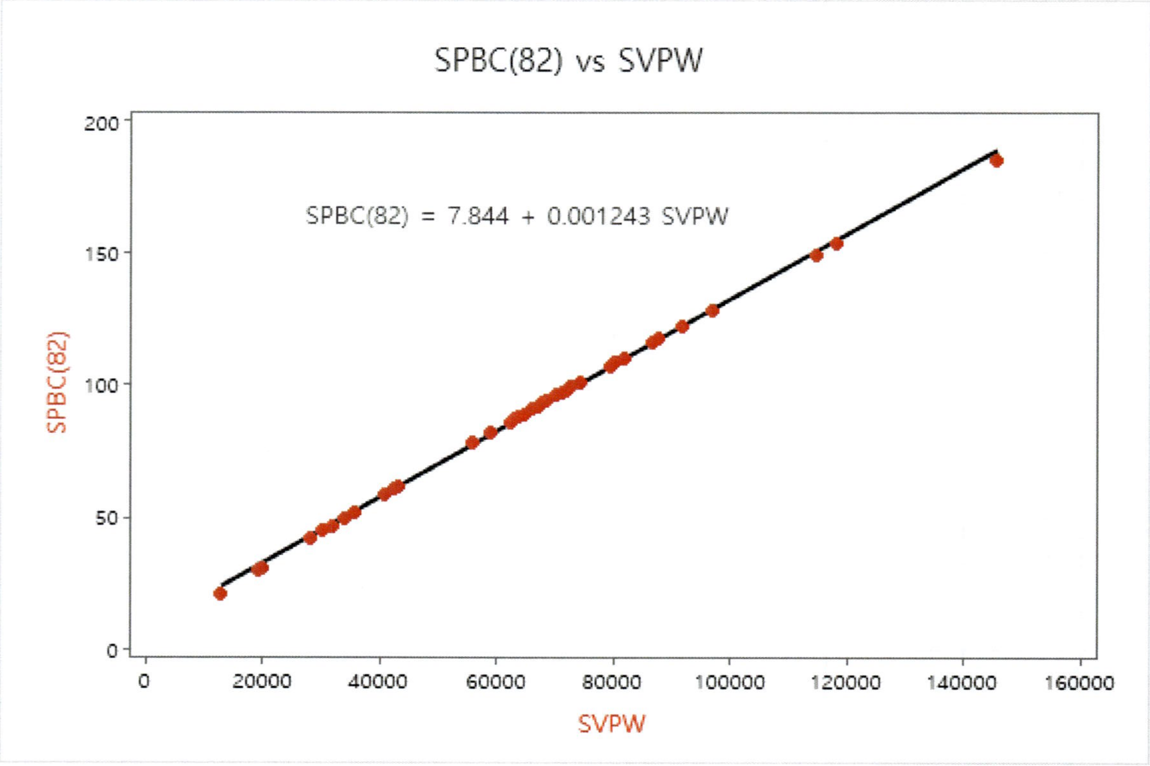
SPBC(82) vs SVPW
SPBC(82) = 7.844 + 0.001243 SVPW
SPBC(82)
SVPW
200
150
100
50
0
0
20000
40000
60000
80000
100000
120000
140000
160000

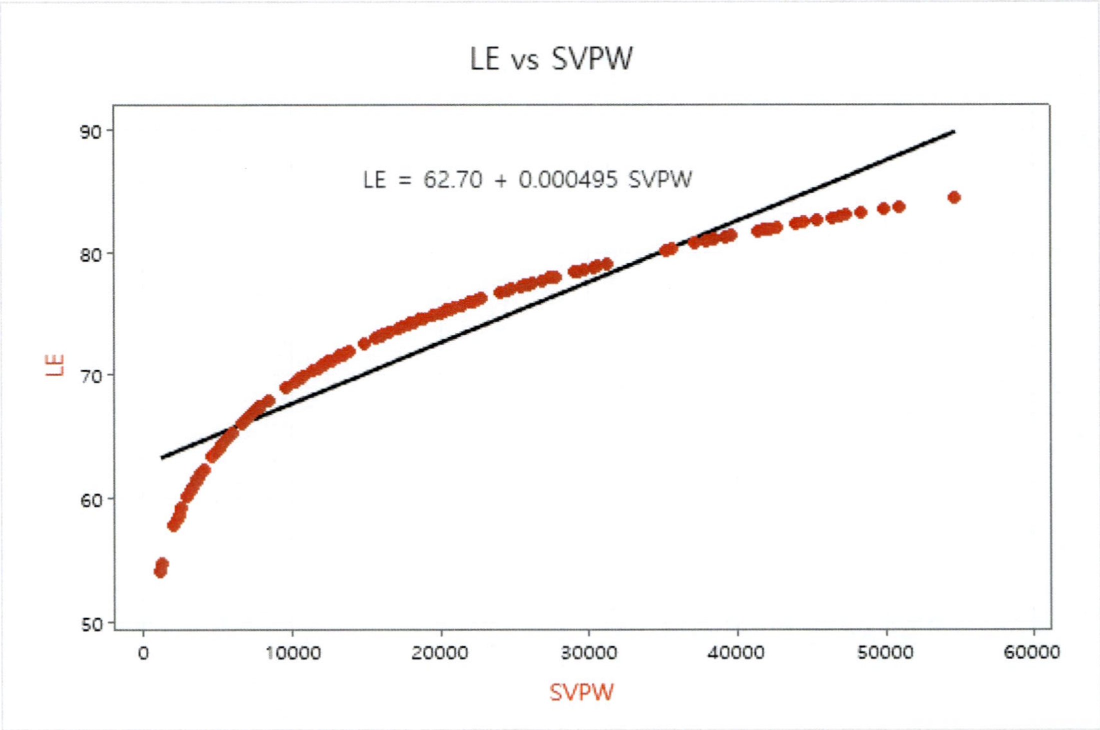

Fig. 4.16 SVPW associated with SPBC (82) & LE

4.3.14 Depth of credit information (DCI)

Finally, international credit rating agencies published the DCI index (ranging from 0 to 8) to measure information affecting national credit ratings. In this regard, the higher the value, the easier it is to access international finance. However, if the national credit index drops, there will be pressure for early repayment of existing debts.

Macroscopically, if the DCI is low, then the country's international competitiveness is weakened. This can negatively affect the domestic economy and lead to an economic recession. Moreover, when the economy is in recession, production and demand decrease, prices and wages fall, and unemployment rises. Ultimately, this will reduce workers' household income and stress their physical and mental health.

As of 2018, 40 countries, including the United States, had the highest score of 8, whereas the Congo had the lowest 1. Examples of the DCI scores by country are shown in Table 4.16.

Table 4.16 Example for depth of credit information index, 2018

Countries	United States	Germany	United Kingdom	China	Republic of Korea	Norway	Sweden	Gabon	Congo, Rep.
DCI	8	8	8	8	8	6	5	2	1

Depth of credit information index (0 = low to 8 = high):

Depth of credit information index measures rules affecting the scope, accessibility, and quality of credit information available through public or private credit registries. The index ranges from 0 to 8, with higher values indicating the availability of more credit information from either a public registry or a private bureau to facilitate lending decisions.

Source: World Bank, Doing Business project (doing business.org).

Impact of DCI on LE

Table 4.16.1 shows that DCI affects 8% of LE as a single independent variable. In addition, Fig. 4.17 indicates that the higher the national credit index, the higher the LE. Therefore, a high national credit index means that the national economy revitalizes the country's competitiveness without depending on foreign support. Through such revitalization, the standard of living will increase, contributing to national health in the long term.

Table 4.16.1 . Multiple regression models of predicting the DCI and LE

(N = 128)

Term	Coefficients	SE Coef	T-Value	P-Value	VIF	R^2
DCI	1.381	0.425	3.25	0.001	1	0.078
R-sq	R-sq(adj)					
7.80%	7.06%					

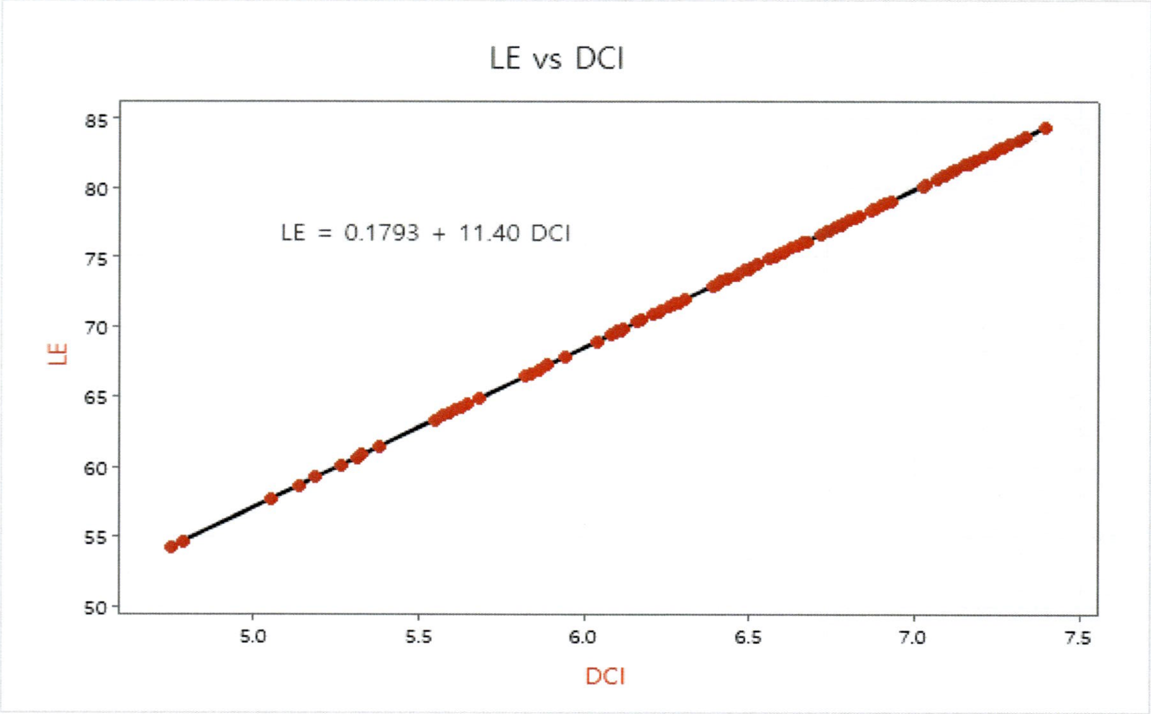

Fig.4.17 DCI associated with LE

4.4 Application factors of SPBC

4.4.1 Establishment of short-, medium-, and long-term plans

We can create short-, medium-, and long-term plans for reaching 100 years of age in one-, five-, and 10-year increments, respectively.

(1) Short-term plans

Short-term plans can occur in one-year increments. For example, planning can be established in January and evaluated in December. This has the advantage of assessing the national health level at the end of every year and making the appropriate improvements. However, there is also the cumbersome disadvantage of performing annual health checkups and evaluating the national health level based on various data.

(2) Medium-term plans

Medium-term plans can occur in five-year increments. Healthcare should be regularly monitored for abnormalities at the individual level and any inconsistencies and issues at the national level. For example, if an environmental factor that harms human beings occurs due to a lack of BSS, a prompt response is necessary. However, it is important to note such instances and establish appropriate health-related plans to remedy the situation over the medium term.

(3) Long-term plans

Long-term plans can occur over a more extended period of up to 10 years. In this regard, a long-term health management plan can be created, with periodic evaluations to ensure that the individual is adhering to the proposed suggestions, including the goal of reaching a healthy 100 years of age. Thus, for example, healthy individuals in their 30s can re-evaluate their health in their 40s and make the necessary improvements.

4.4.2 PLI: Income, hygiene, drinking water, and use of the ISS

Suppose that a country has set a goal of achieving a LE of 100 years of age. In this case, we should establish national health projects to manage SEFs such as individual income levels, BSS, and SMDW. The details of these variables are as follows.

(1) Individual income levels

Individual income levels are an essential factor in the provision of healthcare. It is also vital for improving the quality of life and maintaining a healthy standard of living. Specifically, when individual income levels are high, then we can obtain appropriate healthcare. However, when such income levels are low, medical expenses create burdens for individuals. Therefore, the government should help pay for healthcare, especially for those who cannot afford such costs.

(2) BSS

As stated earlier, infectious diseases can occur when BSS is not provided. Hence, it is important to offer such services, especially in developing countries. This can greatly reduce the incidence of infectious diseases and improve the health of both citizens and workers, the latter of which can have a positive impact on labor productivity and other related aspects that affect the country as a whole.

(3) SMDW

As mentioned earlier, SMDW is a critical health factor that can negatively affect the health of individuals if poorly maintained. Thus, developed countries should support countries and regions that lack drinking water facilities and related infrastructure.

(4) Using the ISS estimation formula

At this point, the ISS estimation formula is based on PLI and CLSS to estimate the age. Then, nine SEFs are evaluated and compared based on the highest score of 100%, as described earlier. Moreover, we assess the degree of goal achievement according to the calculation results in the ISS formula.

4.4.3 Social environment of mixed CLSS: GII, IUI, and UP

Regarding the social environment of mixed CLSS, GII, IUI, and UP are the critical factors. Therefore, the government should address these factors as soon as possible, directly affecting LE and SPBC.

(1) Gender equality

As mentioned earlier, the gender equality index is calculated by quantifying equal employment opportunities and securing equal social status for men and women. For instance, if a woman loses her job due to childbirth, the resulting stress will lower her mental health and quality of life, thus reducing her LE. Conversely, if men and women have equal opportunities to enter, including leadership positions, women's mental health and quality of life would significantly improve.

(2) IUI

Reliable information beneficial to health and health management can easily be obtained through the Internet. Such information will improve the short-term management of healthcare at the individual level and increase the LE and SPBC. Thus, governments should continue to monitor and ensure that individuals have easy and affordable access to these valuable SEFs.

(3) UP

An extensive UP means that people living in large cities have a higher change experience than those in rural areas. People living in large cities tend to experience economic, socio-cultural, demographic, and environmental changes. Economic change refers to how people living in rural areas migrate to large cities in search of work, and thus, can improve their income levels. In addition, socio-cultural change in large cities occurs with the high quality of life and an affluent lifestyle of modern society. Demographic health change can refer to the phenomenon in which the probability of infectious disease increases due to the population concentration. Finally, environmental pollution relates to air pollution, water and soil pollution, noise, and vibration. Since these changes can have a detrimental effect on health levels, social health policy that can supplement them is necessary.

(4) Use of the ISS estimation formula

The ISS estimation formula focuses on the current PLI and CLSS in SEFs which each index is evaluated based on the variable's highest scores. Then, the results of the performances are compared and feedback according to the degree of reaching the goal of 100 years of age.

4.4.4 Hospital visits: GHE and HEPGDP

Although a healthy 100-year-old goal is established and implemented by considering all 14 SEFs variables, numerous health-related issues must be considered, including cardiac arrest, cerebral hemorrhage, obesity, osteoporosis, hypertension, diabetes, etc. Meanwhile, there are diseases such as COVID-19, severe acute respiratory syndrome, cholera, tuberculosis, and AIDS. If such issues develop before reaching 100 years of age, then the country's attention and financial resources should be invested in prevention and treatment. In this regard, the higher GHE, the greater the alleviation of diseases. In addition, the HEPGDP should be high so that essential health and medical personnel can be hired and medical equipment and facilities built. Such investments are critical for achieving a healthy 100 years of age.

4.4.5 Achievement of the health level and SPBC feasibility review

Even if there is no history of chronic or acute diseases, the health levels of individuals, including their eating habits, lifestyles, mental health, community environment, and stress, should be regularly evaluated through, for example, annual health questionnaires or physical examinations. Such an approach can also check the individual's weight, visual acuity, and the presence (or absence) of abnormalities through biological samples such as blood, urine, feces, etc. Subsequently, we can establish customized treatment and health management plans to increase SPBC.

4.4.6 Healthcare system based on CLSS

In the previous section, we explained establishing and implementing a roadmap for achieving the healthy 100-year-old goal. However, emergencies and diseases, especially among the elderly, have a certain unpredictability in this process. Therefore, healthcare systems should ensure that patients receive medical attention within 30 minutes regardless of their location.

Finally, Fig. 4.20 presents a healthcare system in which human beings live to 100 years. In this regard, the medical delivery system is established by first dividing the region into large-, medium-, and small-sized cities, including local communities. The details of each category are as follows.

(1) Large cities

The respective departments of geriatric rehabilitation medicine can recruit health and medical personnel such as rehabilitation specialists, physical therapists, occupational therapists, rehabilitation nurses, and social workers. Such personnel can provide the following programs for the elderly:

- Senior stroke programs:
Gait for hemiplegic patients
Functional improvement of hemiplegic patients
Cognitive rehabilitation and speech therapy
- Geriatric neurology:
Stroke rehabilitation, dementia, Parkinson's disease, sleep disorders, headache, numbness, hand tremors, dizziness, and facial paralysis
- Geriatric internal medicine:
Hypertension, diabetes, hyperlipidemia, osteoporosis, lung disease, and geriatric heart disease.

For example, let us suppose that a geriatric oriental medicine department is necessary. In this case, the department can provide treatment for stroke rehabilitation (e.g., acupuncture, cupping, and moxibustion) and pain (e.g., backache, shoulder pain, and joint pain). In principle, the cost of the medical treatment would be free of charge since the government bears the majority, with 10% of the medical expenses covered by the individual's co-insurance.

(2) Small- and medium-sized cities

Small- and medium-sized cities usually include general public hospitals (approximately 500 beds), with specialists in each field and health prevention projects carried out in parallel. Meanwhile, it is crucial to legislate nurses' medical practice scope if it is challenging to secure professional doctors. In addition, since emergency patients are challenging to reach, we should implement rural and remote island regions, a system for transporting patients by the Coast Guard or by hospital-based helicopters.

Moreover, it is crucial to expand public hospitals in small- and medium-sized cities by introducing a local doctor system and increasing the number of beds. For example, a general hospital with more than 500 beds must be established in countries with no hospitals in small- and medium-sized cities. In addition, public hospital operators should integrate their hospitals into university hospitals and local medical centers.

(3) Local communities and villages

Fig. 4.18 presents a healthcare system. General clinics that provide primary treatment should be established in local communities and villages. In this regard, the medical delivery system can be divided into large-, medium-, and small-sized cities, including local communities.

Health & Hospital visit (chronic, infectious diseases etc.)

Regional:	Metropolitans
Hospital Type:	Public Specialized hospitals
Medical Course:	Specialized hospitals by field
Medical Expense:	Burden 10% of health medical cost
Specialized Field:	3rd~2nd medical treatment Specialized hospitals Infectious Hospitals

▲▼

Regional:	Small and medium cities
Hospital Type:	Public medical hospitals
Medical Course:	2nd~1st treatment and prevention
Medical Expense:	Free of medical cost
Specialized Field:	Infection hospital Specialized hospitals

▲▼

Regional:	Community
Hospital Type:	Public Health centres
Medical Course:	Primary health care services
Medical Expense:	Free of health cost
Specialized Field:	General clinic Health Clinic

Fig. 4.18. The healthcare system based on large-, medium-, and small-sized cities

4.4.7 Health resource mobilization

At this point, a healthcare system can be established by analyzing and evaluating PLI and CLSS to predict SPBC. However, it is first necessary to mobilize/manage the national and local health and medical resources to realize this plan. The details of this process are as follows.

(1) Input

As shown in Fig. 4.21, input includes human resources, facility resources, information, and medical demand. However, if the country's average LE is 82 years old and the goal of living to 100 years of age is implemented, then we must include the following resources:

Ⓐ Healthcare human resources

Medical personnel are employed, such as elderly health experts, caregivers, geriatric specialists, geriatric nurses, physical therapists dedicated to the elderly, clinical pathologists, geriatric psychiatrists, dentists, and cardiocerebrovascular specialists.

Ⓑ Specialized healthcare facilities

Specialized healthcare facilities are nursing homes, geriatric hospitals, and health promotion and recreation centers for the elderly. In addition, we can build walking paths to promote the mental and physical health of the elderly. In some regions, everybody can access them 365 days a year.

Ⓒ Health finances

We should secure the health finances of the elderly through national and local governments and social donations. We can even finance such resources through general taxation, loans, and consumption taxes. Although the insurance method is utilized in most cases, those in the low-income class have a limited ability to pay premiums. Thus, the tax approach is preferred.

Ⓓ Health information

Health information is widely advertised and accessed through television, telephone, and broadcasting so that the elderly can use such information to improve their quality of life and health.

Ⓔ Medical demand

Medical demand can be divided into adults, the elderly, children, mothers, emergency patients, and infected patients. Hence, it is important to regularly check the supply and demand status of hospital beds, notify the public of blood supplies, and establish "central and local control towers" for immediate treatment of patients. By actively responding to such medical demands, LE and SPBC can be increased.

(2) Management process

The management process of health and medical resources can be divided into planning, organization, recruitment, command, and evaluation. The details are as follows:

Ⓐ Planning

If an 82-year-old wants to achieve a healthy LE of 100 years, what type of planning process should they follow? In this case, the planning should naturally focus on maintaining a high quality of life with appropriate healthcare. At this point, let us briefly explain a health and medical plan that can directly affect LE.

This plan should be based on the fact that the national government is responsible for public healthcare. For example, without asking how the 82-year-old has lived thus far, the state or local government should establish a health protection system to achieve a healthy lifespan. In addition, when a disease occurs, a geriatric specialist must immediately initiate emergency measures, hospitalization, and medical treatment. Finally, a rehabilitation system must be in place that allows former patients to return to their daily lives.

Ⓑ Organizations

Organizations should have a medical system that can adapt to changes in the health and medical environment, and make it easier for the elderly to access the healthcare system. Thus, prioritizing when an emergency patient arrives at a medical institution or hospital is the first thing. For example, cardiocerebrovascular patients must reach the hospital within 30 minutes. In this regard, we should make policies to mobilize hospital-based helicopters, ambulances, and private vehicles.

Ⓒ Staffing

Human resources should hire various specialists, nurses, and healthcare workers to provide treatment during emergencies. For long-term inpatients, caregivers and occupational therapists are necessary. Additionally, qualified senior life advisors should be appointed to provide helpful advice to the elderly after recovering from illness or disease.

Ⓓ Management

Management focuses on improving the quality of life through diet and regular healthcare. For example, drinking water can be made by purifying tap water, and stores can stock bottled water for purchase. Such management can also prevent diseases in advance through periodic questionnaires, examinations, and biological samples. Meanwhile, exercise programs for the elderly can be promoted through walking activities and fitness centers.

Ⓔ Evaluation

To ensure that the implemented plan is effective, it is crucial to conduct regular evaluations. Such evaluations should consider their strengths and weaknesses. In addition, the projects that need to be revised and supplemented can be based on the feedback of quantity and quality.

(3) Output

Output is the final part of the process that confirms the goal of achieving 100 years of LE. The first step is to determine if the 82-year-old has made a short-term plan for living another ten years, i.e., the goal of 92 years of age. In other words, during this period, we can implement healthcare management to emphasize physical health through PLI and CLSS.

The second and final step is to determine if it is possible to live beyond the age of 93 and reach the goal of 100 years of age. Hence, it is crucial to examine the individual's medical history, including health promotion, physical exercise, and mental reflection based on the SEFs as mentioned earlier. Although this stage can be challenging to complete, it is a process whereby individuals can determine their SPBC according to certain SEFs.

Resource Mobilization and management process to centenarians

▼

Input

- **Geriatrics Health Professional personnel:**
  Nursing care provider, gerontology doctor, and geriatric disease nurse
- **Geriatrics Healthcare Professional facilities:**
  A nursing home, geriatric hospital, recreation centre, and geriatric tower
- **Geriatrics Health finance:**
  National and local government finance, and social donation
- **Geriatrics Health information:**
  Health information for the elderly, living and security for old age
- **Geriatrics medical demand:**
  Adjustment of supply & demand for hospital beds and emergency

▼

Management process

- **Planning:** Establishment of a public health care system for the elderly
- **Organization:** Systematization of the elderly emergency system
- **Staffing:** Supply and mobilization of medical personnel to the elderly
- **Management:** Food, health management, quality of life improvement
- **Evaluation:** Evaluation and feedback on elderly projects by cycle

▼

Output

- **82 to 92 aged:** Physical health promotion and management
- **93 to 100 aged:** Mental Health Promotion and Management

Fig.4. 19. The process of resource mobilization and management for centenarians

(4) Output: A case study for SPBC

SPBC (82) estimated in this book is shown in Additional File 1 (The Human Mortality Database, 2021). Globally, the country with the highest number of 82-year-olds who live to be 100 is still Japan. Next, is France, so if SEFs increase on the premise that other factors are constant, achieving this milestone on a global scale is possible.

In addition, SPBC (90) estimated in this book is shown in Additional File 2 (The Human Mortality Database, 2021). Globally, the country with the highest number of 90-year-olds who live to be 100 is still Japan. Next is Luxembourg. Therefore, we identified that if SEFs increase on the premise that other factors are constant, achieving SPBC is possible.

Therefore, SPBC (82) and SPBC (90) are impacted by nine factors: GNI, SMDW, BSS, UP, GII, IUI, HEPGDP, SVPW, and FTMTS.

We identified SPBC as impacted by nine factors (GNI, SMDW, BSS, UP, GII, IUI, HEPGDP, SVPW, and FTMTS). From a socioecological perspective, nine factors impact SPBC in those aged 82 and 90 years.

Additional file 1. A list as the data assessment of SPBC (82) for study 39 countries

Countries	2018 (A) †			2000 (B) ‡			SPBC (82) ±		
	Female	Male	Total	Female	Male	Total	Female	Male	Total
Japan	7708	1552	9260	325798	174911	500709	237	89	185
France	1962	430	2392	101651	54841	156492	193	78	153
Canada	1090	275	1365	57956	33727	91683	188	82	149
Chile*)	255	72	327	16138	9506	25644	158	76	128
Iceland	6	4	10	486	332	818	123	120	122
Spain	1513	385	1898	105825	56766	162591	143	68	117
U.S.A	8458	2366	10824	592176	343628	935803	143	69	116
Slovenia*)	32	6	38	2430	1025	3455	132	63	110
Israel****)	96	64	160	8900	5920	14820	108	108	108
Australia	473	152	625	36294	22163	58457	130	69	107
Rep. of Korea	519	100	620	42851	18818	61669	121	53	101
Italy*)	1750	447	2197	143451	78918	222369	122	57	99
Finland	160	32	192	13881	5698	19579	115	56	98
Greece*)	286	107	393	24455	15952	40407	117	67	97
United Kingdom	1651	418	2069	138105	75972	214077	120	55	97
Luxembourg	10	1	11	778	368	1146	129	27	96
Norway	160	47	207	14105	7984	22089	113	59	94
Belgium	215	50	265	19002	9572	28574	113	52	93
Portugal	284	80	364	24932	14656	39588	114	55	92
Switzerland	202	53	255	17927	10079	28006	113	53	91
Estonia	24	3	27	2328	724	3052	103	42	89
Denmark	162	34	196	14208	7998	22206	114	43	88
New Zealand***	62	33	95	6997	3895	10892	89	85	87
Sweden	325	88	413	29335	18353	47688	111	48	87
Netherlands	392	83	475	36493	18491	54984	107	45	86
Ireland*)	71	20	91	6900	4135	11035	103	48	82
Germany*)	1498	290	1788	164601	65581	230182	91	44	78
Austria	134	29	163	14689	6331	21020	91	46	78
Latvia	27	7	34	4093	1370	5463	66	51	62
Poland	339	74	413	46151	21130	67281	73	35	61
Lithuania	35	8	43	5328	2060	7388	67	39	59
Slovakia*)	31	8	39	4994	2644	7638	62	30	52
Croatia	28	7	35	4904	2090	6994	56	34	50
Belarus	68	13	81	13092	4202	17294	52	30	47
Hungary*)	73	23	96	14223	7039	21262	51	33	45
Czechia	60	15	75	12216	5697	17912	49	26	42
Russia**)	1121	176	1297	328068	85740	413808	34	21	31
Bulgaria*)	33	14	47	9694	5995	15689	35	23	30
Ukraine***)	322	50	372	137277	42377	179654	23	12	21

†: The number of aged 100 in 2018
‡: The number of people aged 82 years in 2000
±: (A) / (B) *10000

*) The number of aged 100 in 2017;The number of people aged 82 years in 1999
**) The number of aged 100 in 2014;The number of people aged 82 years in 1996
***) The number of aged 100 in 2013;The number of people aged 82 years in 1995
****) The number of aged 100 in 2016;The number of people aged 82 years in 1998

Additional file 2. A list as the data assessment of SPBC (90) for study 39 countries

Countries	2018 (A) †			2009 (B) ‡			SPBC (90) ±		
	Femal	Male	Total	Female	Male	Total	Femal<	Male	Total
Japan	7708	1552	9260	183316	64237	247553	420	242	374
Luxembourg	10	1	11	217	76	294	461	131	374
Canada	1090	275	1365	29576.53	12208	41785	369	225	327
Chile*)	255	72	327	7275.95	3010	10286	350	239	318
Israel****)	96	64	160	3294	1966	5260	291	325	304
France	1962	430	2392	58314.05	21905	80219	336	196	298
Rep. of Korea	519	100	620	15957	5160	21117	325	194	294
Greece	284	100	384	8957	4575	13533	317	219	284
U.S.A	8458	2366	10824	277367	120862	398229	305	196	272
Italy	1530	395	1925	51362	19588	70950	298	202	271
Spain	1513	385	1898	50520	19442	69962	299	198	271
Iceland	6	4	10	238.3	134	372	252	298	269
Slovenia	39	5	34	1021.63	266	1287	382	188	264
Portugal	284	80	364	9730	4138	13868	292	193	262
United Kingdom	1651	418	2069	58067	23413	81480	284	179	254
Ireland*)	71	20	91	2572	1031	3605	276	194	252
Australia	473	152	625	17438	7896	25333	271	193	247
Finland	160	32	192	5966	1825	7791	268	175	246
Belgium	215	50	265	8061	2821	10881	267	177	244
Norway	160	47	207	6162	2463	8625	260	191	240
Netherlands	392	83	475	14752	5067	19819	266	163	240
Denmark	162	34	196	6013	2437	8450	269	140	232
Germany*)	1498	290	1788	60306	17468	77773	248	166	230
New Zealand***)	62	33	95	3024	1154	4177	205	286	227
Sweden	325	88	413	12502	5718	18220	260	154	227
Switzerland	202	53	255	8277	3476	11753	244	152	217
Estonia	24	3	27	1034	235	1270	233	130	214
Latvia	27	7	34	1393	329	1722	193	211	197
Austria	134	29	163	6402	2110	8512	209	137	191
Slovakia	30	6	35	1356	511	1867	221	117	187
Poland	339	74	413	16680	5383	22063	203	137	187
Croatia	28	7	35	1480	495	1975	186	145	176
Lithuania	35	8	43	1935	552	2487	183	144	175
Bulgaria*)	33	14	47	1876	952	2828	178	144	167
Belarus	68	13	81	4059	999	5058	168	126	160
Czechia	60	15	75	3783	1287	5070	159	117	148
Hungary	66	21	87	4433	1470	5903	149	143	147
Russia**)	1121	176	1297	83556	15169	98727	134	116	131
Ukraine***)	322	50	372	29227	6776	36003	110	74	103

†: The number of aged 100 in 2018

‡: The number of people aged 90 years in 2009

±: (A) / (B) *10000

*) The number of aged 100 in 2017;The number of people aged 90 years in 2008

**) The number of aged 100 in 2014;The number of people aged 82 years in 2005

***) The number of aged 100 in 2013;The number of people aged 82 years in 2004

****) The number of aged 100 in 2016;The number of people aged 90 years in 2007

4.4.8 Assessment of the health level based on PLI and CLSS

The assessment of the impact on SPBC and LE through CLSS and PLI are as follows (Fig. 4.22).

First, it is necessary to determine whether reaching 100 years of age can be achieved. For example, if the LE is 82 years, extending the lifespan by 18 years. Thus, it is crucial to evaluate how healthy the 82 years of age are and whether we can achieve the goal planning levels of SEFs every year.

Second, we must conduct an evaluation every five years to determine what PLI and CLSS achieve levels of this goal.

Next, after ten years, i.e., age 92, it is essential to determine whether the individual's health levels and illnesses during that period. In sum, this health assessment focuses on the physical aspects of PLI and CLSS.

In addition, we must conduct a health impact assessment after the age of 92. This can be done by reflecting on the PLI of one's life and CLSS based on the SEFs as mentioned earlier. However, if the individual and CLSS aspects feel they have failed to reach this goal, it is crucial to analyze the problem, find the possible cause, and present an alternative to help meet the initial plan.

Finally, we should conduct a field evaluation to achieve the overall goal of reaching 100 years of age. Since this evaluation is directly related to the life of the individual and health levels of countries, it can help reconfirm the final goal and the target quantity of SEFs in the process.

Therefore, we can achieve humanity's goal of a 100-year-old healthy lifespan through improvements in the health in PLI and CLSS and the implementation of short- and long-term plans of SEFs.

However, the following question is raised: What measures should be taken if we cannot achieve this goal? The response is to continuously revise and supplement the approach through feedback on the quantity and quality of SEFs.

In addition, ultimately, if it is impossible to achieve the target quantity of SEFs, we can lower the target amount. However, due to the nature of healthcare characteristics, this is not desirable. In other words, it is vital to continue to aim for this goal despite the difficulties.

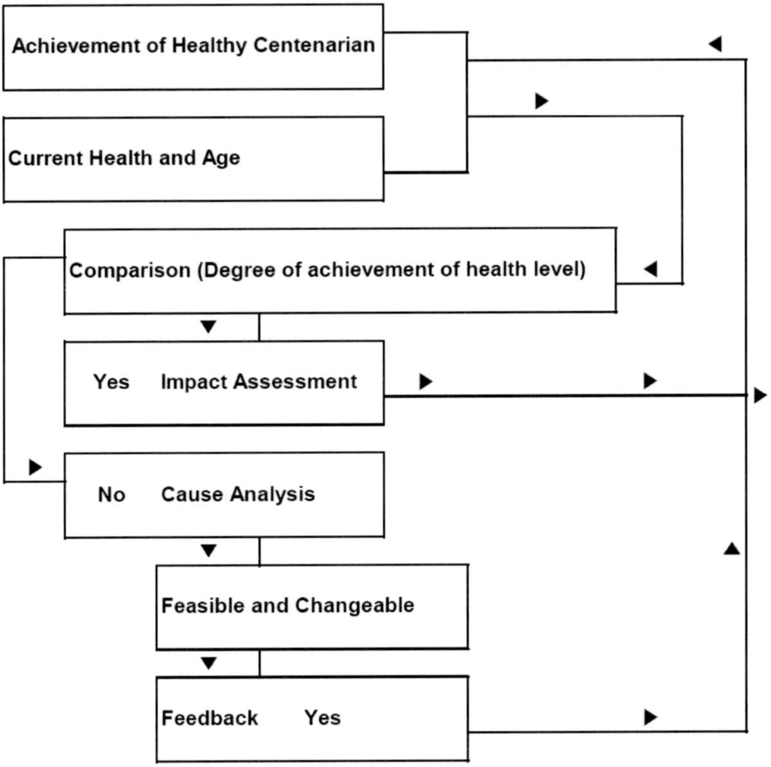

Fig. 4.20. Assessment of the health level based on PLI and CLSS

References

The Human Mortality Database (HMD): Department of Demography at the University of California, Berkeley, USA, and at the Max Planck Institute for Demographic Research in Rostock, Germany. https://www.mortality.org/. Accessed July 16, 2021

United Nations (UN). Human development report: Old-age pension recipients (% of statutory pension age population). http://hdr.undp.org/en/indicators/123806. Accessed on July 8, 2021.

United Nations (UN). Human development report: Population with at least some secondary education (% ages 25 and older). http://hdr.undp.org/en/indicators/23806. Accessed on July 28, 2021.

United Nations (UN). Human development reports, gender inequality index (GII), http://hdr.undp.org/en/data. Accessed July 16, 2021.

WHO. Safely managed drinking water: Thematic report on drinking water 2021. https://data.worldbank.org/indicator/SH.H2O.SMDW.ZS. Accessed July 16, 2021.

World Bank (WB). GNI per capita, Atlas method, (current US$). World Bank national accounts data. https://data.worldbank.org/indicator/NY.GNP.PCAP.CD?view=chart. Accessed July 16, 2021.

World Bank (WB). Incidence of tuberculosis (per 100,000 people). World Health Organization, Global Tuberculosis Report. https://data.worldbank.org/indicator/SH.TBS.INCD?view=chart. Accessed July 16, 2021.

World Bank (WB). Services, value-added per worker. Derived using World Bank national accounts data and OECD. https://data.worldbank.org/indicator/NV.SRV.EMPL.KD. Accessed July 26, 2021

World Bank (WB). World development Indicators.People using at least basic sanitation services (% of population). https://data.worldbank.org/indicator/SH.STA.BASS.ZS. Accessed March 22, 2021

WHO. Indicator metadata registry list. Current health expenditure (CHE) as percentage of gross domestic product (GDP) (%). https://www.who.int/data/gho/indicator-metadata-registry/imr-details/4950. Accessed March 18, 2021

World Bank (WB). Life expectancy at birth, total (years). United Nations Population Division. World Population Prospects: 2019 Revision. https://data.worldbank.org/indicator/SP.DYN.LE00.IN Accessed July 16, 2021

World Bank (WB). Development research group. Gini index (World Bank estimate). https://data.worldbank.org/indicator/SI.POV.GINI?end=2019&start=1967&view=chart. Accessed March 22, 2021

World Bank (WB). Fixed telephone subscriptions (per 100 people). International Telecommunication Union (ITU) World Telecommunication/ICT Indicators Database. https://data.worldbank.org/indicator/IT.MLT.MAIN.P2. Accessed March 22, 2021

World Bank (WB). Urban population (% of total population). United Nations Population Division. World Urbanization Prospects: 2018 Revision. https://data.worldbank.org/indicator/SP.URB.TOTL.IN.ZS Accessed March 20, 2021

World Bank (WB). Depth of credit information index (0 = low to 8 = high). https://data.worldbank.org/indicator/IC.CRD.INFO.XQ Accessed March 16, 2021

Kim JI, Kim G. & Choi Y. Effects of air pollution on children from a socioecological perspective. BMC Pediatrics. 2019; 19, 442.

Kim JI. Association between social factors of health ageing and longevity: Determinants of the longevity index (LI) in OECD Countries. *Ageing International.* 2014; 39(2), 97–105.

Kim JI. Social factors associated with centenarian rate (CR) in 32 OECD countries. *BMC International Health and Human Rights.* 2013; 13(1), 16.

Kim JI. Association between social factors of health ageing and longevity: determinants of the longevity index (LI) in OECD countries. *Ageing International*. 2014; 39(2), 97–105.

Kim JI, Kim G. Factors affecting the survival probability of becoming a centenarian for those aged 70, based on the human mortality database: Income, health expenditure, telephone, and sanitation. BMC Geriatrics. 2014a; 14(1), 113.

Kim JI, Kim G. Labor force participation and secondary education of gender inequality index (GII) associated with healthy life expectancy (HLE) at birth. *International Journal for Equity in Health.* 2014b; 13(1) 1–8.

Kim, JI, Kim G. Country-Level Socioeconomic Indicators Associated with Healthy Life Expectancy: Income, Urbanization, Schooling, and Internet Users: 2000–2012. *Social Indicators Research.* 2016; 129, 391–402.

Kim JI, Kim G. Social Structural influences on healthy aging: Community-level socioeconomic conditions and survival probability of becoming a centenarian for those aged 65 to 69 in South Korea. *The International Journal of Aging and Human Development.* 2015b; 81(4), 241–259.

PART 5

A SOCIETY WHERE PEOPLE LIVE TO BE CENTENARIANS

Part 5 constitutes this book's final position. Among the 39 countries evaluated, SEFs of SPBC (82) influence ranking the power (R^2) of regression analysis is presented. In addition, conclusions and evaluations of these nine variables' impact are presented. Specifically, this part illustrates interviews with 130 centenarians (ages 100 to 108), based on nine SEF indicators from an SPBC (82) perspective. Finally, Part 5 presents a combination that drives the optimal result among the nine SEF factors.

CHAPTER 5

IMPLICATIONS FROM THE INTERVIEWS WITH CENTENARIANS

The previous chapter presented examples from PLI and country-local society support (CLSS), focusing on the significant SEFs discussed thus far. In a society where 100-year-olds live, determining the factors that affect their lifespan is crucial. Based on those findings, making recommendations on a national scale becomes possible.

Therefore, Chapter 5 analyzes whether strong influence occurs when certain SEFs are combined and whether each country type has an optimal type of SEFs. Finally, the chapter presents the task and future direction of SEFs in SEPC (82).

5.1 Ranking impact factors between SPBC (82) and SEFs

We can confirm ranking the impacts of SEFs on the SPBC (82) in 39 countries. The results are summarized in Table 5.1.

For SPBC (82), BSS ranked first among the nine variables. It was followed by HEPGDP, IUI, FTMPS, SVPW, GNI, SMDW, UP, and GII. For their SEFs, the correlation was more significant than 47%, and the explanatory power of influence was greater than 22%.

Among SEFs, the difference in correlation coefficient and influence (R^2) between the leading BSS and lower GII was approximately 8%. Thus, these SEFs in SPBC (82) are equally important with almost no large gap.

Table 5.1. Ranking of impact correlations coefficient on the SPBC (82) and SEFs

Variables		Correlations coefficient	p-value	R^2	Ranking
	BSS	0.554	0.000	0.308	1
	HEGDP	0.544	0.000	0.296	2
	IUI	0.535	0.000	0.286	3
	FTMPS	0.493	0.001	0.243	4
SPBC	SVPW	0.491	0.002	0.241	5
(82 to 100)	GNI	0.487	0.002	0.237	6
	SMDW	0.484	0.002	0.234	7
	UP	0.481	0.002	0.232	8
	GII	-0.471	0.003	0.222	9

5.2 The SEFs affecting centenarians

In this chapter, to confirm how the nine indicators of SEFs—influenced by the SPBC (82) in 39 countries—are implemented in the lives of centenarians, we synthesized interviews with 130 centenarians. We also confirm the application and utilization in the lives of the centenarians and provide implications. The reconstructed nine indicators of SEFs are introduced below based on the synthesis of interviews.

5.2.1 BSS

Concerning the BSS of SEFs, we confirmed that in most of the centenarians we met, they faithfully practiced personal hygiene management as PLI throughout their lives until they became centenarians. In addition, they had experienced health promotion through the social welfare system of their countries.

"There is a public bath within a few minutes' walk from the residence. In some cases, you go to the local public baths with your family. When your family can't go together, a full-body bath service is available at least once a week with the help of the visiting caregiver at the Local Public Senior Welfare Center.

If I were alone, I think this must have been difficult.

Also, a visiting caregiver visits my house about once a week to do simple cleaning and prepare side dishes. I am always grateful. Without them, it would have been tough to even clean, let alone to wash or bathe.

In addition, I set up notifications by entering the hygiene-related items on my phone on a weekly and monthly basis. For example, I usually record the days I go to the local public baths or the days my sanitation caregiver comes so that I don't forget.

I am always happy and healthy because I have help with my hygiene."

The BSS is the first critical element among the nine factors of the SPBC (82). As highlighted in the interview, for the elderly with reduced mobility, caregivers have been visiting their private homes to assist with physical hygiene and housework. Thus, we could conclude that such from a PLI perspective and CLSS resulted from maintaining health care through BSS and increased the probability of reaching the centenarians. Therefore, the main factor in PLI appears to be the result of maintaining a healthy lifespan, especially among the centenarians with the support of CLSS.

5.2.2 HEPGDP

Regarding the HEPGDP of SEFs, the centenarians we met were talkative and healthy at the time. However, various centenarians overcame severe diseases in their 80s. This instance is as follows.

> "Around age 80, I had a significant illness that required surgery. At the time, I thought I was going to die. However, I healed after the surgery, and I have lived healthily into my 100s.
>
> I had a friend who had a similar disease to me and had to give up surgery for financial or other reasons along the way, but all of them passed away. If I hadn't had the surgery then, I would have certainly died.
>
> As I was living, I saw several cases where some people around the age of 80 or 90 gave up surgery in case of a disease that required significant surgery and died several times.
>
> I didn't do that, so I think that's why I'm still living."

HEPGDP is the second most crucial element among the nine factors of the SPBC (82). As highlighted in the interview, the probability of becoming a centenarian increased depending on whether significant surgery was performed or not. Thus, it confirmed that centenarians should support the economic power to overcome severe disease.

5.2.3 IUI

Regarding the IUI of SEFs, the centenarians we met did not directly use the Internet but watched documentaries and movies through Internet TV with their families.

"I don't use the Internet myself. Family members mainly use it at home. However, if I need something or have a question, my family often finds information and provides it.

Most of the data is mainly about health. Recently, my grandson, who lives with me, saw a typical health-related study that I had misunderstood and corrected on the Internet.

I also learned how to use hearing aids correctly through the Internet.

I often watch Internet TV in my spare time because it is difficult to find broadcasts. I mostly enjoy watching historical documentaries.

In addition, there is a community only for the elderly in the Internet space.

My Internet skills are limited, but I meet my peers and juniors here, chatting and talking with each other and having a good time as if meeting and speaking at the senior center."

The use of the Internet enhances communication and facilitates the transfer of necessary medical information. Previous research by Kim & Kim (2016) has identified that the Internet is a significant factor in prolonging a healthy life expectancy. Consequently, Internet use is a significant factor influencing rank three in SPBC (82). In addition, necessary medical services and health information are variables that prolong healthy life and influence reaching the age of 100.

5.2.4 FTMPS

Regarding FTMPS of SEFs, among the centenarians we met, those who have retained good hearing were living their lives happily while talking directly to family and acquaintances over the phone.

> "Because I am old, I have limited mobility, so it is difficult to meet my acquaintances or go to the Senior Center. In addition, the children live far away, so it isn't easy to see them except during the holidays.
>
> So, when I feel lonely, I tend to call my acquaintances or children and talk a lot.
>
> We mainly talk about small things such as news and jokes about each other's lives through the phone. However, after talking on the phone like this, they met in person and talked for a long time, which helped me mentally.
>
> Recently, I used the cell phone that my son gave me as a gift, and I also talked to my grandchildren."

This interview suggests that communicating with friends and family over the phone can help improve the life satisfaction of centenarians. Furthermore, it confirmed that the chance of conversation disappears as the range of movement becomes narrower due to aging. The telephone is one of the excellent means to compensate for this. Furthermore, communication with individuals one likes can increase the probability of becoming a centenarian.

5.2.5 SVPW

SVPW is a significant variable that increases personal income by creating added value per person concerning private gain. An increase in the income level bridges the gap in the health level of the elderly. Therefore, we can confirm that the added value of income improves the living satisfaction and health of the elderly.

> "The amount of crops produced by paddy fields of the same area has increased significantly over the past few decades. In addition, the price of agricultural products has risen considerably, resulting in a significant improvement in per capita farm household income. Thus, agricultural profits have also increased, and government support has been added.
>
> In the past, when I was unable to move, I just stayed at home or used a cane, but now I use an electric wheelchair to visit a nearby acquaintance's house or go directly to a Senior Center.
>
> Unfortunately, an electric wheelchair is not easy to buy with a government subsidy alone. However, the income of the farmhouse has increased so that the elderly can ride an electric motor. Thus, my mobility became more leisurely, so I started walking again, which I had never done before."

Since state support is inherently limited, an increase in individual income is an essential element. The increase in added value per capita eventually generated additional revenue for individuals, which, coupled with state support, increased the probability of maintaining a healthy life and becoming a centenarian.

5.2.6 GNI

The GNI of SEFs confirmed that 80% or more of the 130 centenarians we met had income levels above the middle class. Here is a summary of their interviews regarding the income of centenarians.

> "I have not felt any financial burden in my life so far. I see myself as middle class. I am not rich, but I do not think that I am living a tough life. Children and other family members are living without difficulty. I don't drive, but I have a car for other family members to use when I need it.
>
> I have a fixed income, and I own quite some real estate, such as rice fields. In addition, I have a personal caregiver and can get help immediately, and I enjoy chatting with the caregiver or playing card games. If I had lived difficult life, I don't think I could have lived this long."

This case suggests that income is highly correlated with health, even regarding centenarians. Income is a significant variable in the health level gap due to unequal living standards. Conversely, if the income level is high, it can help pay for health costs and support a healthy life, thus elevating life satisfaction.

5.2.7 SMDW

SEFs' SMDW was an essential factor for the 130 centenarians interviewed. Interestingly, the majority of centenarians did not drink tap water and were mainly drinking bottled water. The following is a summary of their interview related to drinking water for centenarians.

> "In the past, we mainly used the town's underground water for drinking due to poor water supply. It's not that I didn't drink tap water, but I used to boil it all the time. As I remember, the underground water was spotless, and it is still clean.
>
> But these days, I heard that there is a sanitation problem, and I think it is cumbersome to use the underground water every time.
>
> So I buy cheap and convenient bottled water and drink it. Nowadays, we use bottled water for food, and we drink bottled water in almost every situation."

As seen in the interview, SMDW drank tap water and groundwater when young, but now they drink quality water. Moreover, unlike other beverages, bottled water can prevent excessive sugar and sodium intake. Through this, the survival probability of becoming a centenarian could have increased.

5.2.8 UP

In SEFs, population urbanization was an essential factor. For centenarians in interviews, we have focused on the distance to reach general hospitals in case of emergency. Interestingly, the majority of 100-year-olds lived in the vicinity of public hospitals. Therefore, the discussion with centenarians related to urbanization is summarized as follows.

> "The nurse at the public health center frequently checks my health over the phone and visits me about once a week for a simple check-up, such as a blood pressure test. They also give a lot of health advice.
>
> I live in the city's suburbs. There is a general hospital where you can get medical services in at least 20 minutes by car.
>
> In the past, it wasn't easy to go to the hospital. Because the road was rough, I wouldn't have even thought of it. However, a newly paved road has opened as a straight street, and the distance to use the hospital is closer."

Urbanization of the population has advantages and disadvantages in terms of health. The advantage of urbanization is that a general hospital can provide appropriate treatment in an emergency close to home. In addition, because the health care system is well equipped, it is possible to receive health checks and use medical services in an emergency. Therefore, we suggest that higher the UP and proximity to the hospitals, higher is the SPBC.

5.2.9 GII

A majority of the 130 centenarians were interviewed regarding gender discrimination and their experiences throughout their lives. Centenarians did not experience gender discrimination in their youth in the past or had overcome gender discrimination in their lives. The following is a summary of their interview related to gender discrimination of centenarians.

> "Our family has never experienced gender discrimination.
>
> Although it was a patriarchal family, we shared the household chores and helped each other instead of 'what men do' or 'what women do.' We enjoyed working together, earning money, and doing business together.
>
> We think we have lived a happy life while acknowledging the different aspects of our lives."

It is important to note that women's equal access. Economic participation in society can increase household income and promote health and welfare. If such involvement increases SPBC, it indirectly affects public health because that healthcare expenditure can gain by increasing its GDP in the short-to-medium term.

5.3. Humans can live 100 years based on PLI and CLSS for SEFs

The centenarians have overcome the onset of diseases throughout their lives and have reached the milestone of 100 years of age in relatively good health. Therefore, from a micro perspective, physical and mental health had been maintained through PLI, whereas from a macro perspective, they have been maintained social health through CLSS.

A society in which humanity lives to 100 years based on PLI and CLSS in SEFs is shown in Fig. 5.1. For instance, the (+) direction of the X-axis represents the extension of a healthy lifespan by promoting physical and mental health. However, the X-axis's negative (−) direction represents poor physical and psychological health due to insufficient PLI. In addition, it assumes that the (+) direction of the Y-axis represents the extension of a healthy lifespan through CLSS promotion and healthy social life. Conversely, the Y-axis's negative (−) direction refers to poor social health due to insufficient CLSS.

First, suppose that the PLI on the X-axis maintains a positive (+) direction, while the CLSS on the Y-axis also continues in a positive (+) order. In this case, the people's health level is (1) [Healthy].

Second, suppose that the Y-axis moves in a positive (+) direction because the people's social health level is maintained with good CLSS. Hence, the Y-axis moves in a positive (+) approach, but the X-axis moves in a negative (−) direction. In this case, the people's health level is (2) [Moderate].

Third, suppose that the X-axis moves in a positive (+) direction, but the Y-axis moves in a negative (−) focus due to the lack of CLSS. In this case, the people's health level is (4) [Moderate].

Finally, suppose that all of the lines on the XY-axis move in the negative (−) direction due to insufficient CLSS and PLI. In this case, the people's health level is (3) [Unhealthy].

These findings indicate that only continuous and sufficient CLSS and PLI can contribute to SPBC. Additionally, it is possible to overcome the intermediate health levels of (2), (4) [Moderate] with sufficient PLI and CLSS. But the overall goal is to achieve a healthy level of (1) [Healthy] to reach 100 years of age.

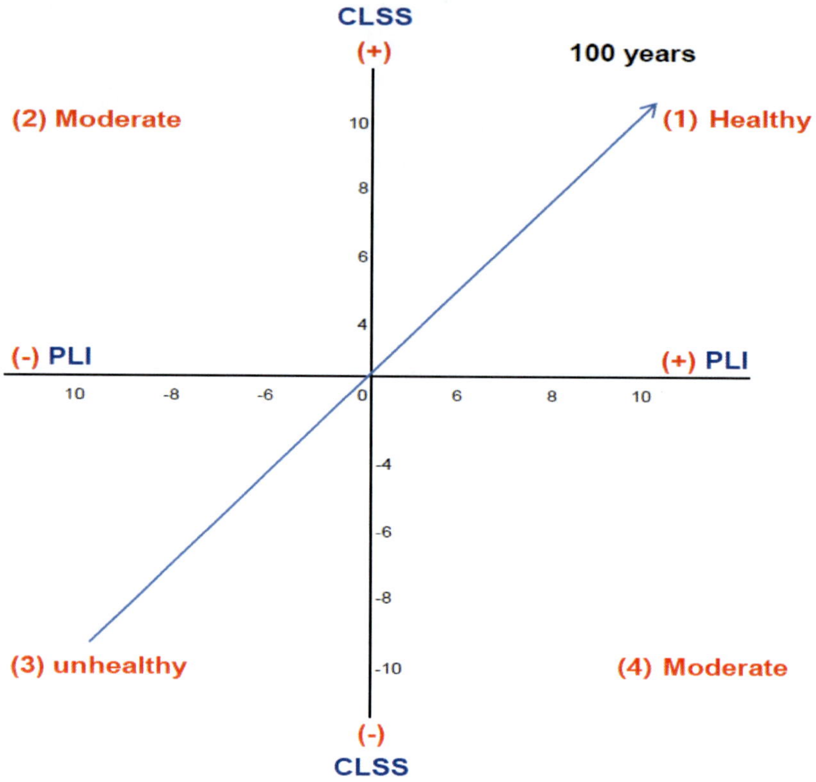

Fig. 5.1. Relationship between PLI, CLSS, and health

5.4 Impact when combined with SEFs in SPBC (82)

5.4.1 GNI, UP, and SMDW

The influence of SMDW alone on SPBC (82) is 23.4% (see Table. 5.1). However, when combined with GNI and SMDW, it has a 33% impact. When combined with UP, SMDW increases to 35% (Table 5.2). Thus, we should develop policy alternatives to increasing SPBC (82) according to the SMDW and other SEFs such as GNI, UP, and SVPW.

Table 5.2 Multiple regression models of predicting the SPBC (82) and SEFs

SEFs	Coefficients	SE Coef	t-value	p-value	VIF	R^2
SMDW	2.6	1.18	2.2	0.034	1.24	0.328
GNI	0.000549	0.000245	2.24	0.031	1.24	
SMDW	2.61	1.17	2.23	0.032	1.22	0.332
SVPW	0.000301	0.000131	2.3	0.027	1.22	
UP	0.967	0.464	2.08	0.045	1.28	0.321
GNI	0.00054	0.000251	2.15	0.038	1.28	
UP	1.008	0.444	2.27	0.029	1.2	0.336
SVPW	0.000307	0.000129	2.37	0.023	1.2	
UP	1.074	0.425	2.53	0.016	1.12	0.352
SMDW	2.83	1.11	2.55	0.015	1.12	

Figure 5.2.1 shows the effects of UP and GNI on SPBC (82), while Figure 5.2.2 shows the impact of UP and SMDW on SPBC (82). Countries with a high SPBC (82) for SMDW generally receive 100% of their drinking water from safe and sanitary water sources. Conversely, in countries with low SPBC (82), 70% of the drinking water supply comes from clean water sources.

UP is a variable with an influence of 35% (R^2 = 0.352) when combined with SMDW and up to 49% when combined with BSS and FTMPS (Table 5.2, 5.5). Population urbanization is a major socio-ecological factor that increases the probability of survival to 100 years when combined with other SEFs with a healthy lifespan.

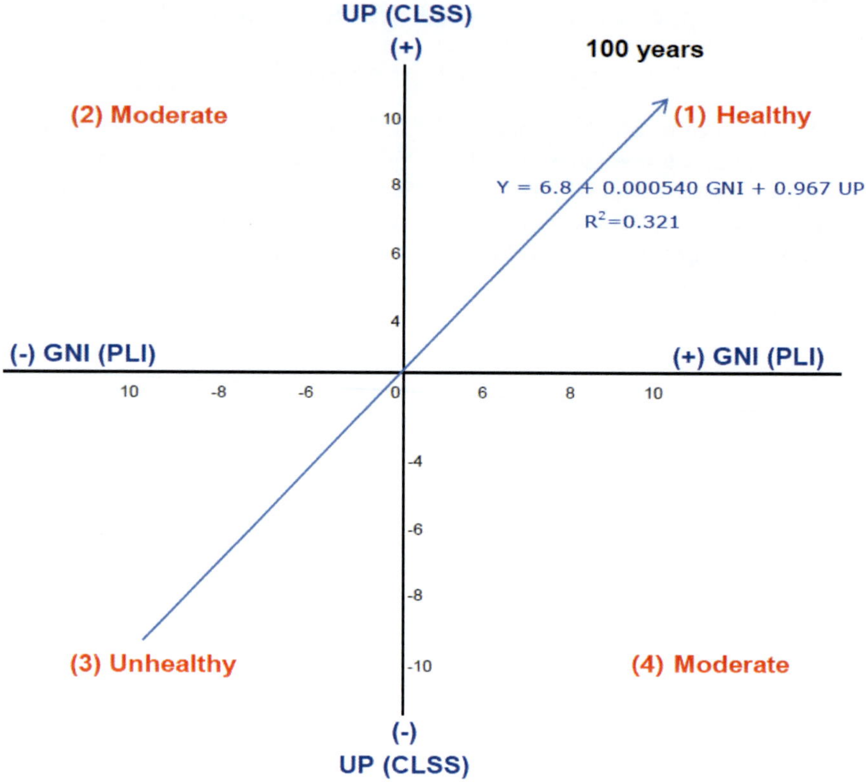

Fig. 5.2.1 Relationship between GNI and UP in SPBC (82)

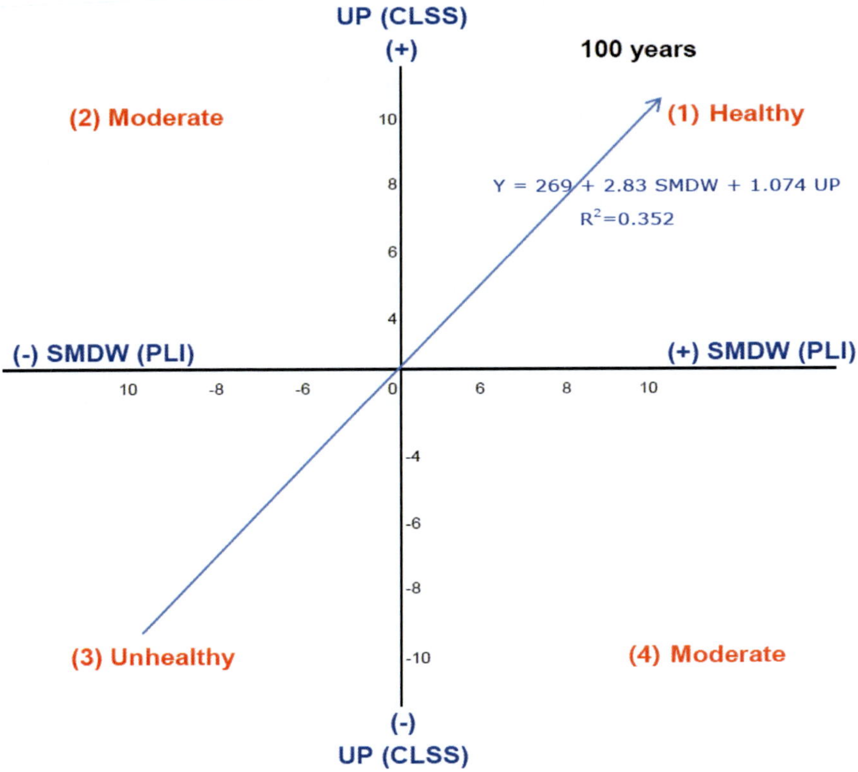

Fig. 5.2.2 The relationship between SMDW and UP in SPBC (82)

5.4.2 BSS, SVPW, and UP

The influence of the BSS alone on SPBC (82) is 31% (see Table. 5.1). However, when combined with GNI and FTMPS, it has a 40% impact (Table 5.3). Furthermore, when combined with HEPGDP, it increases to 41%; and IUI, UP, and SVPW increase to 42% (Table 5.3). Thus, we should develop policy alternatives to increasing SPBC (82) according to the BSS and other SEFs such as GNI, FTMPS, HEPGDP, IUI, UP, and SVPW.

Table 5.3 Multiple regression models of predicting the SPBC (82) and SEFs

SEFs	Coefficients	SE Coef	t-value	p-value	VIF	R^2
BSS	4.77	1.5	3.18	0.003	1.14	0.402
GNI	0.000537	0.000222	2.42	0.021	1.14	
BSS	4.71	1.51	3.12	0.004	1.16	0.404
FTMPS	0.855	0.354	2.41	0.021	1.16	
BSS	4.2	1.58	2.67	0.011	1.28	0.412
HEPGDP	5.59	2.21	2.53	0.016	1.28	
BSS	4.34	1.54	2.81	0.008	1.23	0.416
IUI	1.264	0.492	2.57	0.014	1.23	
BSS	4.93	1.45	3.39	0.002	1.1	0.418
UP	1.037	0.397	2.61	0.013	1.1	
BSS	4.85	1.46	3.32	0.002	1.11	0.418
SVPW	0.000305	0.000116	2.62	0.013	1.11	

Figures 5.3.1 and 5.3.2 present the results of increasing SPBC (82) by increasing BSS, HEPGDP, BSS, and SVPW in SEFs. In the case of BSS, if HEPGDP and SVPW are raised, we can extend a healthy lifespan, the quality of life can be increased, and people can become centenarians.

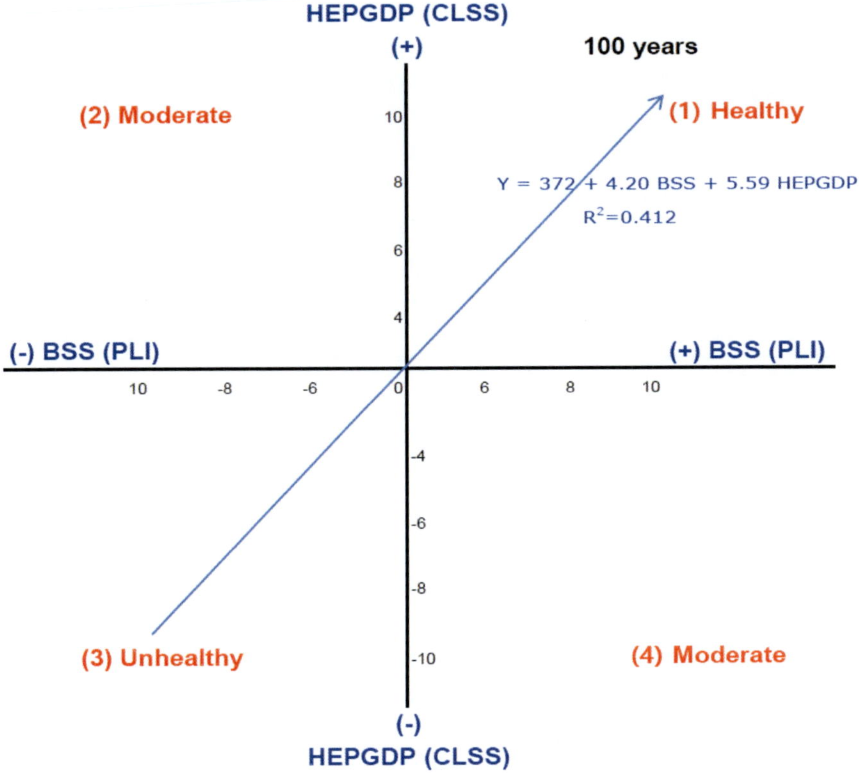

Fig. 5.3.1 Relationship between BSS and HEPGDP in SPBC (82)

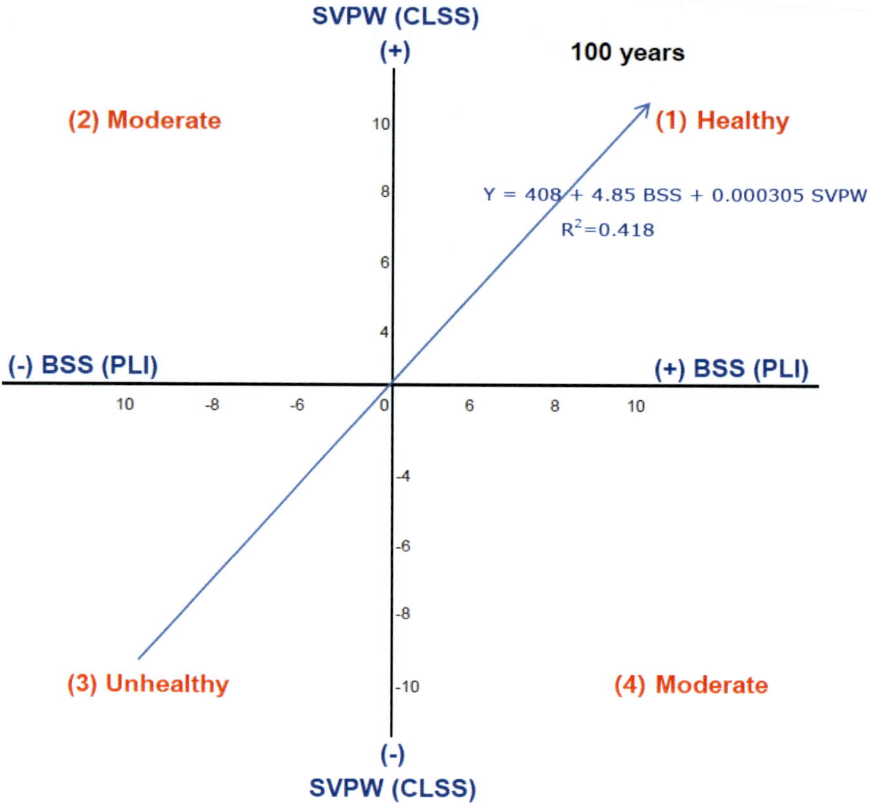

Fig. 5.3.2 Relationship between BSS and SVPW in SPBC (82)

5.4.3 HEPGDP, FTMPS, and IUI

The influence of HEPGDP alone on SPBC (82) is 29.6% (see Table 5.1). However, when combined with SVPW and SMDW, it exerts an influence of 38%; and when combined with UP and GII, it increases to 40% (Table 5.4). When combined with IUI and FTMPS, it increases to 43%; and when only combined with FTMPS and IUI, it rises to 44% (Table 5.4).

Therefore, again, policy alternatives aimed at increasing SPBC (82) should include both HEPGDP and other SEFs such as UP, GII, IUI, and FTMPS.

Table 5.4 Multiple regression models of predicting the SPBC (82) and SEFs

SEFs	Coefficients	SE Coef	t-value	p-value	VIF	R^2
HEPGDP	6.25	2.24	2.79	0.008	1.23	0.375
SVPW	0.000272	0.000127	2.13	0.041	1.23	
HEPGDP	6.36	2.21	2.88	0.007	1.2	0.378
SMDW	2.44	1.12	2.17	0.036	1.2	
HEPGDP	6.59	2.11	3.13	0.003	1.13	0.401
UP	1.002	0.41	2.44	0.021	1.13	
HEPGDP	6.79	2.07	3.28	0.002	1.1	0.402
GII	-168.7	67.2	-2.51	0.017	1.1	
HEPGDP	6.15	2.08	2.95	0.006	1.16	0.425
IUI	1.347	0.473	2.85	0.007	1.16	
HEPGDP	6.8	2.01	3.39	0.002	1.08	0.426
FTMPS	0.959	0.335	2.86	0.007	1.08	
FTMPS	1.022	0.326	3.13	0.003	1.04	0.442
IUI	1.574	0.444	3.55	0.001	1.04	

Figure 5.4 indicates that—as a result of analysis in 39 countries—the elderly who reached centenarians had low GII and high HEPGDP. Consequently, they had increased SPBC (82) and became centenarians. Therefore, if GII is low and HEPGDP can raise, the elderly's healthy lifespan can be extended, their quality of life can improve, and their probability of reaching 100 can increase.

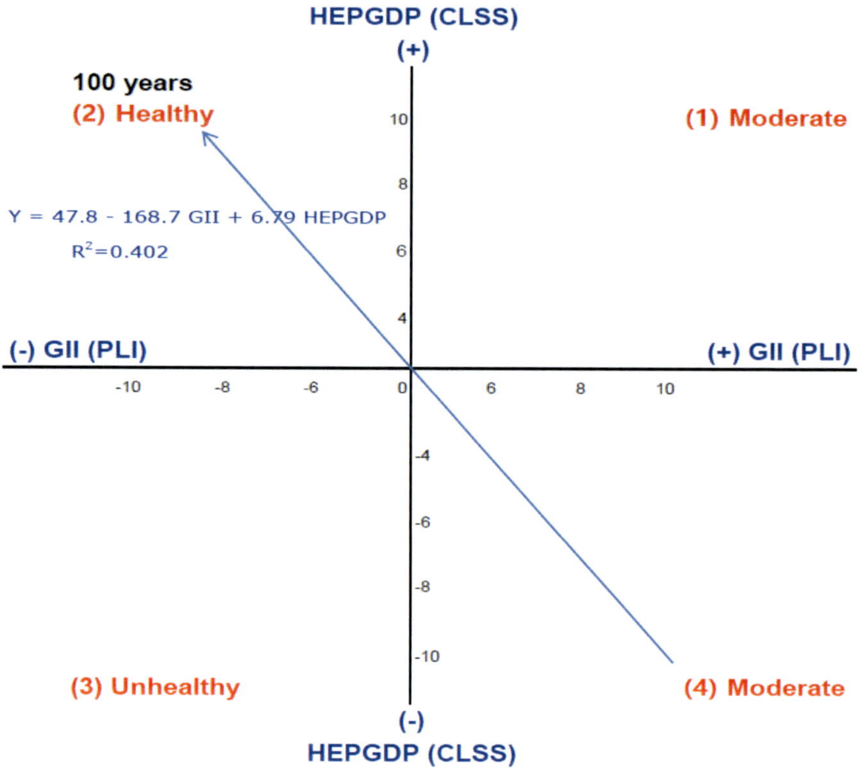

Fig. 5.4 Relationship between GII and HEPGDP in SPBC (82)

5.4.4 FTMPS, BSS, IUI, UP, and HEPGDP

The influence of FTMPS and BSS on SPBC (82) is 40% (see Table 5.3). However, when combined with FTMPS and UP, it exerts an influence of 49% (Table 5.5). When combined with IUI, it increases to 50% (Table 5.5); and when only three combined with FTMPS, IUI, and HEPGDP, it rises to 53% (Table 5.5). Thus, again, policy alternatives aimed at increasing SPBC (82) should not only include FTMPS and BSS but other SEFs such as UP, GNI, IUI, and HEPGDP.

Table 5.5 Multiple regression models of predicting the SPBC (82) and SEFs

SEFs	Coefficients	SE Coef	t-value	p-value	VIF	R^2
FTMPS	0.75	0.339	2.21	0.034	1.18	
BSS	3.74	1.5	2.5	0.017	1.26	0.478
GNI	0.000471	0.000213	2.21	0.033	1.17	
HEPGDP	4.48	2.17	2.07	0.046	1.35	
BSS	3.65	1.52	2.4	0.022	1.31	0.481
UP	0.846	0.391	2.16	0.038	1.16	
FTMPS	0.762	0.335	2.27	0.029	1.17	
BSS	3.18	1.56	2.05	0.048	1.39	0.488
HEPGDP	5.04	2.11	2.39	0.022	1.29	
FTMPS	0.744	0.335	2.22	0.033	1.18	
BSS	3.88	1.46	2.66	0.012	1.22	0.492
UP	0.922	0.381	2.42	0.021	1.12	
FTMPS	0.806	0.329	2.45	0.019	1.16	
BSS	3.16	1.52	2.07	0.046	1.37	0.502
IUI	1.2	0.462	2.6	0.014	1.23	
FTMPS	0.856	0.311	2.76	0.009	1.09	
IUI	1.201	0.438	2.74	0.01	1.17	0.528
HEPGDP	5.01	1.96	2.56	0.015	1.21	

Figure 5.5 shows that the elderly who became centenarians in 39 countries increased SPBC (82) when FTMPS and IUI were high, HEPGDP was high, and the highest effect ($R^2 = 52.8$).

In other words, the most excellent synergistic effect was shown when FTMPS, IUI, and HEPGDP were combined. If the ratio of FTMPS and IUI increases in terms of PLI, and the percentage of HEPGDP is rising in terms of CLSS simultaneously, improve the quality of life and increase the probability of reaching centenarians.

Therefore, it is necessary to consider the selective strategies of SEFs to achieve SPBC (82) for each country type, which is as follows.

Developed countries with high GNI need to strengthen information and communication factors such as FTMPS and IUI. However, countries with low GNI should select and implement elements that solve the most basic drinking water and sanitation problems, such as SMDW and BSS.

For example, high-ranked influences in the SPBC (82) are sanitation, telephony, and the Internet. However, basic sanitation and drinking water do not emerge as issues in developed countries. However, it is a significant factor in underdeveloped countries that we must address first to extend a healthy lifespan.

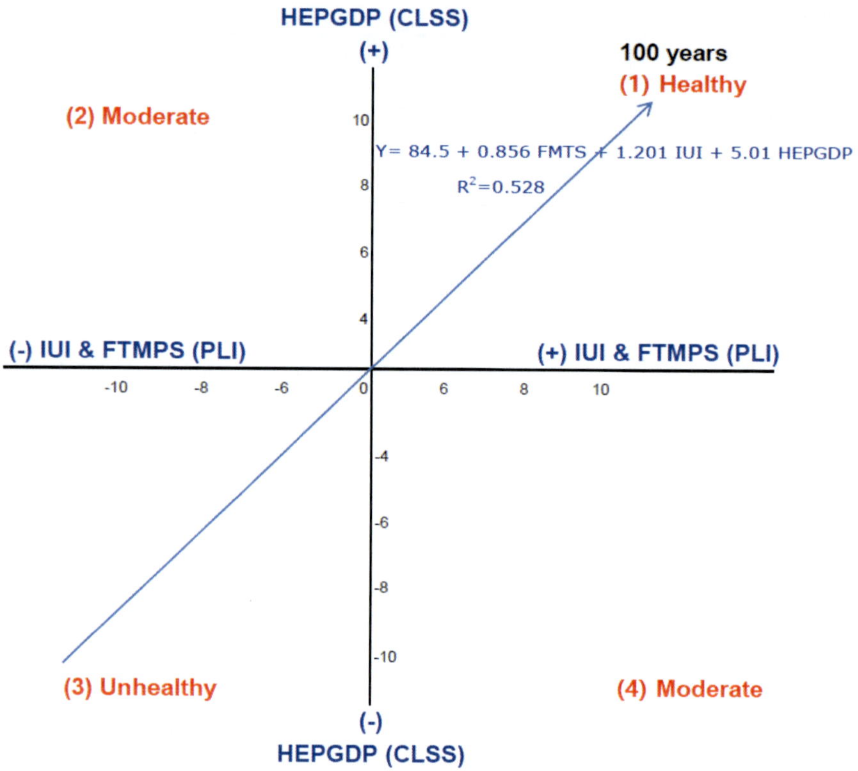

Fig. 5.5 Relationship between IUI and FTMPS and HEPGDP in SPBC (82)

5.5 Summary: Impact of SEFs on SPBC (82)

The primary issue of this book focuses on the human potential to become centenarians. From SEFs, nine variables of PLI and CLSS influence SPBC (82). It is crucial to select and implement the appropriate variable for each country in consideration of the influence of the nine variables.

First, however, it is essential to grasp the current reality of each country. By estimating the ISS from birth to life expectancy, each country's current situation and expected age level are identified. Then, two or more influential factors that can overcome this are selected and implemented.

Following this, each country's life expectancy is analyzed according to the estimation formula of ISS, and the most influential variable is decided and executed by selecting two or more of the nine variables that influence reaching 100 years of age.

Each country sets goals for a healthy lifespan. Each country's health care plan is established, implemented, evaluated, and analyzed in the short and long term. Through annual feedback, the degree of achievement of the estimated healthy life expectancy is checked. The accomplishment of continuous goal correction and long- and short-term performance will be a society in which humanity will live to be 100 years old.

References

Kim JI. Association between social factors of health ageing and longevity: Determinants of the longevity index (LI) in OECD countries. Ageing International. 2014; 39(2), 97–105.

Kim JI. Social factors associated with centenarian rate (CR) in 32 OECD countries. BMC International Health and Human Rights. 2013; 13(1), 16.

Kim JI, Kim G. Factors affecting the survival probability of becoming a centenarian for those aged 70, based on the human mortality database: Income, health expenditure, telephone, and sanitation. BMC Geriatrics. 2014a; 14(1), 113.

Kim JI, Kim G. Labor force participation and secondary education of gender inequality index (GII) associated with healthy life expectancy (HLE) at birth. International Journal for Equity in Health. 2014b; 13(1), 1–8.

Kim JI, Kim G. Country-level socioeconomic indicators associated with healthy life expectancy: Income, Urbanization, Schooling, and Internet

Users: 2000–2012. Social Indicators Research. 2016; 129, 391–402.
Kim JI, Kim G. Social structural influences on healthy aging: Community-level socioeconomic conditions and survival probability of becoming a centenarian for those aged 65 to 69 in South Korea. The International Journal of Aging and Human Development. 2015b; 81(4), 241–259.
Kim JI, Kim G, Choi Y. Effects of air pollution on children from a socioecological perspective. BMC Pediatrics. 2019; 19, 442.
Kim JI, Kim G. Effects on inequality in life expectancy from a social ecology perspective. BMC Public Health. 2018; 18, 243.
Kim JI, Kim G. Relationship between the remaining years of healthy life expectancy in older age and national income level, educational attainment, and improved water quality. The International Journal of Aging and Human Development. 2016; 83(4), 402–417.
Kim JI, Kim G. Socio-ecological perspective of older age life expectancy: income, gender inequality, and financial crisis in Europe. Globalization and Health. 2017; 13, 58.
Kim JI, Kim G. Country-level socioeconomic indicators associated with survival probability of becoming a centenarian among older European adults: Gender inequality, male labor force participation, and proportions of women in parliaments. Journal of Biosocial Science. 2017; 49(2), 239–250.

COMPLETING THIS BOOK

From prayers to the gods to making artificial organs, the origins of human longevity have been continuously developed. The SFEs of longevity are like living organisms. Various factors identified will become more critical in the future.

Some will remain important for an extended time, and others will become less important. The Internet, which could not be considered a factor of longevity 100 years ago, has become one of the most closely related to longevity. It suggests that for humanity 100 years from now, unknown, unimaginable factors may emerge as new longevity factors.

In addition, it will be a critical study for society to identify the factors for longevity in the present age. Because each SEFs does not arise suddenly one day but occurs through gradual evolution, like a smoke signal changes to a telegram, a telegram to a telephone, and a phone to a mobile phone.

Therefore, if you recognize the current SEFs, predict prediction, and prepare for future changes, it will provide a remarkable gift of longevity to the future development of human civilization. This book is intended to help us determine, from an international perspective, previously vague factors of longevity, how they influence human life, and how we may use them now and in the future.

Finally, I wish all readers a healthy and happy voyage beyond the age of 100, and I hope that this book will be helpful by your side.

Author, Professor, JONG IN KIM, PhD